Liz Harfull is passionate about telling the stories of regional Australia, its people, communities, history and traditions.

Liz grew up on a small farm near Mount Gambier, which has been in the family since the 1860s. She became an award-winning rural journalist and communicator and director of a leading national public relations agency.

In 2006 Liz walked away from corporate life to write books. Her leap of faith was rewarded two years later with *The Blue Ribbon Cookbook,* which captured the stories and traditions of South Australian country shows and show cooks and became a surprise bestseller. It won a Gourmand World Cookbook Award in Paris. Since then she has written two national bestsellers, *Women of the Land* and *The Australian Blue Ribbon Cookbook,* as well as *Almost an Island: The story of Robe,* about her favourite seaside town on the windswept Limestone Coast.

Today Liz lives in the Adelaide Hills, juggling a busy writing career with travelling around Australia to visit the places and meet the people that inspire her writing.

www.lizharfull.com
/lizharfullauthor
@LizHarfull

City Girl
COUNTRY GIRL

The inspiring true stories of
courageous women forging new
lives in the Australian bush

LIZ HARFULL

ALLEN&UNWIN

SYDNEY·MELBOURNE·AUCKLAND·LONDON

First published in 2016

Copyright © Liz Harfull 2016

All rights reserved. No part of this book may be reproduced or transmitted in any form or by any means, electronic or mechanical, including photocopying, recording or by any information storage and retrieval system, without prior permission in writing from the publisher. The Australian *Copyright Act 1968* (the Act) allows a maximum of one chapter or 10 per cent of this book, whichever is the greater, to be photocopied by any educational institution for its educational purposes provided that the educational institution (or body that administers it) has given a remuneration notice to the Copyright Agency (Australia) under the Act.

Allen & Unwin
83 Alexander Street
Crows Nest NSW 2065
Australia
Phone: (61 2) 8425 0100
Email: info@allenandunwin.com
Web: www.allenandunwin.com

Cataloguing-in-Publication details are available
from the National Library of Australia
www.trove.nla.gov.au

ISBN 978 1 74237 981 4

Internal design by Simon Paterson, Bookhouse
Set in 12/17 pt Sabon Pro by Bookhouse, Australia
Printed and bound in Australia by Griffin Press

10 9 8 7 6 5 4 3 2 1

MIX
Paper from responsible sources
FSC® C009448

The paper in this book is FSC® certified. FSC® promotes environmentally responsible, socially beneficial and economically viable management of the world's forests.

Dedicated to the memory of my mum, Elaine Harfull: a city girl who married a country boy and (almost) never looked back

CONTENTS

Introduction ix

PART I: LONG LIVES WELL LIVED
Elaine Harfull, Mil Lel, South Australia
Grace Gilmore, Eight Mile Creek, South Australia

1 The Boy in Blue	3
2 Life at Mil Lel	14
3 For the Love of Grace	21
4 Till Death Us Do Part	27

PART II: LOVE IN A FOREIGN LAND
Doris Turner and Wendy Bonini, Manjimup, Western Australia
Giuliana Vincenti, Carmel, Western Australia

5 Child of the Forest	37
6 The New Chums	53
7 The Outlaw Returns	67
8 Tall Timber Dancing	75

PART III: THE LITTLE TOWN THAT COULD
Marnie Baker, Harrow, Victoria
Sherryn Simpson, Connewirricoo, Victoria

9 The One Nun Story	93
10 New Life and Almost Death	112
11 A Beaut Bloke	121
12 Lessons for the Teacher	129
13 Connewirricoo	139
14 The Ripple Effect	151

Part IV: Resilient Spirit
Daljit Sanghera, Bookpurnong, South Australia

15 A Long Way from Home	159
16 Trusting Your Luck	168
17 To the Riverland	174
18 When Giving up is not an Option	179

Part V: Here I Am, Here I Stay
Annabel Tully, Sarah Durack and Wendy Tully, Quilpie, Queensland

19 Creative Cowboys	201
20 Grass Castle Legacies	220
21 The Fence of Hope	242

Acknowledgements 257

INTRODUCTION

I'm sitting down to write the opening lines of this book a year to the day since my mum died. She is constantly in my thoughts, not just because I miss her terribly, but because she was the inspiration for this collection of stories about women who have come from very different places to make a new life in rural Australia.

Mum was a city girl. She spent most of her life in Melbourne until one eventful evening when she met a country boy on leave from the Royal Australian Air Force. It was wartime and society had been turned on its head, throwing together people who might otherwise never have crossed paths at all. Less than a year after the war ended, my parents married in a celebration kept discreet because clothes and food were still rationed. Mum had to save coupons for her dress and the reception was a modest repast of cold meat, savouries and trifle. After an adventurous honeymoon in the wilds of Gippsland, they took up residence in a dark, limestone farmhouse at Mil Lel near Mount Gambier, with no electricity and practically no plumbing.

It was the beginning of a very different life for an independent woman who enjoyed a respectable job as a bookkeeper in the city, a dashing wardrobe of the latest fashion, and the social whirl of going out to dances with her sister and friends several nights a week. While the farm was not that isolated, Mum found herself an arduous journey and a whole world away from Melbourne. Over the coming years she learnt to milk cows, stook hay and drive a tractor, playing an active part on the farm while raising four children. In between, she also learnt to match her mother-in-law's skills at making Dad's favourite cakes and puddings, hand-stitched all the babies' clothes, transformed the old farmhouse into a bright, modern family home, and volunteered to do her bit for a host of local community organisations.

In many ways, my mum's story is not unique, and nor are those of the other women featured in this book. Thousands of women have faced similar challenges after leaving behind the city, or another country. A whole new generation are experiencing them now. If reality television shows that help farmers find wives and the sale of rural romance novels are any indication, many more women are dreaming of following in their footsteps and falling in love with a tall, rugged country bloke wearing RM Williams boots and a wide-brimmed Akubra hat.

But behind the stylised, romantic visions that people have of the Australian bush can lie a very different truth. Loneliness and isolation, the lack of essential services and facilities often taken for granted in the city, and the vagaries of drought and floods challenge any woman, whether she is from the city or country bred. Then there are the long back-breaking days of hard work, with few days off, and the constant financial struggles for many farm families, coping with the ups and downs of commodity prices and the demands of fad-following city consumers.

Mum says that in the early years she would cry whenever she left Dad to visit her family back in the city, and she would cry again when she left her family to return home. I'm guessing a piece of her was always missing, no matter where she was, and I'm guessing this because that's how I felt, too. In my early twenties I reversed the trend, married a city boy and took up an urban life 400 kilometres away. The marriage didn't last but my city life made me appreciate the things I had taken for granted while growing up in the country.

Things like the freedom we had as children to wander the farm and the neighbourhood. Spending our days outside in fresh air and open spaces, riding our ponies to visit friends, and using our imaginations to make up our own games. Sitting in the back of an old ute, bouncing across a paddock, the wind making waves in the coat of our border collie, Boofa, struggling to contain his excitement at the prospect of work to be done.

Things like the closeness of the community which made it impossible to go to the post office to collect mail or to pick up something at the local farm supplies store without allowing extra time to chat about the weather and how the crops were looking, and exchange news about the family and mutual friends. Neighbours dropping in cakes and casseroles at times of tragedy and loss, practical symbols of their care and concern. The camaraderie of community celebrations and knowing almost everyone crowded into the local hall and showground. The nonchalant wave of passing drivers acknowledging even complete strangers.

And then there was the traditional country baking and preserving—tastes, smells and experiences that led me to write two books about show cooking. Afternoon tea before setting off to bring the cows in for milking, with home-baked scones and cake, often shared with neighbours who dropped in, knowing the routine. Tommy the Caltex Man, who came every month to fill up the fuel tank in a ritual that stretched back decades, always timing the run so he could share a cuppa, too. And the supper tables at community events in the hall—trestle tables groaning with ginger fluff, strawberry sponges, corned beef and mustard pickle sandwiches, and homemade sausage rolls.

On our farm there was always a menagerie of animals. The border collie waiting patiently at the back door, not bothering to even lift his head if Dad emerged wearing his town boots and hat. George the cockatoo barking like a dog whenever a vehicle pulled into the yard. The bulls roaring over the back fence when they sensed the herd of cows nearby, and the calves that slobbered over your jeans and pulled at your fingers with raspy tongues as you tried to feed them from a bucket. The cats sitting in a circle at your feet at the top of the haystack, waiting for mice to appear as you lifted each sheaf of oats. And the horses—patient Prince who taught me and my sister how to ride, gentle Rusty who thought it funny to sneak up behind my brother and blow in his ear, and Toby the rescue horse, the first horse of my very own, who waited for me to get off the school bus every day.

Life on a farm connects you to the rhythms of nature and the changing seasons. The smell of fresh-mown pasture when haymaking starts in the spring, and discovering a batch of mewling kittens hidden in the shed. The setting sun glancing off paddocks of bleached stubble after the harvest is over, and the croaking of frogs from the swamp as a summer storm approaches. The dancing clarity of an autumn night sky crammed full of stars, undimmed by intrusive streetlights. Coming in from the crisp winter chill to the comforting warmth of a wood stove and a huge pot of lamb, vegetable and barley soup simmering on the back.

These are the things my mum came to love, too, as more than sixty years of marriage passed, and she watched her children, grandchildren and great-grandchildren grow. Mum knew that I was planning to tell her story, and I thought deeply about the best way to approach it. In the end, I decided to treat her the same as every other woman in the book, and tell it in the third person. Mum's story focuses mainly on her life before I came along, but when I do make the odd appearance,

INTRODUCTION

I have stayed true to her overwhelming preference and used my full name, Elizabeth. Mum didn't think of her life as anything exceptional, but she was quietly proud at the idea of being part of the book. There is much more I would have asked her, but she died unexpectedly after a very short illness and the opportunity was lost.

Recognising that has made me all the more determined as a writer to do what I can to capture the lives of other women, the quiet, seemingly small lives, well lived, and so often overlooked, who make up the rich fabric of our rural communities. Women such as Annabel, Daljit, Marnie, Sherryn, Wendy, Elaine and Grace.

Liz Harfull
19 June 2015

Part I
LONG LIVES WELL LIVED

1

THE BOY IN BLUE

Elaine Schwennesen hated the Big Dipper, its bone-rattling swoops that left your stomach back on the last rise, the ear-piercing shrieks that rose over Luna Park. She really wasn't sure how she had been talked into going. Bushfires had caused havoc across Victoria for weeks in what was proving to be a hot, dry summer but she and her sister Reay were shivering with cold and the park was crowded with servicemen on leave who seemed a little the worse for wear. Now her best friend Maree was 'rolling her eyes' at one of them.

Maree had taken an instant fancy to Arthur who was out on the town with three of his mates, all flight engineers in the Royal Australian Air Force. They were camping at the Melbourne Showground on the other side of the city where the RAAF No. 1 Engineering School was based, and had come into a hotel near the Swanston Street Station for a slap-up meal to celebrate completing an engine-fitting course. Afterwards they hopped on a tram to the seaside suburb of St Kilda and its popular amusement park.

Thousands of summer holiday-makers had passed through the gaping mouth of the iconic Mr Moon gate since the park opened thirty-two years before, but it was even more popular during what seemed like a never-ending war that encouraged people to seize pleasure when they could. It was January

1944, and the conflict had been going for almost four-and-a-half years, although things were finally looking up. Just that morning the front page of *The Argus* was reporting Allied advances in Italy, German retreat in Russia, and the Japanese being forced back by the Australians in New Guinea.

Looking at the group of young men gathered around them, Elaine focused her attention on the handsome boy with dark blue eyes made even bluer by his RAAF uniform. He seemed sober, and in the raucous setting of Luna Park looked especially quiet and dependable. 'You had better come along and look after us,' she told him.

Lyall Harfull was not about to turn down the opportunity to spend more time with the tall, slim brunette. A few weeks shy of her nineteenth birthday, she was wearing a soft blue dress with flowers embroidered on the sleeve and a demure, buttoned-up collar. Later on, in the custom of the day, she would give him a photo of herself wearing that dress, signed very properly 'To Lyall with best wishes, from Elaine'.

At the end of the night Lyall walked her to the tram, and then unbeknown to Elaine and her sister, he and his mates jumped on the back. 'They thought we were nice girls and they wanted to see that we got home safely,' Elaine would tell her children years later, when they asked her to relive the magical moment that lit the spark that became their family.

The next day Lyall took Elaine up into the nearby Dandenong Ranges with a party of friends for a ride on the Puffing Billy steam train. 'It was stinking hot and he was dressed in these lovely shorts. He used to look nice in his shorts. And he sat down under this tree and ate lots of watermelon,' Elaine said.

After watching them together, one of Lyall's friends turned to him at the end of the day and predicted, 'You're going to marry that girl.'

❖ ❖ ❖

Alma Elaine Schwennesen was born in a small private nursing home in the central Victorian goldmining town of Bendigo, where her father worked as a butcher. The year was 1925 and the month was February, but after that the facts are a little unclear. According to details registered by her father, she arrived on 27 February. According to her mother, she was born three minutes after midnight on 28 February and that is the date on which her birthday was always celebrated. In fact, Elaine didn't even realise it was in doubt until thirty years later when she required a copy of her birth certificate to apply for a passport.

Never known by her first name, which she hated, Elaine was the first of four children born within five years to Bruce Schwennesen and Vida Marriott. Originally from Denmark, her father's family were tailors at Talbot, a once-thriving town in the heart of the Victorian goldfields. She remembers her Grandfather Schwennesen as being a hard, cold, 'nasty' man, but she was deeply fond of her Grandpa Marriott, who was a staunch Methodist, went to church three times on Sundays and looked after the Sunday school. A travelling salesman for part of his life, at one stage he also owned the Federal Dairy in Bendigo and he had worked in the mines as a younger man.

When Elaine was only a few years old, her family moved to Frankston, on the southern side of Melbourne. Her father found work as a butcher and there always seemed to be food on the table, even during the worst years of the Great Depression. Occasionally, there was a little spare money for special treats. The whole family would sometimes walk to the grocery shop on the corner and buy a large bag of honeycomb. 'And if they were in season, we would get peaches on a hot night and come home and have them with ice-cream,' Elaine recalled.

After living in three different rental houses in the one street, they fetched up in a place on top of a hill, opposite the railway line. It had a big garden, with a creeping vine growing over the fence and a side gate through to their landlords, the Rogerson family. Elaine had very fond memories of those years and their neighbours, particularly Mrs Rogerson. 'She had one arm and a hook for the other and she taught me to knit. She was like a second mother to us.'

By the age of six, Elaine was good enough at knitting to make her own school jumper, navy blue with a thin light blue stripe around the bottom—a feat that staggered the man selling Griffiths tea when he came to call on his rounds one day and was invited to inspect it. She proved to be good at remembering numbers, too, after a gifted teacher at the school put her class through a daily exercise in which he would write five rows of five numbers on the blackboard, then rub them out and ask the students to write them down unaided. And she loved to dance. She and Reay were both sent to the Vesper School of Dancing, which ran lessons every Saturday in the Frankston Mechanics Hall. Elaine learnt highland and tap dancing, becoming so proficient that, at age ten, she was chosen to lead the opening number at the school's annual revue.

Elaine was in grade four at the Frankston State School when she caught diphtheria from a boy who sat next to her in class. The disease was extremely contagious and rife in parts of Melbourne, where whole schools were shut down at that time in an attempt to stem the spread. Called in at night because she was delirious with a soaring temperature, the family doctor recognised the symptoms and sent immediately for an ambulance which carried her away to the Fairfield Infectious Diseases Hospital. Within days, Elaine was joined by Vida, Reay and youngest brother John, despite her mother's attempt to disinfect the house by sealing cracks around the doors with newspaper and burning sulphur.

The rest of the family recovered within a few weeks, but Elaine was kept at Fairfield for three months and two days. The fact that she remembers the amount of time so precisely is telling. Her experiences through the illness remained among the most distressing of her long life. Perched above the Yarra River at Fairfield, the hospital was opened in 1904 to treat patients with potentially deadly ailments such as typhoid, cholera, smallpox and poliomyelitis that killed thousands before vaccines were developed. Elaine was put upstairs in Ward 2. From there she could see another ward downstairs full of even sicker children. 'At night time we could look down on this from the balcony where our beds were and see them wheeling the little kids that died out to the morgue. Often two and three a night, wheeled out covered in sheets.'

Elaine had never been away from home before and she missed her family terribly. Once Vida was discharged, she was only permitted to make one visit and they were not allowed to hug, or even touch. Elaine was kept behind a wire cage, with her mother standing no closer than a few metres. No doubt such draconian measures were considered necessary and the hospital may well have been applying the best practices of the day to help their patients get better and reduce the risk of infection, but it was a traumatic experience for the young girl.

If a child at the hospital was discovered to have lice or fleas, everyone in the ward was completely submerged in a phenyl bath. And if a child wet the bed, one of the nightshift nurses thought the best deterrent was to smack them hard on the bottom with an open hand. Elaine had kidney problems before the diphtheria and was unfortunate enough to have this happen more than once.

The invalid diet they had to eat was pretty terrible, too. 'Our food came on a trolley and was usually a gluey mass by the time we got it,' Elaine said. 'We had tripe for lunch every day, and then rice or sago for dessert, and for tea we had milk and bread at three o'clock and then nothing else before we went to sleep. The doctor would come and swab our nose and throat every day [to check if patients were clear of infection], and we would be given two pieces of fruit after that, which was the highlight of our day.'

Elaine was not given a clean bill of health until the doctors removed her tonsils, and the swabs cleared.

She was about eleven when her father became seriously sick, too. He contracted double pneumonia and pleurisy, so the doctor suggested he should move to a drier climate and give his lungs a chance to recover. The Schwennesens settled on the tiny dairy farming community of Leitchville, not far from the River Murray, between Kerang and Echuca.

They took on a local bakery business and moved into a house with a small shop at the front, on the road leading to the railway station. Bruce baked bread at a separate premises off the main street, in an enormous Small and Shattell oven that still stands today, an historic curiosity in the centre of a new bakery. He delivered the bread by horse and cart to neighbouring areas, while Vida made the smallgoods at home. 'Mum would cook things like cinnamon slices, Napoleon cake, lamingtons and all sorts of other cakes. She would cook these in a wood stove in our kitchen and the whole table would be covered,' Elaine recalled.

The school at Leitchville only went as far as year seven, so to finish her education Elaine was sent to Bendigo, where she boarded with her mother's parents, the Marriotts. During the week she attended the Bendigo Girls' School, as it was known then. The first school of its kind in Victoria, it was set up in 1916 to teach the domestic arts to teenage girls as part of their formal secondary education. When Elaine went there in the late 1930s, it was very much about turning out the 'perfect housewife'—someone who could keep a spotless house efficiently and economically, sew and mend clothes, and cook tasty meals for her husband and children.

As part of the curriculum, she was taught strict rules for everything from dusting and polishing to hanging clothes out to dry, and the preferred order in which to iron the components of a man's shirt—shoulders first, then the back, then the sleeves, the front panels and finally the collar and cuffs. The campus also had its own small cottage so the students could practise their housekeeping skills. Elaine applied these lessons every day during her married life, and did her best to pass them on to her daughters, too. At least once a week, the students would plan and cook a three-course meal which was served to the general public in the school's purpose-built dining room. Recipes more often than not came from the Presbyterian Women's Missionary Union Cookbook, which remains a much-loved bible in many Victorian households more than a hundred years after it was first published.

Elaine seemed to enjoy her time at the school, but she was only part way through her secondary education when Grandpa Marriott died, in odd circumstances. 'One night I tried to say goodnight to him as usual, but said "goodbye" instead, even when I tried again,' she explained. He was late getting up the next morning so Elaine was sent to wake him. She found him dead in his bed. The discovery upset her so much that she panicked and ran down the street in her nightie to an aunt who lived nearby. After the funeral Elaine boarded with other relatives, who shared their house with her dreaded Grandpa Schwennesen and his wife.

While Elaine was finishing her education, the family moved back to Melbourne where her father bought a delicatessen at Glen Iris. Elaine worked with him for a while after returning from Bendigo, but when World War II broke out she found a job using her mathematical skills as a book-keeper for one of Melbourne's best-known menswear businesses, Fred Hesse Pty Ltd. Named after its owner, by then the business had three stores in the city, offering both bespoke tailoring and ready-to-wear clothing marketed with the catchy slogan, 'Be thrifty and dressy, be clothed by Fred Hesse' (pronounced

Hess-ie). During the war the company also became military tailors, making uniforms for officers.

Elaine worked in the main office, at the Elizabeth Street premises, under the steely eye of Miss Jenkins, who later also employed Reay. A formidable woman who kept a close eye on her staff, Miss Jenkins insisted on immaculate book-keeping. Elaine was given an adding machine, and she had to account for every single penny. On at least one occasion that put her in a very awkward position. 'There were a lot of nice blokes that worked there, and I had to dob one chap in. He was part of the gang and we all used to go out together, but one day he didn't send up the money for a military hat that he sold, and I had to report him.'

Some customers had accounts but the majority of business was cash sales. Payments would be delivered immediately to the office upstairs via a wire pulley system. Staff working at the cash desk on the sales floor would place the money into a small metal canister attached to the wire, and then send it up to the main office by pulling a cord. Elaine sometimes relieved the staff on the cash desk on the shop floor, and she was also given responsibility for carrying the day's takings to the bank in a small case.

She enjoyed the work and the social life that went with it. Every Monday, Friday and Saturday night, a group of employees would go dancing. There were plenty of choices given it was wartime and social dances were popular with the thousands of American and Australian troops in transit through Melbourne or visiting on leave.

On Monday nights 'the gang' would usually head to the Earls Court Ballroom in St Kilda where their employer sponsored a variety program with singers accompanied by dance bands, broadcast live on Melbourne radio. Afterwards, they would have supper together somewhere in Acland Street. There would be more dancing on Friday night, usually at St Kilda, and then on Saturday nights the girls would 'dress up to the nines' and head to somewhere like the Caulfield Town Hall where there were regular cabaret balls.

Elaine was a good dancer and never short of partners. She even learnt the latest American craze, the jitterbug, with its twists and spins and tosses, that in its most exciting moments saw her flying through the air and rolling over her partner's head. After meeting Lyall at Luna Park, Elaine didn't go dancing quite so often. He wasn't that keen on dancing but he loved going to the cinema so he often took her to the pictures when he could get leave.

Within weeks of their meeting, Lyall was called home to work on the family farm. Labour was in short supply and his parents and only brother, Ross, weren't coping without him. Lyall loved being in the RAAF, the camaraderie, the lifelong friendships he made, his work as an aircraft engineer, even the food and the routine. In between training in Melbourne, he was based at the flying training school at Mallala, north of Adelaide, maintaining Avro Ansons for the learner air crews, and he was just about to be promoted. But farming was considered an essential service for the war effort, so the RAAF discharged him and, reluctantly, he headed home.

Shortly afterwards Elaine paid her first visit to the farm, accompanied by her fourteen-year-old brother, John, as an unlikely chaperone. They boarded a train at Spencer Street Station and travelled as far as Hamilton in western Victoria, where they caught a bus to Mount Gambier, about 140 kilometres further on, just over the South Australian border. Now the state's largest regional city, Mount Gambier at that time was a small country town of only a few thousand people, surrounded by farmland. Most farmers ran dairy cows, which thrived in the cool climate. A high rainfall and rich soils produced plenty of pastures, which the cows happily converted into plenty of milk.

Milking cows was part of the Harfull farm enterprise, too, along with growing oats and breeding working horses. The farm was in the rural district of Mil Lel, about eight kilometres to the north of the town, where Lyall's grandfather took up a small parcel of land in the mid 1860s. A shipwright's sawyer who worked in the naval dockyards at Portsmouth in England, John migrated to South Australia with his pregnant wife and their young daughter in 1853. He headed south to Mount Gambier sometime in the late 1850s, not long after the township was officially proclaimed, and set up a carrying business. Using horses and a wagon, he moved produce and supplies between local stations and ports along the coast, as far east as Portland and west as Robe.

The farm was bought with money earnt from the business and saved under the judicious eye of his wife, Marina, who also applied her skills as a midwife in between raising nine of her own children. Meanwhile, John's expertise with a saw and adze stood him in good stead when it came to putting up post and rail fences, building a house and clearing the land, which was heavily forested with eucalypts and blackwoods, and ferns almost as tall as a man on horseback. Lyall's father, William, who was born on the farm in 1868, loved telling the pioneering stories of those days and so did his son. Elaine soon became familiar with them, too.

Apart from meeting Lyall's family, during that first visit Elaine also had the chance to experience something that was very much a focal point of the Harfulls' lives. The house was always filled with music. His mother, Amy, was a gifted amateur pianist and vocalist who performed at local concerts, both as a soloist and accompanying other singers. She also played the organ for services at the local Presbyterian and Anglican churches. Ross followed in her footsteps when he was quite young, and Lyall took up the button accordion, playing his first gig at the age of eleven when the musicians booked for a school dance failed to turn up. He and Ross became well known all over the district for providing the music at old-time dances, and when the war started they were part of a concert party that travelled across the region raising money for the Red Cross.

Well before the days of television, and even after it, sitting down in the evening with family and friends to play music was a favourite pastime for all the family. A few days after Elaine and her brother arrived, the Harfulls entertained their likewise musical friends, the Fletts. A few days after that there was another musical evening, this time with the Chambers family from the farm across the road. Everyone who could played and there was no doubt a pause at some stage for a fine supper of home-baked treats served with plenty of tea.

After ten days, Elaine and John returned to Melbourne. The visit obviously went well because the following Easter, less than a year after they met, Elaine and Lyall became engaged. Before making it official, they travelled to Bendigo so the prospective groom could meet Elaine's extended family. Her Grandmother Schwennesen approved. 'I never thought you would have the brains to marry anyone like him,' she told Elaine, forthrightly.

Lyall and Elaine were married a year later on a showery day in April 1946, in the Presbyterian Church at Elwood. It was close to the bride's family home and it also happened to be under the jurisdiction of a minister who had recently served the Mount Gambier community. Her sister Reay and friend Ivy were bridesmaids, and her oldest brother, Bruce, was groomsman. Lyall's best man was his cousin John Thomson, resplendent in his RAAF pilot officer's uniform after returning safely from service in Europe. Ross played the organ, recording in the daily journal he kept most of his life that 'everything went very well'. Afterwards everyone gathered at a nearby hall for a simple evening meal of cold meat, savouries, cakes and trifle.

2

LIFE AT MIL LEL

The honeymoon that followed Lyall and Elaine's wedding might well have been the end of the marriage. It certainly gave Elaine a taste of the adventures she could expect in the future with Lyall, who loved exploring out-of-the-way places on back country roads. For their honeymoon, he decided to take her on a caravanning trip to Gippsland. One overnight stop was the old goldmining town of Walhalla, in a deep valley on the southern edge of the Victorian alps. The road in was narrow, winding and very steep, with precipitous drops. More than a few times Elaine was convinced they would end up at the bottom of one. When they finally pulled in to the virtual ghost town, the few remaining inhabitants turned out to stare in wonder. They were the first people anyone could recall who were brave, or foolish, enough to tow a caravan into Walhalla.

On another night they pulled up in a forest. Lyall climbed out of the car and started looking around. When Elaine asked him why, he told her he was just checking which way the trees might fall if the wind picked up. Startled at this hidden danger, the city girl tried not to feel too nervous about the prospect of being squashed while she lay asleep in her bed, and must have been wondering why they were not staying at a genteel hotel. Then the kerosene stove in their little caravan broke down.

The next morning a local timber feller came to the rescue and cooked them a hearty breakfast of steak, eggs and chips.

After a fortnight or so, surprisingly unscathed, the newly-weds headed back to Mil Lel and the start of Elaine's life as a farmer's wife. They arrived in time for tea, in the middle of a thunderstorm and heavy rain. Two days later they were officially welcomed by the district at a special social and dance held at the Mil Lel Primary School; there was no hall in those days so the school often served as the community gathering point. During the evening there were supper and speeches, and the young couple were presented with an elegant oak pedestal.

Lyall didn't have much opportunity to dance with his wife that night, even though the party continued until the small hours, because he was part of the band providing the music. She didn't mind too much, which is just as well given the pattern repeated itself at many other dances over the years. But that doesn't mean she didn't dance; there was always plenty of other willing partners.

During those first few days on the farm, Elaine also survived what was known as a tin-kettling. About forty people showed up on a Tuesday night to observe this nerve-wracking tradition, which was still very much alive in rural communities like Mil Lel in the 1940s. It involved friends and neighbours welcoming newlyweds to the district by showing up at their home and banging together pots, pans and any other metal objects they could lay their hands on.

Officially, the couple had no warning. People would wait until they were nicely settled for the evening, sneak up to the house and then make as much noise as possible. Unofficially, they often had at least some idea it was going to happen so they could make sure there was food and drink on hand to share with the revellers afterwards. Only the year before, during Elaine's first visit, there had been another tin-kettling in the district which apparently got a little out of hand. A wagon was overturned, a horse let loose, and a man was spotted dressed up in some of the new wife's clothes!

Lyall and Elaine's new home was an old farmhouse, which Lyall inherited from his Uncle Jack when he was only fifteen, along with half of the original family farm. A bachelor who bred horses and was a keen member of the local hunt club, Jack named the property Oakbank Farm, after the home of the famous Great Eastern Steeplechase in the Adelaide Hills. The land was always run as an integral part of his brother William's share on the other side of the block, but Jack built his own house and moved there after William and Amy married in 1910. He later returned to the home farm to be cared for by them in his old age, and his house was rented out.

Solidly constructed of local limestone, it had a verandah across the front and a central passageway leading from the front door, with two rooms on either side. All the rooms had high ceilings, fireplaces and dark timber architraves and doors, which seemed to suck out the light despite generous sash windows. There was a small porch at the back, and the toilet was in the garden.

In between the oat harvest, threshing grain and their frequent gigs as musicians, the Harfulls worked hard to spruce up the house as much as possible before the wedding. Lyall and Ross bought some chairs, a hall stand and a double bed at an auction. They fixed the kitchen chimney and painted the master bedroom with kalsomine, a lime-based wash that came as a powder and was then mixed with water. Then, while the newlyweds were on their honeymoon, Amy and Ross finished setting it up, buying a new kapok mattress and blankets for the bed.

Lyall and Elaine had been resident for about a fortnight by the time the kitchen was painted and a tap had been installed to provide cold running water. That was the extent of the plumbing in the entire house. There was a bathroom and a laundry on the back porch, but it took almost a year before the pipes for cold water were laid there, too. However, Ross helped Lyall fit out the laundry with a new set of concrete wash troughs, purchased for £3 and 5 shillings, and a copper for washing clothes in hot water. Hot water for the kitchen and bathing was heated in a square copper urn that sat on top of an old Metters wood stove in the kitchen. The urn had handles on either side so it could be carried to the bathroom and emptied into the bath.

Mains power was not connected to the farm until 1961. In fact, for the first four years there was no electricity of any sort. Kerosene lamps lit the house, and there was no way to chill food. Elaine and Lyall's oldest child, Roger, was three and his sister, Valerie, about eighteen months old when the first electric light was fitted in 1950, powered by a 12-volt generator set up across the yard in the dairy. Cables fed the supply to two large batteries stored on the back porch.

Elaine had to wait another two years to get a washing machine; however, Lyall did lash out and buy her an Australian-made Silent Knight refrigerator for the princely sum of £71. The generator only ran for a few hours at night and wasn't capable of handling too much demand, so the fridge was kerosene powered, but at least it boasted a small deep-freeze section. Elaine celebrated by making ice-cream. In a rush of technological advances, a few months later the house finally got a telephone, which hung on a wall in the hall. It was a shared extension of the phone at Amy and William's house, but at least it was a phone. People from properties further out, who were not so lucky, would frequently drop in to use it.

These new luxuries were possible because Lyall took the step of setting up his own dairying enterprise. In the first year of marriage, he was given just £5 a month 'in lieu' of wages for his work on the farm, but that and his earnings from playing music were not enough to live on and improve the quality of life for his family now that they had two young children. So he built a cowshed about a hundred metres across the yard from the house, and in December 1949 started milking a herd of twenty cows, which was pretty typical for the time. The milk was put into ten-gallon metal cans and carted just across the road to the Mil Lel Cheese Factory.

Well known for producing high-quality mature cheddar, the factory was established in 1889 by John Innes and his remarkable sisters, Janet and Lizzie, to make cheese and butter. The women took over ownership of the business five years later, with Janet acting as manager. According to an obituary in the local newspaper, to hold the position she needed a certificate to operate the factory's steam boiler. Obtaining a certificate usually involved sitting an examination, however Janet was allowed to side-step this process because of her 'long experience', becoming the only woman in South Australia with such a qualification.

The Innes sisters stopped making cheese in the mid 1910s and the small weatherboard building sat idle until they eventually agreed to sell it to Jack Frost in 1925. A talented businessman and cheese-maker, who learnt the craft from his father, Jack walked away from a promising career managing a highly successful factory because he wanted to run his own enterprise. His decision caused an uproar at the time, with many people predicting he would regret it, but Jack turned the business into one of the most successful cheese-making operations in Australia.

After starting with only sixty gallons of milk a day, by the mid 1930s Frost had built a new state-of-the-art facility which was processing 1600 gallons a day, including milk from the Harfull farm. By the time Lyall became a supplier, Mil Lel mature cheddar was being exported overseas and winning major awards, and the factory was making 600 tonnes of cheese a year. In 1951, Jack sold the business to the Kraft

Walker Cheese Company Pty Ltd, a major national business best known as the makers of Vegemite. The purchase figure wasn't disclosed, but weeks before the sale the factory had been passed in at auction after bids went as high as £40,000.

The factory did more than provide an income for the Harfulls. It housed the district post office, and ran a well-stocked general store where Elaine could buy fresh bread and groceries, without having to tackle the rough gravel road into town. It also gave her some close neighbours, helping to reduce the sense of isolation after living in city streets for most of her life. The Frosts lived in an old weatherboard house next to their business, and Jack built two new houses directly opposite Lyall and Elaine for his sons. After they sold the factory to Kraft, the new manager, Gordon Judd, moved in with his wife, Jill, and their six children. They became lifelong friends.

It all added to the vibrant social life of the small community, where there seemed to be a dance every week, and a host of activities centred around the school and various sports clubs, on top of the busy round of private parties and family gatherings. Then there was the annual show to look forward to in October, where Elaine was soon roped in to help on the sweet stall, and the 'Christmas tree night' in December which marked the end of the school year, with musical performances, the presentation of school prizes, gifts for all the children and supper. Both traditions are still going strong seventy years on.

But despite the many social opportunities, there is no doubt the first years at Mil Lel were challenging for Elaine. No matter where she was, she felt like part of her was missing. She made at least one extended trip back to Melbourne every year to see her family, although Lyall could often only stay a few days because of his responsibilities on the farm. Sometimes he would drop her off at the bus stop in Mount Gambier, or he might drive as far as Warrnambool or Hamilton and put her on the train. She would cry during the trip at the prospect of being away from him. Then she cried again when she left her parents, because she hated parting from them, too, especially her mother who had been diagnosed with diabetes which was starting to affect her eyesight. She would eventually go completely blind.

Elaine's family did their best to compensate by frequently coming to stay on the farm. Sometimes they came for extended visits, and on other occasions they took the luxurious option of flying in for the weekend on one of Ansett Airways' new Douglas DC-3s. After boarding at Essendon aerodrome, they would settle into its blue leather seats and, providing the flight was not too rough, enjoy the novelty of a meal served by an air hostess. The Harfulls would be waiting at the other end to collect them. Not far from the farm, the Mount Gambier aerodrome was the base for a RAAF air observers' school during the war and had excellent facilities compared with many other country towns.

During those first few years there seemed to be hardly any time at all when the Harfulls were not either on a trip to Melbourne or juggling visitors from the city. If it wasn't family, including various cousins, uncles and aunts, it was Lyall's mates from the air force. Elaine's youngest brother, John, often spent most of the summer on the farm, establishing a pattern that would be repeated by his children and all the other city cousins for the next thirty years or more.

Then came the remarkable day when Elaine discovered a childhood friend from Melbourne was living in the Mount Gambier area, too.

3

FOR THE LOVE OF GRACE

Elaine and Grace Bissett came to know each other in Sunday school. Grace can't quite remember their age at the time, but they were old enough to have started taking an interest in boys. 'They used to have a fete at the church every year, and one of the things they did was sell postcards to us kids, and we would write on them and address them to a boy, and someone would deliver it,' Grace says. 'Elaine was keen on a boy called Gordon and I was keen on his younger brother. That was one of the last things I talked to Elaine about. I couldn't remember Gordon's name, but she remembered it straight away.'

Grace grew up in the Melbourne suburb of Glen Iris where Elaine's father ran a delicatessen for a short while. After the war started, they would sometimes catch up briefly in the city during their lunch hours. By then Elaine was working at Fred Hesse's. As soon as she reached the age of eighteen, Grace enlisted in the Women's Auxiliary Australian Airforce (WAAF). She spent the next three years at the Victoria Barracks on St Kilda Road working as an office clerk, and would often go into the city during her lunch hour. 'I would sometimes run into Elaine down near the GPO. We were both stressed for time because I had to be at the Barracks and she had to be at work, so we couldn't talk for long,' Grace recalls.

Then the two friends lost track of each other. Unbeknown to Elaine, Grace married the son of farmers just a few kilometres up the road from the Harfulls. Ray Gilmore was also in the RAAF. He was a flying officer and the wireless operator in a Liberator bomber crew when Grace met him. The second pilot, Ron, was going out with one of Grace's best friends, Bonnie, who kept saying to her, 'You must meet Ray. I think you'd like him.'

Bonnie and Ron were engaged before Grace finally met the mysterious Ray. When she first spotted him standing in the doorway of a shop with Ron, waiting for the girls to hop off a tram, she wasn't impressed. 'He was an officer, and I had no time for officers. I was only a corporal and they used to take it out on you.'

Turning to Bonnie, she said, 'You never told me he was an officer.'

'Well, it's too late now, he's seen you,' her friend replied.

The party of four headed off for dinner together, and that was that. Grace and Ray announced their engagement in March 1945 and married two months later, while the rest of Melbourne was celebrating Victory in Europe Day, following Germany's unconditional surrender.

It was the following year before Grace and Ray were both discharged from the services and headed for Mount Gambier. They moved to Kongorong, south-west of the town, where relatives of Ray's managed the store. They were meant to be moving into a small farmhouse, but the tenants in residence had refused to move out. 'So we lived in one room in the store,' Grace says. 'Uncle Alb offered Ray five dollars a week and keep if he would work for him and drive his truck up to the Mount every day.'

Meanwhile, Ray's parents built a new house on their farm at Attamurra, a few kilometres north-east of the town and only about six kilometres from the Harfulls. When it was finished enough to be habitable, they offered their son the old home—a small cottage made of corrugated iron. 'The kitchen was the dining room, too. Then there was the lounge, and off that was our bedroom, which was a fairly big room, and the other room was the boys' bedroom. There was a lean-to verandah out the back and a wash house, with a copper in it. I think it even had a dirt floor. I had two big galvanised tubs that were my wash troughs. The toilet was down the yard. The house was on top of the hill and you had to go well down the hill to get to it.'

There was no plumbing or electricity at all in the house. Water was carried in from a tank outside, and the dishes were washed in big bowl on the kitchen table. On bath night, a portable tub was set up on the kitchen floor and filled with water heated in the wash-house copper. Lighting came from kerosene lamps until Ray bought a small engine and set it up in a nearby shed to produce 12-volt power. 'When you heard it going putt putt putt, everyone made for bed because it was running out of fuel and the lights were about to go out.'

Grace was living at Attamurra when, according to Elaine, they bumped into each other in the main street of Mount Gambier. Seventy years on, Grace struggles to recall the details, but she remembers that Elaine was pregnant at the time with her first child, Roger, who was born in August 1947. Her own first child, Trevor, born in December 1946, was only a few months old.

Once the women reconnected, the two families spent a great deal of time together. By then, Ray had bought his younger brother's truck and was earning a living by collecting milk from farms seven days a week, and delivering it to cheese factories at Yahl and OB Flat as well as Mil Lel. In those days, most districts had their own dairy factories so milk didn't have to be carted far, given it was stored in tin-plated cans and there was no refrigeration. Ray would finish his rounds and then, quite often, he would go and help Lyall with the milking.

While the two men worked in the dairy, Elaine and Grace caught up at the house. After they had been fed, the children were put to bed. By then the Gilmores had three sons, who were tucked into the Harfulls' double bed so the adults could enjoy their own meal without interruption. Then the Gilmores would return the favour, with the Harfulls going to their place. Sometimes they would play cards but mostly they just shared meals and talked. The evenings would never end too late, because everyone had to be up early in the morning.

These informal gatherings became far less frequent in the late 1950s when the Gilmores were awarded a soldier-settler's block about forty kilometres away at Eight Mile Creek. Situated on the coast near Port MacDonnell, the Eight Mile Creek Soldier Settlement Area covered thousands of hectares of mostly peat swampland. Urged on by the local council, the state government believed it was possible to turn what was essentially 'hopeless' ground covered with impenetrable ti-tree scrub into rich pasture country.

Apart from the scrub, there was another major obstacle—water, and lots of it. Much of the area was inundated most of the year, if not permanently. Prospects lifted in the late 1930s when the regional drainage authority set to work building a network of drains to carry the water out to sea. Inspecting progress in 1947, the South Australian Minister of Lands described it as a revolutionary program, and 'the greatest reclamation and land development work of its kind yet undertaken in Australia'. By 1949 the main drains were in place and an estimated 450 million litres of water was flowing through them every day. It wasn't enough. The land was still very wet in winter and spring, and not easy to coax into production, especially for servicemen with limited farming experience.

One of thirty-two blocks created with the modest ambition of carrying sixty cows each, the Gilmores' farm became available because its original occupier couldn't make a go of it. Even for Ray, coming from a farming family, it was challenging, despite claims by the government that there was no problem that 'hard work and less complaints' wouldn't overcome. Grace remembers struggling to find clumps of dry ground to stand on while they were feeding hay out to the cows in winter. The water lying in the paddock was so deep it ran over the top of her rubber boots.

Clearing the land and keeping it free of cutting grass proved a nightmare. Even with caterpillar tracks instead of wheels, tractors frequently became bogged and local roads were often impassable. In winter and spring, a tractor had to be used to drag the school bus to its destination. A 1953 newspaper carried reports that the children were being jolted so badly during this exercise that it 'affected them physically and mentally'. Normal methods to improve roads were clearly not working, so it was time for 'extraordinary measures', the school insisted.

On the plus side, the new inhabitants at Eight Mile Creek moved onto properties with brand new stone houses, unlike soldier-settlers further west around Allendale and Mount Schank who initially had to make do with RAAF huts relocated from the Mount Gambier aerodrome. However, none of the settlers had access to mains power. Grace had a twelve-volt washing machine which was powered by their car. 'I had to start the car to run it,' she says. Eventually Ray installed a 32-volt generator in the dairy, which they hooked up to the house, and things improved considerably.

Very much hands-on with the milking and caring for the herd, Grace spent most of her time outdoors working alongside Ray because their children, Trevor, Norman and Byron, were all at school. Things changed when the twins, Sharon and

Lincoln, arrived in 1959, but Grace was still responsible for the farm books and would work outside whenever she could.

Despite the rain and the howling southerly gales blowing straight from Antarctica across a flat landscape devoid of trees, Grace loved the life. 'It was hard work, but it never worried me because when I was growing up I always said that I would like to live in the country. In those days I imagined a beautiful home and beautiful big trees around me. I don't think I ever imagined a dairy farm or anything like that, but I adjusted quite well. I enjoyed it. The only thing I didn't like was leaving my mother, who was alone. That was the only thing I regretted.'

That situation resolved itself in 1964 when Mrs Bissett came to live with her daughter, who cared for her until she died in 1969. In later years, Grace and Ray were in the rare position for many farmers of being able to consider early retirement. Then eleven days after his sixtieth birthday, Ray had a massive stroke. Grace cared for him at home, too, and gradually over the next five years his speech and mobility improved to the point where they were able to do some of the travelling they had planned.

4

TILL DEATH US DO PART

Elaine never spent as much time in a dairy as Grace. In the first few years of married life, Lyall was milking the family herd alongside his brother, Ross, up at the home farm and her help wasn't needed. By the time Lyall set up on his own, Elaine had two young children to care for, so she concentrated on transforming the old farmhouse and applying the lessons learnt at the Bendigo Girls' School.

Like so many women in the 1950s, she felt enormous pressure to be the perfect wife and mother, living up to the images depicted in women's magazines of the day. The house had to be tidy and spotlessly clean. Tasty meals must be ready to go onto the table as soon as Lyall came inside from working out on the farm. An excellent seamstress, she spent hours smocking babies' clothes and sewing, making outfits for herself and all her children. She turned out everything from coats to ballgowns, including copying a black velvet dress by iconic London designer Mary Quant, right down to its crocheted white collar.

Determined to create a bright, modern home, Elaine oversaw the construction of a new bathroom, and a combined dining room and lounge, separated by a bench from the kitchen. She did most of the decorating on her own, including plastering the very high ceilings in the original part of the house. To reach them, she placed a chair on a table, and then a stool on top of the chair. Lyall came home one day to find her unconscious on the floor after falling from this precarious platform, the plaster dry in her hands.

Elaine also applied the skills from her years at Hesse's and took on the farm book-keeping. The amount of paperwork grew as the milking herd expanded, because individual records were kept for every cow, tracking the history of their mating and calves and their milk production. With her brilliant memory for numbers, she could recite unprompted the statistics for almost every cow, even when the herd reached close to one hundred.

She wasn't always quite so proficient when it came to preparing the paperwork at the end of the financial year. Mr Plate, the farm's tax agent, would always put off calling them until he received a final notice, warning they would end up in court if their annual tax return wasn't lodged within fourteen days. 'Mum would store every piece of paper in a pillowcase in a cupboard, and when she got the dreaded phone call from Mr Plate, out it would come,' Valerie recalls. 'She would sit at the table and all the stuff that was rubbish would be thrown on the floor, so there would be this growing pile, and then there would be these more orderly piles on the table.'

With the deadline looming, Elaine would repeat frantically, 'I'll just have to go to gaol, Lyall. I'll just have to go to gaol.' Valerie became a chartered accountant and rural financial counsellor helping people avoid this scenario, in part, she asserts only half jokingly, because of this childhood experience.

In summer, Elaine's focus switched to bringing in the harvest. Rich volcanic soils and reliable spring rainfall made the Mount Gambier area ideal country for growing oats, which the Harfulls fed to their working horses and dairy herd as either hay or chaff. After leaving school at the age of twelve, Lyall earned money with his own team of Clydesdales, ploughing land and sowing crops for farms around the district.

He kept at least one harness horse right up until the 1970s, just because he loved handling them—born in 1962, Elizabeth learnt how to harness a horse to a cart or gig before she learnt how to ride a bike.

Harvesting oats for hay was a labour-intensive business. Right up until 2005, the Harfulls used binders to cut the oats and bundle them into sheaves. The sheaves then had to be stooked into small teepee-like structures of twenty or so sheaves each. After a few weeks curing in the sun to develop the sugars in the stem and dry the hay out thoroughly, it was loaded onto a large flat dray, one sheaf at a time, using pitchforks to toss up each sheaf and place it carefully so the load would hold together on its way back to a yard near the house. Then it was unloaded one sheaf at a time and rebuilt into a haystack, shaped like a picturesque cottage in golden straw, with a pitched roof to deflect the rain. Building these stacks so they had tight, round corners to hold them firm and keep out the mice was an almost-forgotten art and Lyall was very good at it.

Elaine often helped with the stooking, taking the children with her. When they were not playing, they would sleep among the sheaves while she worked. Sometimes, she would operate the binder, which had a little iron seat perched at the back. From there she could reach a series of levers that set the height of the blades so they avoided small stones or rough patches, and the height of the wooden arms that swept the oats onto a canvas. She also had to keep an eye on the knotting mechanism that tied the string around each sheaf, making sure that it was tying them correctly and that the twine didn't run out. And most importantly, she had to operate the cradle that collected the sheaves, using foot levers to release it so they fell in neat lines across the paddock.

Elaine spent plenty of time in the kitchen, too, cooking to fuel the harvest workers with dozens of scones, sponge cakes, tomato and cheese sandwiches sprinkled with salt and white pepper, corned beef served with new season potatoes, and every week a roast, cooked in the wood oven which was kept going no matter the temperature outside. She was an excellent cook, and besides the workers, there was often a stock agent or the fuel delivery man or a neighbour, who just happened to arrive at the right time for afternoon tea. Farmers dropping off milk at the factory would often come by in the mornings knowing full well that she baked bread first thing every day. 'She would make two big, double high-top loaves, so four loaves when you pulled them apart, but the family would often end up with just one,' recalls Valerie.

In early autumn, once the harvest was over and the cows had stopped producing milk before the birth of their next calf, Lyall and Elaine would take the children on holidays. Lyall bought a caravan shell and fitted it out with a double bed, two bunk beds, a table and cupboards that he made himself. Then Elaine painted and decorated it with bright curtains and bed covers.

Sometimes they would head just over the border to Portland for the weekend, where Lyall would share memories of his own childhood summers spent in a boarding house near the foreshore, with his mother. Most years they wandered Victoria, dropping in to visit the Schwennesens in Melbourne and the Marriotts in Bendigo. Lyall often planned trips so he had an excuse to take in anything powered by steam—riverboats, railways and traction engines. More than a few days were lost tracking down old engines left behind in the bush where timber mills once stood. Elaine was not always happy about these lengthy diversions, which her husband sometimes snuck in despite her protests.

One year they decided to take the caravan as far as Sydney, pulled by a second-hand 1934 Plymouth that Lyall acquired in the early 1950s as the family car. It was one of Roger's favourite holidays, not because of the destination but because of the adventures along the way. 'Somehow we managed to get tangled up in a circus that was moving camp in a long line of vehicles, and then we found ourselves in the middle of the famous Australian Redex reliability road trial, with people lining the roads to see it pass through.' To Elaine's mortification and the children's endless amusement, someone shouted out, 'Come on, Mum. You'll win it yet!'

Then came a period that Elaine didn't talk about very much. In July 1958, she had been pregnant for about three months when she lost the baby. It was one of at least two miscarriages that darkened their hopes of expanding the family, until January 1962 when Elaine gave birth to Elizabeth. The following year Elaine was startled to find out she was pregnant again. Another daughter, Fiona, was born in June 1964.

The pattern of her days changed again in the mid 1970s, when she and Lyall decided it was time to give up milking cows. By then Roger was married to Anne and their first child had arrived. The small farm had another family to provide for, and the future of dairying was looking very bleak. Milk prices were poor and thousands of Australian dairy farmers had already walked away from the industry after markets collapsed when Britain decided to join the European Common Market in 1973.

Talking over the problem together, they decided the logical solution was to turn their hand to something the Harfulls had been doing for generations—growing oats and cutting chaff. There might only be a handful of working horses still in existence but the Lower South East was home to thousands of ponies, trotters and racehorses, and they all needed to be fed.

That autumn, Lyall and Roger spent days sowing more of the farm to oats so they would have enough hay to supply a modest number of customers. When summer came, they employed extra people to bring in the harvest, and Elaine found herself in charge of hiring labour. As trade built steadily, she also took on the job of serving the customers who came to the farm, and maintaining the books that tracked every sale. With Miss Jenkins's training holding firm after thirty years, she made sure they balanced right down to the last cent. She was still helping with the bookwork a few weeks before her death at the age of eighty-nine.

❖ ❖ ❖

It is cold—the kind of deep, damp, bone-chilling cold that people expect of winter in Mount Gambier. The sky is heavy and grey, the light dull and flat. Inside the hospital room the warmth of a decades-old friendship has shifted the season to long ago summers. Elaine is in hospital with pneumonia and the prognosis is not good, so Grace has come to say her goodbyes.

Elaine has barely spoken or even been conscious for a day or two, but she wakes when Grace gently calls her name and takes her hand. Her eyes light up in a way her family never thought to see again. 'I'm a bit of a mess, Grace,' she says, pushing the words out in short breaths. The two women start to talk, sharing treasured memories stretching back to their girlhoods in Melbourne, how they met, the boys they liked, their chance meetings during the war. Grace searches for names. More alert now than she has been in days, Elaine prompts her friend. She even finds the strength to laugh.

Roger, Valerie, Elizabeth and Fiona are in the room, and they are astonished. Grace's visit has been transformative. There is a sense of great privilege witnessing this unforgettable moment, the joy on their mother's face, and the power of the friendship between these two strong women who have led such parallel lives: city girls who found love in wartime and gave up their cosmopolitan ways to marry country boys. In between learning how to drive tractors, milk cows and do the farm bookwork, they made homes, raised families and cared for invalid husbands. Till death us do part, in sickness and in health, they both pledged, and they stuck true to the promise.

Elaine died in June 2014, outliving her husband by almost eight years. Lyall had died a few months after their sixtieth wedding anniversary and she never stopped missing him. Dreading the idea of having to move into aged care, she was luckier than most. She was fit enough to stay in the family home they created together, watched over by her children, grandchildren and great-grandchildren.

Most weeks she went into town to do a few errands and go to church, and on a regular basis she picked up the phone and had long chats with her friend Grace. In her younger days, they had been known to go on for as long as two hours, husbands and children and approaching meal-times forgotten until someone caught their attention and reminded them of the time. 'I miss that telephone call from Mil Lel,' Grace says.

Part II
LOVE IN A FOREIGN LAND

5

CHILD OF THE FOREST

Doris Turner had a reputation for remaining calm in a crisis. Having lived through two world wars and the Great Depression by the time she was in her early forties, she was usually quick to see the humour in any situation and rarely lost her temper, no matter how much her patience was tried by husband Ted and their eleven children. Her daughter Wendy cannot recall seeing her cry. The first sight of her new home in the Australian bush broke that resolve—at least for a moment.

It was the end of a stinking hot day in March 1949 when the Turner family arrived at the farm they had purchased sight-unseen, from the other side of the world. Doris was in the front seat of the truck, nursing her eighteen-month-old baby daughter, Mavis. Her husband, Ted, was on the back with the rest of the children. Hot, tired and bedraggled, they perched on bales of hay as the truck rattled over the last ten corrugated kilometres of gravel road. The vehicle's wooden tray had been hosed down in an unsuccessful attempt to get rid of the smell of pig manure, but that didn't worry them so much. The Turners were used to farm animals. The heat was another thing, and the flies, and the all-pervading dust that had settled over their Sunday-best clothes, donned so they would look their finest for such a momentous occasion.

The Turners had left the immigrant camp at Point Walter in Perth early that morning, excited to be on the final leg of their journey. A slow train took them south to Bunbury, where they climbed onto a bus for the next 130 kilometres to Manjimup. The trip seemed to take forever as the bus rattled over gravel roads, stopping occasionally in the middle of nowhere to drop off bags of mail. There was no cooling system, and everyone sighed with relief when they were allowed to get off in Bridgetown for refreshments.

As the bus passed through established orchards near the town, the children spotted apples trees, branches heavy with bright red fruit waiting to be picked. Closer to Manjimup, farms were still being carved from the bush. To the Turners' English eyes, the landscape was bleached of colour. Turning into the driveway of their new home, they passed ghostly stands of dead eucalypts, ring-barked but not yet cleared, and pasture bled white-gold by the sun. There was no sign of life, until the ground shifted in a tawny blur as hundreds of startled rabbits ducked for cover.

Hardly able to take it all in, eleven-year-old Wendy and her siblings looked up the rise to a small weatherboard building just below the brow of the hill. 'There's the shed, but where's the house?' one of the girls asked. Then the truth dawned.

❖ ❖ ❖

Early April and it's show time in Kalamunda, a picturesque town in the Perth Hills. Wendy Turner, now Bonini, is standing in the kitchen that serves the historic red-bricked agricultural hall, making cups of tea and doling out homemade cake and sandwiches. Now in her late seventies, she has been on her feet for days. Not only is Wendy a keen participant in the traditional amateur competitions that have been held in the hall for more than a century, she is a member of the Kalamunda and Districts Agricultural Society committee that stages them. Apart from attending all the planning meetings, she has been on hand for the past three days to help feed volunteers as they convert Kostera Oval into a showground, set up the hall and its exhibits, and coordinate the judging process for hundreds of items. It's a mammoth task for the small committee that involves working as late as midnight to make sure everything is ready. On top of that Wendy has spent hours preparing her own entries, baking and preserving, and organising pot plants and flower arrangements for the competitive classes.

Wendy was drawn into this world by her daughter, Giuliana, who has been the society's president for seven years. Married to a local orchardist and a more than competent cook, Giuliana often wandered into the hall as a spectator to check out the traditional displays of cookery, handicraft, plants and produce that remain a highlight of most country shows. Every year she noticed the same names on the prize cards in the baking and preserves classes, and decided to see if she could add her own to the collection. Wendy thought it was a great idea and entered something, too. They both went home with prizes for their first attempts, and like generations of men, women and children before them, they became hooked on the experience. Since then Giuliana's daughter, Kiara, has also joined their ranks.

The Kalamunda show may be smaller than its iconic city cousin, the Perth Royal, but it's the premier event for the local shire and people turn out in their thousands every year. Patrons start pouring in through the main gates as soon as they open on Friday evening. Many of them return the following day for the full program, which always ends with a spectacular fireworks display. Despite temperatures climbing to almost 40 degrees, by mid morning on the Saturday the crowd is starting to swell and the hall is busy.

In the secretary's office just off the main auditorium, Pam Edwards is fielding last-minute queries and coordinating the giant task of typing up the results and calculating prize money. The stakes aren't huge—the majority of classes offer only two or three dollars as first prize, but competitors tend to enter more than one class so working out how much they are due in total is a big job in itself. No-one wants to be show secretary—myriad tasks stretch over many months, and how well they are done can make or break an event. But Pam is an old hand, and things are going smoothly so far. Across the passageway, the kitchen is cool and quiet, too. Most of the volunteers are yet to come in, so Wendy takes a moment to sit down and reflect on her family and the place where she grew up.

Wendy's story is deeply rooted a long way from here, in the ancient woodlands, bogs, heaths and commons of the New Forest. Covering a vast area in southern England, this area of extraordinary natural beauty was given its name almost a thousand years ago when it was designated a royal hunting ground by William the Conqueror. Renowned for its wildlife and free-roaming ponies, much of the New Forest is still protected as a national park which draws millions of visitors every year.

Wendy's family on her mother's side comes from Brockenhurst, one of the larger villages, where it's still not unusual to see ponies and donkeys wandering up the high street. Her mother, Doris, was an Anstey. The Ansteys have been associated with the village since the Middle Ages when, according to family lore, one of them was given a patch of land by a local lord of the manor as reward for saving his life during the Crusades.

The earliest descendant that Wendy remembers personally is her grandfather, Charlie. His father worked as a signalman on the railway but with a reputation for being good at handling horses, Charlie chose a different path. By the time he was twenty-one he was employed as a coachman at Langdown Lodge, a modest country house at Dibden, on the eastern edge of the New Forest. Working as a housemaid in the same establishment was a Dorset lass, Jeanetta Davis.

Charlie and Jeanetta soon married and found work together about twenty-five kilometres away, in the picturesque village of Sway at a private residence called Arnewood Towers. A country house with forty or so rooms, it was well known for the remarkable architectural curiosity that stood in its grounds. Sway Tower was built by Andrew Thomas Turton Peterson, a barrister who made his fortune practising law in India before retiring to England in the 1870s. A keen amateur architect, he was obsessed by two things—the little appreciated potential to create buildings out of concrete, and spiritualism, the then-fashionable idea that you could communicate with the dead.

The two worlds collided in 1879 when Peterson laid the foundations for an elegantly slender 66-metre tower made almost entirely out of Portland cement. Working through a medium, he claims to have been guided by the spirit of long-dead English architect Sir Christopher Wren, the genius behind St Paul's Cathedral in London. Peterson devoted seven years of his life and a staggering £30,000 to proving the value of concrete by creating what was then the world's tallest non-reinforced concrete structure. The heritage-listed tower is revered today as a landmark building of its time and one of England's most unusual architectural follies.

Jeanetta and Charlie lived in the gatehouse, or lodge, that Peterson built at the entrance to his property. Jeanetta was the cook and housekeeper at the big house. When the owners were away in London, she and Charlie moved in to keep an eye on things. Meanwhile, they started a family. Their eldest daughter, Lillian, was born in 1902, followed by Doris (Wendy's mother) in 1903, and then several years later, a son, Jack, who only survived until the age of five, after contracting polio and then pneumonia. Another son, Alec, known as Sonny, came along in 1912.

When Doris was a child, Arnewood Towers was home to a young family, with two children similar in age to Doris and her sister. They had a nursemaid who would often take all four children out to play on the nearby common where some of the forest's famous ponies often grazed. One day when Doris was about four, the older girls decided it would be fun to run under the stomach of one of the horses. Doris followed, but ran between the pony's back legs instead, and the startled animal kicked her in the head. The injured little girl was taken to a nearby hospital, where they operated on her crushed skull and inserted a steel plate. It was still there, causing considerable medical interest, more than eighty years later when Doris was x-rayed in the Bunbury hospital south of Perth.

Family life was turned on its head with the coming of World War I. Although he was by then in his early forties, and married with a family, Charlie was called up as the casualty lists mounted to the millions and the military authorities became desperate for reinforcements. He became a dispatch rider in the British Army, serving on the Western Front where he carried messages between command posts and the troops on the front line.

Doris remembered with stark clarity the day when word arrived that her father was missing in action, believed dead. They were told that he was riding alongside another man when a shell exploded, tossing Charlie high into the air. The other man escaped with his life and reported what had happened. The news devastated Jeanetta, who wondered how on earth she was going to manage without him. She was no longer working at Arnewood Towers and she had two young daughters to raise.

But Charlie survived. He was pulled from the shell hole by his horse, which was standing above him with its reins dangling within reach when he regained consciousness. A group of soldiers found him and took him to a French hospital. He was not badly injured, but he had lost his memory. It took him about two weeks to work out who he was and then he returned to his unit. A most relieved Jeanetta received a second letter to say her husband had been found and was alive.

Recalling fondly the man she knew well as a child, Wendy says: 'He used to make me laugh with his stories. "You know, those French girls in the hospital never wore underwear, and here they were bending over scrubbing the floor. What a view!" he told me.'

As soon as she turned fourteen, Doris went into service at the manor house, like her mother before her. She was given responsibility round the clock for looking after a three-year-old girl and a brand new baby. Every morning she would bathe the infant, dress him and take him downstairs for a brief visit with his mother before returning to the nursery. Wendy saw for herself the level of care her mother would have given the child when she watched Doris bathe her own children.

'Mum always had a big white apron, always starched. She would put this on for bath time for the baby, and on the table would go the bath, and the water just right, and the cotton wool and the towel laid out. And we would sit there and watch while she washed the baby. She washed the head and rinsed it, and then she'd get the cotton wool and wipe the eyes, and then a little bit of cotton wool and do the ears and the nose, put some powder on its bottom, check it all over and then put its nappy on, and she always had them in long gowns until they were about four months old. Then the baby went into its cradle and was put into the bedroom.'

Wendy's father, Edward 'Ted' Turner, also came from the New Forest. Ted was born into a reasonably well-off family with market gardens at Bashley, not far from the banks of the Solent. Ted's father died from cancer when he was only eleven, and his mother soon married again. Her second husband apparently took control of his wife's inheritance and quickly spent it. 'It was the law in those days—the husband owned everything when you got married so you had no say in it. He took all the money and kicked all the boys out of the house before they even turned fourteen,' Wendy explains, the bitterness in her voice no doubt a reflection of something she heard in her father's tone when he recounted this period of his life. 'My dad said it was lovely being wealthy but dreadful being poor.'

In desperation, as soon as he turned fourteen in 1916, Ted signed up for a five-year stint in the famous Coldstream Guards, whose duties include keeping an eye on royal residences in the United Kingdom. Even though the regiment accepted such young recruits, they were not permitted to take part in active combat until they were eighteen so Ted was spared the horrors of the Western Front. By the time he was old enough for combat, the war was over. Instead, he got to stand on guard duty at the gates of Buckingham Palace, resplendent in scarlet jacket and a towering bearskin hat.

Ted found this a dubious honour. 'They weren't allowed to move. To go to the toilet, they had an oilskin bag strapped to their legs and they had to wee into it,' explains Wendy. There was one incident in particular that Ted never forgot. He was on duty, standing in the rain and cold, when two little Cockney boys came up. They looked up under his helmet and one of them said, 'You poor sod.' That was exactly how Ted felt. 'He hated the army—he couldn't get out quick enough,' Wendy says.

As soon as his five years were up, Ted returned to the New Forest. His stepfather wouldn't take him in so he found somewhere to board and made his own way, growing vegetables on a small area of land belonging to an uncle.

Ted met his future wife a few years later when he was recovering from appendicitis. She was friends with his sister Amy, who took Doris along to visit him in hospital. They had attended the same village school, but even though there was only a year's difference between them, neither recalled knowing the other. Wendy isn't certain, but she thinks they married within six months, as soon as her mother turned twenty-one. Doris's parents believed Ted wasn't good enough for their daughter and refused to attend the ceremony, but his family were there, with Amy acting as bridesmaid.

Even though the young married couple set up home only metres from the Ansteys, Doris was pleased to be away from Jeanetta who she found very controlling. After Doris married, she would walk the long way round to avoid her parents' house when she went to visit her girlfriend, knowing that her mother would be sitting in the upstairs window keeping an eye out. But times were very hard, with Ted and Doris taking in Amy as well as Ted's brothers because they had nowhere to live and no money. Wendy says it was typical of her parents, who were generous to a fault, especially when it came to family.

'Mum used to feed everyone, all the neighbours' kids . . . and Dad always put his children first. He was a market gardener and his brothers were market gardeners, and they used to come to dinner on a Sunday and Mum always cooked a roast. We would all be shelling peas to help Mum get ready. Uncle Arthur sat down for lunch one day and he says to my dad, "Here!" he says. "Ted," he says. "What's with feeding these kids all these peas? You could get one and six a pound for them at the market. Why waste them on your kids?" And my dad said, "My kids come first. I give them the best of anything I've got!" And that's why he never had anything.'

Things changed for the better in 1938 when the Turners moved into a brand new farmhouse on Wootton Farm Estate, on the edge of the tiny hamlet of Wootton, just up the road from the market town of New Milton. Their dramatic change in circumstances came about because of the generosity of a wealthy relative. One of Ted's aunties had promised his father when he was dying that she would make sure his children were looked after if she ever came into money. She made good the pledge when her husband died, leaving her a fortune from his earnings on the London Stock Exchange. She gave Ted and each of his four brothers the choice of buying either a farm or a hotel. All of them chose to buy land and earn their living as market gardeners.

Ted selected a four-hectare block on a new estate off Bashley Common Road, created by the recent subdivision of an old farm. With the money left over he built a fine house and fitted it out with 'all the mod cons'. The single-storey bungalow had red-brick walls, a tiled roof and large bay windows to let in plenty of light. There were four bedrooms, a large lounge, sitting room and kitchen with hot water, gas and electricity. The aunt even provided new furniture for the house and a bicycle for each of the children. By then there were six. Lorna, the eldest, was about twelve years old, followed by Iris, Doreen, Janet, Peter and then the baby, Elizabeth Edith Wendy Turner, always known as Wendy, who was eight months old. About three years after the move came John, then Faith and Richard, followed by Mavis, the last child born in England.

Wendy recounts with frequent gales of laughter what seems to have been a mostly idyllic childhood, despite tensions within the extended family, limited money and the impact of another war. Her earliest memory revolves around a very large cabbage. She was sitting in a royal blue pram being wheeled back from the market garden by Doreen and Janet. 'They got this big Savoy cabbage for Mum and they stuck it in front of me. I'm sitting up in this pram and all I could see is the green light coming through the cabbage leaves so I started eating the cabbage so I could see what was going on, and they all thought it was hilarious.'

Wendy and Peter, her elder brother by two years, formed an inseparable gang of three with John. They enjoyed enormous freedom, treating the New Forest as their own private backyard—an expansive adventure playground where they spent countless hours exploring the ancient woodland, heaths and bogs, building cubby houses and climbing trees, catching minnows in the rivers and streams, munching on nuts and berries harvested from the forest and hedgerows, and getting into the occasional scrape. 'We used to get up very early, have our breakfast and then go out and feed the rabbits, feed the chickens, feed the ducks, feed the geese, do all our jobs and then we had the rest of the day to do whatever. We had a wonderful time,' Wendy says.

Peter was always in charge. He was well liked by other children and a natural leader who easily convinced his younger siblings to go along with most of his schemes. 'He was a great organiser. He would say to me and John, "Now I want you to go and collect thistles for my rabbits, and I want you to collect the oats," and you did whatever he said.'

Wendy can really only remember one refusal—and that was when Peter suggested John give up his coat to protect three goats they were walking back to the farm. In a memoir he wrote many years later for his family, John recalled: 'We got the goats but on the way home it started to get dark and the wind had come up along with driving rain. The wind was so strong it practically took my breath away . . . I thought, bugger the goats, so that was one time I didn't do what Peter asked.'

Entrepreneurial from a young age, Peter was constantly coming up with ideas to make money. One of them was breeding rabbits and pigeons to sell at a local farmers' market. Only about eight years old at the time, he would pack them into boxes and take them on the train. His customers were other children who didn't get to enjoy the birds for too long. They were homing pigeons and flew back to Peter, who would sell them again the next week.

Even the idea of confronting a German invasion of Britain didn't faze him. He had plans to lure the enemy into one of the treacherous bogs in the New Forest, where they would sink without a trace. And he scouted out a hiding place under an old bridge. 'There were two big sleepers, enough room for each of us to lay along,' says Wendy. 'Peter had one side and I had the other with John. And across the front was another sleeper that made a sort of shelf. We were going to store our food there.' After water rats ate their initial supplies, Peter confiscated his mum's biscuit tin. 'I reckon its probably still there today,' Wendy adds.

Pausing to think about her brother, who died in 1989 at the age of fifty-four, she confesses: 'If it wasn't for Peter, my childhood would have been very dull. He was older and he knew best but he always looked after me and didn't mind a girl tagging along. I used to climb trees, and do everything the boys did—swing on ropes, swing over ditches with leap-frog poles. And we used to make bows and arrows and spears.' Great training for Wendy, who at the age of thirteen became the South of England champion javelin thrower in school sports.

A favourite pastime for all the children was building dens, or cubby houses, using tools and ropes from their father's shed. Wendy remembers a major project one summer which involved all the neighbours' children. 'We spent all summer making this den in the forest, with sticks all around, tied together. We spent hours on it. Peter took Dad's good tin from the roof of his shed and put it across the top, and then we put clumps of soil on top of that. And then we heaped it up with bushes so it was camouflaged. We collected dead grass and bracken and all sorts of soft things to put on the floor. We worked and worked.'

There was plenty of fun when they were younger, too. Even with so many children to care for, Doris would regularly make time to play with them. One of Wendy's favourite memories is walking down to the woodland where there was a bank of earth. Doris would help them scoop out little shelves and then line them with moss to create a shop. The shelves would be stocked with beech nuts and acorns, and other bits and pieces scavenged from the forest floor, which the children would pretend were groceries such as sugar, ice-cream and even chocolate cakes. Then Doris would become the customer while the children served her, delighted with their salesmanship.

A special treat was spending a day in the forest with their father, instead of going to school. He would put some apples or swedes into a hessian sack so the children had a snack while they walked. 'Can you imagine telling a kid today that they would be eating a raw swede? Dad grew a lot of them, and they are quite sweet and they would last us all morning,' says Wendy. Carrying the youngest child on his shoulders, Ted would lead them to the river so they could catch minnows in jam jars and then let them go. They had butterfly nets and would try to trap different species for a collection pinned on boards at home. Like many children of the day, they collected birds' eggs, too, carefully putting a small hole in one end and blowing out the centres before storing them in a box padded with cotton wool. In the summer, Ted would show them where berries grew—the small blue-black fruit of the whortleberry, blackberries and sweet wild strawberries which grew in large patches along a nearby railway line. In winter, he taught them how to track deer and rabbits in the snow.

'Dad taught us everything about the forest. We knew all the animals, we knew all the birds, the butterflies and the fruits, and what we could and couldn't eat. We knew that we could eat the sorrel, and we would pick big purple clovers, pull the stems out and suck the ends because they were full of honey. And in our forest was a very old tumbledown woodman's cottage, and in the garden was a cherry tree. We used to climb up into the tree and eat cherries, then we used to fill up our shirts with them and walk home.'

Wendy was only three when war broke out. With the conflict stretching over six long years, as she grew older she became very aware of the changes it brought to her family and the place where she lived. Strategically well located on the south coast, at the height of the war the New Forest and immediate surrounding area had no fewer than twelve airfields and landing grounds, several key coastal defences, an experimental bombing range, and numerous sites favoured for military training exercises. In the lead-up to D-Day in June 1944, it was crowded with equipment and thousands of troops waiting to embark on the invasion of German-occupied France that would help determine the outcome of the war. Small village roads were widened to accommodate large military transports and areas were cleared for more camps, extra runways and even tank parking bays, which are still visible today.

The Turners lived not far from Holmsley aerodrome, an important base for British and American bombers. At night, the children would lie in their beds listening to the roar of the huge planes as they took off and flew low over the house with their deadly cargos bound for enemy territory. Then in the morning they would see the surviving aircraft straggle home, often visibly damaged. Sometimes the Germans returned the favour and sent bombers to destroy nearby military targets. No bombs landed close to the Turners' home, but John recalled seeing searchlights reaching out into the black night sky and hearing the anti-aircraft guns boom into action when enemy aircraft were captured in their beams. And Wendy clearly recalls seeing the sky light up as bombs fell on the port of Southampton about thirty kilometres away. 'We thought it was Guy Fawkes night,' she says.

In the evenings, the family gathered around the radio to hear the latest news and the stirring speeches of Prime Minister Winston Churchill. 'Even the baby didn't cry. Everything was silent for the news. We were all holding our breath, listening, because at one stage it looked like Germany was going to invade England completely,' says Wendy. After the news came the emotive propaganda of Lord Haw Haw, the pseudonym of a notorious English traitor who broadcast from Hamburg in an attempt to demoralise the British public. While most people laughed it off, Wendy was terrified by his promise that the Third Reich was about the cross the English Channel and invade Britain while she was asleep in her bed.

As the conflict dragged on, several members of the family became directly involved in the war effort. Lorna became a nurse with the Red Cross and Iris joined the Women's Land Army, set up to help overcome labour shortages on farms producing vital food supplies. Even though he worked in the market garden every day, most nights Ted cycled about ten kilometres to Lymington where he was a spotter at Wellworthy's engineering works, keeping a watchful eye out for German bombers. The factory was working at full capacity, churning out piston rings and other components for the British Air Ministry, so it was a likely target.

Meanwhile, adding to the chaos of an expanding family were the number of serving men who frequently stayed with the Turners while on leave, camping on the lounge room floor. They included distant cousins from the United States and Canada, who were stationed nearby. At times the children had to bunk in together—two facing one way, and three the other in the one bed. For a month or so, Doris even took in two children evacuated from London's East End to escape the intensive bombing that decimated much of the city and killed thousands.

Food was scarce in Britain because of the difficulty getting supplies past enemy patrols and the rationing system introduced to make sure the populace didn't starve, but the Turners had a productive home vegetable garden, chickens, rabbits and their own house cow. Ted was not above supplementing the table with the odd deer or pheasant poached from the old royal hunting grounds, and every now and then there was some illicit pork.

Government authorities continually checked how many pigs farmers stocked because under wartime regulations every animal had to be sold direct to the Ministry of Food. But whenever a sow delivered piglets, Ted would hide one before the inspector came round. Once it had grown, the pig was taken to a neighbour's farm to be killed and smoked, and the meat was shared. One day the inspector came to the house and stood in the open door of the kitchen, chatting to a nervous Doris, little realising that half a pig was hanging on the other side. The story entered into family folklore, but it was a sign of the ever-expanding British bureaucracy that eventually pushed Ted into making a momentous decision.

6

THE NEW CHUMS

Ted Turner had contemplated emigrating to Australia since he was a young man. Now married with a large family, it wasn't just about seeking adventure. His landholding was small, money was always short, and he had his childrens' futures to consider. War, and all the rules and regulations that came with it, proved to be the tipping point.

As a farmer Ted found himself responsible to a new Ministry of Food and a county War Agricultural Executive Committee that told him how and what to farm. They even threatened to give his land to a neighbour when he found it difficult to increase production while working nights as a spotter. There were no signs the bureaucracy was decreasing after the war ended—if anything it seemed to be getting worse—so Ted submitted an application to Australia House in London.

One of the first obstacles he had to overcome to qualify for the Australian government's new emigration scheme, and assisted passage for his large family, was finding a sponsor or guarantor. Salvation appeared in the form of relatives who wanted to sell their dairy farm at Manjimup in Western Australia and retire. They would act as guarantors if Ted agreed to purchase their farm, house and livestock for the princely sum of £2000. For an additional £1000 they would even stay on and look after things until the Turners could get there.

Ted accepted the offer and sold the Wootton house and most of his land, only to discover it was going to take more time for the bureaucratic processes to run their course than he realised. The older girls moved in with Iris, who was living in a cottage some distance away, but Ted was desperate to find temporary accommodation for himself and Doris, and their six youngest children, so he called on mates at the Wootton Working Men's Club. In a single weekend, volunteers laid cement foundations and put up a Nissen hut on a small patch of land that Ted still owned. It was very basic but at least it was a roof over their heads. Privacy was limited, with curtains strung on lines the only partition between various living spaces, and the children all slept in the same bed. Their belongings had to be kept in cardboard boxes because there was no storage, and instead of the modern kitchen Doris was used to, there was a coke-fired stove in the middle of the hut to cook on and keep them warm.

The Monday after the working bee, officials from the local council turned up and told Ted to pull the hut down—he didn't have the required planning approvals. Over the coming weeks as Ted tried to straighten things out, five different officials showed up at various times just to check the foundations. Fortunately, his solicitor managed to hold the line for the year or so that it took for the Turners to be allocated tickets aboard one of the government ships heading to Australia. Ted spoke freely of his frustrations to a reporter from the local newspaper who wrote about the family shortly before they set sail. 'Only yesterday someone said it would be rather odd to go to Australia in order to get a house, but at least that is one way of doing it!' he is quoted as saying. 'At least I have the consolation of knowing that we shall be far away from building inspectors where we are going . . . We shall have room to spread our wings there.'

The article appeared with photos of the family taken outside the hut. Forty-six years of age and used to physical labour, Ted is leaning against the wall, blond head bare, cigarette dangling from the fingers of one hand while the other rests in a trouser pocket. He is looking straight at the camera, wearing a determined expression. Just one year younger, Doris stands alongside him nursing Mavis. About five foot six, still slim despite having given birth to so many children, with dark brown eyes and hair, it's hard to distinguish her in age from her oldest daughters—people often mistook them for sisters. Her ready smile isn't apparent in the photo, but the rest of the family make up for it in a separate image. The eldest child, Lorna, is the only one missing—recently married, she and her husband had decided to stay. The rest are crowded together in the garden, looking happy about the prospect of a new life in Western Australia, especially thirteen-year-old Peter who is wearing a cheeky grin.

News of the Turners' impending arrival was soon picked up by several papers in Australia. As one of the largest families to migrate under what was known colloquially as the Ten Pound Pom scheme, they were 'pin-ups' for the success of a concerted effort by the post-war Labor government to attract a minimum of 70,000 immigrants every year by offering free or assisted passage. The government had even set up a new, separate ministerial portfolio for immigration to help drive the initiative and placed it in the hands of Arthur Calwell. He promoted it relentlessly, pushing the slogan 'populate or perish'.

A staunch advocate of the White Australia Policy, Calwell was particularly keen to attract people from Britain. Just twelve months before, he had issued a press statement announcing that the government had organised extra shipping, including the *Empire Brent*. Built in the 1920s as an ocean liner, she sailed the Atlantic before being requisitioned by the Royal Navy. After the war she was sold to the British Ministry of Transport, who set her to work ferrying war brides to Canada. By 1948 she had been reassigned to carry migrants to Australia.

The Turners were allocated berths on the first of four trips made by the *Empire Brent* in 1949. They were scheduled to sail towards the end of winter, from Glasgow on the east coast of Scotland. That meant travelling first of all to Waterloo railway station in London where they caught the famous *Flying Scotsman* to Edinburgh, more than 600 kilometres away. Another train took them to the port where they found themselves among 967 passengers being shepherded aboard, carrying just enough clothes for the journey and a few personal possessions.

The Turners' household goods were packed into large wooden crates and stored in the hold. They weren't taking much because they didn't think it possible. They gave away most of the contents of their house, keeping mainly household linen, some kapok mattresses, a cherished set of Willow pattern china and some cooking utensils. 'Mum found out when she got here that she could have brought a lot more with her, but she didn't know that, you see. Actually, Mum and Dad didn't look into things enough—they just assumed,' Wendy confesses.

The *Empire Brent* set sail for Australia on 8 February. It took six weeks to cover more than 14,000 kilometres to the Western Australian port of Fremantle, travelling no faster than sixteen knots (thirty kilometres) per hour, which was the ship's top speed. On board, the family found themselves split up to accommodate the logistics of squeezing in as many people as possible. Along with all the other males, Ted and the three boys, including four-year-old Richard, were assigned bunks in the hold, a huge open area that looked little different to when the ship had been a troop carrier. Doris and the six girls found themselves in a small cabin above the waterline. They shared it with two other families, separated by temporary partitions. Wendy counted herself lucky because she scored a top bunk with a porthole. 'I was spoilt,' she admits.

As they settled in, the Turners realised most of their fellow passengers were Scottish, which influenced the journey in ways they hadn't expected. Porridge was served for breakfast every morning, with the Scots eating it the traditional way, with salt, much to the children's disgust. In a concession to their English tastes, they were allowed honey and sugar. The distinctive sound of bagpipes often drifted through the ship too. While most of the children failed to appreciate this musical bonus, over the coming days they unwittingly absorbed the rolled R's and burrs of the voices they were surrounded by, leaving the ship with distinct Scottish accents.

The novelty of ship life soon wore thin as the weeks dragged on, although the crew did their best to keep passengers entertained with concerts, fancy dress competitions and movie nights, even if it did mean showing the same small selection of films over and over again. One of them was *The Overlanders*, starring laconic Australian actor Chips Rafferty. It told the story of a family setting out from their cattle station with a large mob of cattle, trying to escape the imminent invasion of northern Australia by the Japanese. Along the way they faced extreme heat and water shortages, crocodile-infested rivers, horses dying from eating poisonous weeds and a stampede. Until seeing the movie, Wendy thought she was heading to a place remarkably similar to the New Forest. It came as a bit of a shock. 'I thought, if that's what Australia looks like, I don't want to go there!' she says.

Things became a bit more interesting for everyone on board when the *Empire Brent* reached Egypt and passed through the Suez Canal, offering exotic views of camels and sweeping sand dunes. Taking advantage of the ship docking at Port Said, Iris, who was twenty-two and the oldest sibling on the trip, went ashore with eighteen-year-old Doreen. They were accompanied by a couple of male passengers, who had to rescue Iris from being led away by a stranger. If that wasn't heart-stopping enough, they only just made it back to the ship before it sailed. But it is the moment when her baby sister Mavis was almost lost overboard that is seared into Wendy's memory. 'They used to stack the life rafts on the deck, level with the rail,' she explains. 'Someone took the baby off me to show her to a friend, and they sat her on a raft. The boat dipped into a wave and she started to roll off, over the side. One bloke grabbed her by the clothes—if he hadn't, she would have gone in!'

Meanwhile, the captain and crew of the *Empire Brent* were having adventures of their own. In the Mediterranean, a passenger became seriously ill and the ship had to make an unscheduled stop at Gibraltar so she could be taken ashore. Another family had to depart at Suez after a five-year-old boy fell from a top bunk and broke his arm while trying to catch a glimpse of the native hawkers pulling alongside the ship. Then in the Red Sea, the vessel made a detour to rescue a lighthouse keeper on the volcanic island of Jabal al-Tair. According to newspaper reports, the Maltese man had been there for twenty-four years and was due to be relieved when he suffered heart trouble. The over-worked ship's surgeon was sent ashore in a lifeboat to see what he could do.

The various delays meant the *Empire Brent* sailed into Gage Roads, the main shipping lane leading into the port of Fremantle, later than expected and had to wait overnight until a berth became available. The delay must have been frustrating for those on board. Anxious for the first glimpse of Australia, the Turners stood at the railing, looking towards the coastline. One of the first things they noticed was huge clouds of smoke, which John thought looked like plumes from an atomic bomb explosion. The cause was a series of bushfires, some started by accident and others part of an official burn-off season that began earlier in the week.

The *Empire Brent* finally docked at Fremantle on 11 March 1949, thirty-two days after leaving Glasgow. Most of the passengers were staying on board for ports on Australia's east coast, but 122 others joined the Turners in going ashore that day. Wendy remembers there being 'a lot of fuss', with the media anxious to catch up with them because of the size of the family. They had just been pipped to becoming the largest family to arrive in Australia under the Ten Pound Pom scheme. That honour went to the Davis family, with thirteen children and a couple of son-in-laws, who had passed through Fremantle on their way to Melbourne in late January. But the Turners were Western Australia's own, and local reporters wanted to tell their story.

From the docks, the new band of migrants were taken by bus to Point Walter, where a migrant holding camp had been set up the year before, overlooking the city of Perth and the Swan River. Wendy loved it. There was a beach nearby and palm trees, and people bought the children ice-creams, quite a luxury in Britain because of ongoing food rationing. 'We had a great time,' Wendy says.

❖ ❖ ❖

Despite basic facilities, the migrant camp was luxurious compared with what the Turners discovered after climbing down from their new neighbour's Maple Leaf truck on the farm at Manjimup in the isolated south-west of the state. The perils of buying a property sight unseen quickly became apparent. Most of the sixty-four hectares had not been cleared and were heavily infested with rabbits. The dairy herd was in a terrible state, made up of scraggly cows that were at the end of their productive lives and gave very little milk. And then there was the old weatherboard house meant to provide a home for eleven people. Although it had been spruced up in anticipation of their arrival, there were only four rooms, there was no electricity, no plumbing and the toilet was out in the backyard. According to John, it was all too much for his normally stoic mother, who indulged in 'a good crying session'.

Wendy does not remember this, and by all accounts Doris's tears didn't last long. After the initial shock had worn off, she apparently decided what was done was done and there was no point in complaining. 'She was a wonderful woman,' Wendy says. 'My mum always laughed, always joked, never got sad. She never got cross—she used to get disappointed but she never got cross. I never ever saw Mum cry in my life but she probably did,' Wendy says. 'My sisters were so upset when they saw the house, and I think Mum was, too.'

One of the first issues that occupied Doris's mind was where everyone was going to sleep. There were only two small bedrooms. Ted and Doris took one of those, the other was assigned to the girls, while the boys found themselves sleeping under a tarpaulin on the front verandah or in the old creamery not far from the house. Less than three metres from side to side, the square timber structure offered just enough room for two small beds and a gramophone. Peter slept on an old wire bed with a horse-hair mattress, while John made do with a kapok mattress placed over some boards suspended between two apple boxes.

Covered in a huge rambling rosebush, the creamery looked picturesque enough, except that it had a gap at floor level all the way around to create airflow. The gap was originally covered with flywire but it had long since rusted away. The boys weren't too worried about this until they discovered a large snake was living under the rosebush. Taking matters in hand, Doris decided she would tempt the snake out with saucers of milk and then kill it. About ten years old at the time, John was ready to help. When the snake appeared as it started to get dark, he armed himself with an axe. 'When he got close, he changed his mind and he threw the axe, and it chopped the tail off. Well, the snake shot straight up in the air and we all ran for our lives,' recounts Wendy. 'It did these big loops and went back into the rosebush.' Not surprisingly, the boys didn't want to sleep in the creamery that night but the next evening Ted came to the rescue, catching the snake with a long length of wire.

The house had two verandahs, one at the front and another at the back which was partially closed in to create a tiny kitchen. There was just enough space to squeeze in a small working table alongside a green-enamelled Metters wood stove, and a larger dining table in front of a long bench, with a kitchen chair at each end.

At the other end of the verandah was another enclosed area, about the same size, that served as the bathroom. It housed a big tin bath but there was no plumbing except for a pipe to remove the waste water. The house had two small rainwater tanks to supply water for drinking and cooking; water for bathing and washing clothes had to be carried up from the creek in large milk cans borrowed from the dairy, and then heated in a copper. In summer, the creek would start to dry up so the water was collected from its deeper pools. It was not unusual for the children to find twigs, leaves, and even leeches and the occasional frog floating past them in the bath.

Six days a week, everyone would make do with a quick wash, standing in a small amount of water—an operation that moved into the lounge room, in front of a big open fire, during the winter. Bath night proper came round every Saturday. The youngest children would go first. Doris would put a small amount of rainwater in the bottom of the bath and use the best Lux soap to wash the babies. Creek water and a splash of Dettol antiseptic liquid were added in batches as the older children took their turns, making do with harsher Lifebuoy soap to wash their hair. 'I used to have long hair, all curls, and Mum used to wash it for me and pour a jug of rainwater over my head,' says Wendy. Ted came last. By then the bath would be full of muddy water smelling strongly of antiseptic.

The outside of the house was creosoted in an attempt to stop the timber being attacked by termites, but it was only partially successful. Doris ended up making a series of intricate rugs woven out of scraps of material to cover holes in the floors, where the damage was the worst. 'Neighbours would come over to say hello and she would tell them not to stand on the mats,' recalls Wendy. 'They thought she was being house proud, but it was because there was a hole under every single one and she didn't want them to break a leg!'

While termites undermined the structure of the house, rabbits were accomplishing the same thing out in the paddocks. 'Our farm was one humungous rabbit warren,' says Wendy. Along with Peter and John, she was given the job of setting more than two hundred rabbit traps every evening and then going round to check them the next morning before school. 'It took me a while to be brave enough to do it, because if you made a mistake you'd lose your finger,' she says.

The infestation was so bad the children caught more than a hundred rabbits every day. Most of them were cooked down in a big copper, skin and all, for the pigs, but a good number ended up on the dinner table. They were skinned and taken up to the house where Doris soaked them overnight in a large bowl filled with water and vinegar. To make up for the monotonous diet, she became extremely inventive about how they were cooked. 'She used to roast 'em, bake 'em, curry 'em, you name it,' Wendy says.

The children were not always impressed. 'Not rabbit again, Mum!' they would chorus.

'Never mind, it'll put a little hop in your day,' Doris loved to reply.

At one stage, the Western Australian government provided poison to help landholders get on top of the rabbit plague. The poison was laced through large batches of apples, also provided by the government. Ted would then feed them out through a hopper, towed behind a horse and cart. The next day the children would head out into the paddock with the horse and cart to collect the dead rabbits, which were dumped into hollows left after tree stumps were removed, and then burnt. This approach to rabbit control brought unexpected benefits because Doris would hijack some of the apples before they were treated. 'They were a soft apple called Cleo, very good for cooking. I can still see Mum—she would have a whole bucketful, peeling them and cutting them up into this big saucepan to stew.'

Apart from trapping rabbits, Wendy, Peter and John also had to help milk the cows before going to school. The farm had a herd of about twenty-five, which Ted worked on improving over the years. The children would climb out of bed at five o'clock. Carrying hurricane lamps, they would collect the farm dog they had acquired and then head out into the paddock to bring the cows in to the dairy where they were milked either by hand or using a portable machine.

Milking was barely finished in time for the children to have a rushed breakfast of Weet-Bix and fresh cream, and then change and catch the school bus that pulled up at the bottom of the long driveway. Doris would head down first with the youngest children to help buy them a little extra time. 'It was about a five-minute walk. We could see the bus coming, and Mum used to send the two little ones first because they would be ready. And the driver would say, "Any more coming?" and then the next one would run down the hill, then the next, then the next one, while the old bus was ticking over. We would always hold the bus up.'

After such an early start, the children would often fall asleep at their school desks. Wendy can also remember struggling initially because the lessons were too advanced. 'They put me in a class and I didn't know what they were talking about because it was out of my league. In England we had huge classes and I sat at the back and didn't learn anything,' she admits. But she soon made two good friends, both named Phyllis, which helped.

In her spare time, Wendy found work harvesting potatoes. At the age of twelve, she earnt eleven shillings during her first harvest so she headed into Manjimup and spent it all on a new dress from the local Woolworths variety store. 'All the clothes I had were hand-me-downs from my sisters. It was the very first new dress I'd ever had in my life,' Wendy recalls, describing it in great detail. It had a square neck and full skirt, gathered at the waist according to the fashion of the day. The white fabric was printed with images of cacti and Mexican men wearing sombreros. 'I thought I was the ant's pants,' she says.

Wendy's memories of her years on the farm are dominated by laughter, frequently at the family's own expense as they adapted to a strange new country. She recalls her mother's first lesson in Australian slang. After helping them to settle in, the neighbours told Doris they would be back the next morning with twelve 'chooks'. Where Doris came from, a similar word was used to described little pigs, so she told Ted to get a big pen ready to hold them. Ted was extremely puzzled that anyone would be so generous as to give them so many pigs, small or not, but he dutifully set to work. The next morning the neighbour drove up in his truck, with some crates on the back. He took one look at Ted's handiwork and told him, 'That's no good, they'll fly out.' Still laughing heartily today at the wonders of a country where it seemed that pigs really did fly, Wendy adds with great understatement, 'We had a lot to learn!'

Another favourite family story relates to Ted's first experience fighting bushfires in February 1950. The fire started just up the road from the farm, and he and John set off with a neighbour. It was a hot day but there was no wind, and the area had been burnt out only a couple of years before so there was very little undergrowth to fuel the fire. Armed only with wet hessian bags, shovels, rakes and a few knapsacks filled with water, volunteers managed to bring the blaze under control just as night was falling. Relieved that the danger was over, Ted sat down to enjoy a well-earned mug of tea and a sandwich. Moments later John was startled to see his father leap into the air. 'I've got a bloody red-hot coal down my pants,' he exclaimed. Yanking down his trousers, Ted discovered instead a very large bull ant, much to the amusement of the locals looking on.

And then there was Peter's adventure with a renegade bull which kept breaking out of its paddock and getting onto neighbouring farms. The neighbour who owned the bull offered its carcase to the Turners if they could catch it and shoot it. Dreaming of steak and roast beef instead of rabbit, Peter volunteered to round up the animal with the help of some friends. Peter was good with horses, training a brumby while only a teenager and working the Clydesdales to plough paddocks, tow logs and feed hay out to the cows.

The boys saddled up and managed to direct the bull into an old stockyard. Then instead of waiting for Ted to come down with his double-barrelled shotgun, Peter decided to use his new single-shot .22 rifle and have a go at shooting the bull himself. It did not go well. The rifle was too small in calibre and Peter not a good enough shot to bring the animal down. All he succeeded in doing was infuriating the bull which broke out of the yards, threw the dog and terrorised Wendy, Richard and Faith who were watching from up on the stockyard fence.

John managed to reach a horse and galloped off for his father who dropped the bull with a single shot.

Ted and the boys rolled the animal onto a makeshift sleigh and used one of the Clydesdales to tow it back to the house yard where it was skinned and butchered. There was no refrigeration, so Ted gave most of it to neighbours, while Doris salted as much as she could for her family. It was an old bull and had been under some stress, so the meat turned out as tough as old boots, fit only for stewing.

The Turners were often homesick, and there was plenty of hard work and very few luxuries, but their helpful neighbours and Ted and Doris's sense of humour stood them all in good stead. 'We used to sit around the table and laugh every night. I have never laughed so much in my life as when I was a kid,' says Wendy. Even the grace recited before meal-times was not sacrosanct. On more than one occasion Ted brought it to a close by asking God to supply at least one of his daughters with a rich husband so he wouldn't have to work anymore. Doris would pretend to scold him: 'Father, how dare you say that. You wicked man!'

7

THE OUTLAW RETURNS

About two years after the Turners moved to Australia, Doris decided it was time to go back to England for an extended six-month visit. Jeanetta was missing her grandchildren and had never seen the newest baby, Roslyn. So after receiving yet another pleading letter from her mother, Doris promised to return with the two youngest as soon as she could. Regulations stipulated that people who arrived under the assisted scheme could not go back to their home country for two years, even for a holiday. When the time eventually came, thirteen-year-old Wendy was recruited to go along, too, and help look after the children.

Wendy was very excited to be back in the New Forest, revisiting her old haunts and catching up with relatives and friends. 'We had a great time. I was allowed to go out with my cousins to the beach and the pictures, and I thought it was wonderful so I wanted to stay. I didn't want to go back to the farm and milking cows,' she says. Doris eventually agreed that Wendy could remain with her grandparents for another year, and set sail for Perth without her.

She had barely said goodbye when Wendy began to regret her decision. 'I was like a prisoner,' she says. 'Grandmother was very old-fashioned and she wouldn't let me do a lot of things after Mum had gone. She wouldn't even let me read books.' Forced to go to bed early and spend considerable time in her upstairs room, Wendy dreamt of escape, especially when her carefree cousins wandered down the road, whistling for her attention. During the afternoons, while her grandfather was at work and Jeanetta was taking an afternoon nap, Wendy would practise climbing out of her bedroom window, onto the roof of the front porch, and then sliding down the drainpipe and jumping as silently as possible onto the front lawn. The only problem was that she couldn't make the reverse climb, so there was no way to get back inside.

A little relief came when a young priest at the Anglican church just down the road began organising dance classes on Saturday nights in the church hall. Two local women provided the music and instruction, teaching popular ballroom dances of the day such as the Veleta waltz. Wendy was convinced her grandmother wouldn't let her go, even though it was a church-organised activity, but the priest made a point of visiting Jeanetta and wangling permission. There was one stipulation—her granddaughter had to be home by eight o'clock. 'The dances only started at seven o'clock, and the worst of it was the boys didn't arrive until an hour later,' says Wendy.

One night a boy offered to walk her home. Knowing there would be trouble if her grandmother saw them, Wendy only allowed him to walk with her for part of the way. As they strolled along, he decided to push his luck further and ask her out to the movies. 'Don't be funny,' she told him. 'My grandmother won't let me out of the house, let alone go to the pictures.' Wendy recalls laughing when he remarked, 'She's very Victorian, isn't she!' But Wendy is honest enough to now admit, 'It was probably just as well because, when I think about it, I was a bit of an outlaw.'

Outlaw or not, Wendy began to wage a letter campaign to her mother, begging to come home. The dilemma was that this time the cost of her passage would not be subsidised. Her parents would have to find £78 for the boat fare, and that was an enormous amount of money for the cash-strapped Turners. Eventually, Wendy's brother-in-law stepped in. 'Otherwise I might still be there!'

Almost two years after returning to England, Wendy was finally on her way back to Australia. Her grandmother found a local married woman prepared to act as chaperone on the ship, but she spent most of the trip drunk and distracted by a male companion so the irrepressible teenager was left to her own devices. Wendy took full advantage of her unexpected freedom. Gregarious, attractive and confident for her age, she was able to pass for eighteen, and soon had young men falling over themselves to buy her exotic treats like her very first Coca-Cola and fresh pineapples. 'I only had one pound to spend that a sister sent me, but I didn't need it. I changed it for two ten-shilling notes, and when I got off the ship I gave one to the purser and one to the fella that served me at the table.'

Settled back on the farm, Wendy was expected to find seasonal work to contribute to the family income. In the early 1950s one of the main options around Manjimup was hoeing and picking tobacco.

Few people remember that Western Australia once had a tobacco industry. Much smaller than its better-known counterparts in northern Queensland and Victoria, and much shorter lived, it was centred around Manjimup. The first commercial crops were planted around 1930, with encouragement from a government keen to find lucrative cash crops to boost the local economy. By the early 1940s, more than 600 hectares were under cultivation in the state's south-west. There was another spurt of growth after the war, powered by the labours of returned servicemen and immigrants from southern Europe where tobacco was an established crop.

A driving force behind the industry in the west was the Michelidis family. Originally from Greece, they set up a cigarette-making business in Perth in the early 1900s. By the time Wendy was looking for work, Michelidis Tobacco Limited was the third largest manufacturer in Australia, producing a range of brands such as President and Golden West cigarettes, Luxor fine-cut tobacco, marketed as 'the Ultimate Smoke for Men who Want the Best!', and White Oak tobacco, which was promoted during the 1933 cricket test series with England as the brand that 'always leaves the Ashes in Australia'. The company was also the largest tobacco grower in the Manjimup shire where they owned nine plantations and employed more than two hundred people. Many were Macedonians who migrated to the area in large numbers between the two world wars, bringing with them first-hand experience in growing and curing the notoriously tricky and labour-intensive crop.

Initially, Wendy joined an older sister hoeing tobacco for a Macedonian bloke who rented the top end of the Turner farm. Battling flies, dust, heat and an aching back, she found the work hard and tedious, the rows of plants seeming to stretch on forever. She persevered, finding a certain kind of rhythm, and then the next season went to work for a Macedonian family with their own small farm north-west of Manjimup. Spring and summer for six years she lived with Jim and his wife, who Wendy called 'Majka', Macedonian for mother. 'I was treated like a daughter,' she says.

Wendy recalls tiring days of demanding physical labour, fuelled by nurturing meals of exotic flavours that she later wove into the meals she prepared for her own family. Her routine started just before dawn when she headed out into the paddock with the other workers to hoe weeds. This filled her days from October to January, and then picking would start in about mid January and continue well into March. 'You couldn't just pick anything, you had to pick the leaves that were going a bit pale, and that usually started with the bottom ones. Never any more than four at a time. You went over and over the crop for weeks, until you got to the top of the plant and all the stalk was bare.'

At half-past eight every morning, Majka would bring them a hearty breakfast of French toast made with eggs from their own chickens, olives, roasted capsicums and hot coffee with sweetened condensed milk. The family didn't have a cow but they grew their own fruit and vegetables, including plenty of red capsicums which Wendy soon learnt were a staple of the traditional Macedonian diet. One of her favourite dishes involved grilling and then dressing the capsicums with olive oil, garlic and basil.

At lunchtime, the workers traipsed back to the house for soup so thick it almost qualified as a stew. One version was made with lamb, risoni, tomatoes and a big handful of fresh mint. For afternoon tea there were sandwiches filled with roasted chillies, eaten out in the paddock, and then for a special treat in the evenings, sometimes there would be steak, served with eggs broken into the juices and scrambled roughly. 'They looked horrible, but the flavour!'

Wendy's mouth waters at the memory. 'It was totally different to the food I grew up on, but in those days I was always hungry and I would have eaten anything. For instance, there was always a dish of hot chillies served with everything. For a start I was a bit timid, and I was the same with olives. The first one I tried, I thought, "How could anybody eat those?" But I acquired the taste.'

The Macedonian family took such a shine to Wendy that after a season or two, they offered to rent her a hectare of land so she could grow her own crop and keep the proceeds. Farmers weren't required to hold a licence to grow tobacco; however, they could only purchase seed from the state agricultural department and the crop could only be sold at the official tobacco auctions held every year in Fremantle. Thinking her boyfriend, Joe, and his mates would help with the hoeing, Wendy took up the offer and then went to the agricultural department, where the staff assumed she was collecting seed for her father.

No doubt they were surprised when she popped up on the front cover of a weekly rural newspaper, which reported excitedly that Wendy had become the state's only woman grower. Still only seventeen years of age, Wendy was described as 'a tall, raven-haired English girl with a cultured voice and a flair for hard work'. Not only was she 'good looking with lustrous hair and a flashing smile' but she could ride a horse, drive a truck and swing a dexterous hoe. 'Wendy knows the anxieties of veteran growers, dreads the thought of summer hail storms which can flatten and ruin a crop in minutes,' they wrote. 'Her hopes are the same as the hopes of other tobacco planters: to have a good leaf pick, a good colour cure, an uninterrupted grading period and a bumper price at the annual Fremantle auctions.'

Wendy knew that growing tobacco wasn't easy—her own father had tried and failed, and many other inexperienced growers who settled in the district as part of a Commonwealth War Service Land Settlement Scheme gave up within a few years. The government set up a training centre at Manjimup for returned servicemen, but according to Wendy it wasn't successful because the Queenslander in charge didn't understand local conditions. Meanwhile, she was being mentored by her Macedonian friends and could count on them for advice when needed. 'The Macedonians, the Greeks and the Slavs had all been growing tobacco here through the war, so they knew what they were doing,' she says.

The first step was preparing the ground. Wendy's small patch of land was prone to flooding in winter so she dug a drain to carry away the excess water. Then the paddock had to be ploughed and harrowed to create a fine, even seed bed. She tried to hire someone to do this, but when that didn't work out she tackled the job herself. Even though she had never driven a tractor before, looking back along the nice straight rows, she was pretty happy with her efforts.

Her initial sense of achievement was short-lived. She had borrowed the tractor and a disc harrow from a young lad who lived about ten kilometres away, on the understanding that she return them for the weekend. Saturday morning came and she set off down the road without raising the discs because she didn't know how. 'I thought it would be okay if I went slowly, but I ploughed the road up—miles and miles of disced road. It wasn't too bad when I was on gravel, but there was one strip of bitumen that the council had just done, and I crossed over it!'

In a completely unrelated problem, a little further down the road Wendy noticed smoke coming from the tractor. She was near a spot mill, set up to process timber from the surrounding forest, so she waved her arms to draw the workers' attention. About ten men rushed over to help. They fixed the problem which related to the battery and a loose wire, and then they noticed the discs and sorted them out, too.

Sometime later Wendy was back working in the paddock when a car pulled up alongside the fence. Two well-dressed men got out and headed towards her. They were from the council and wanted her to visit their office so they could talk about the damaged road. Anticipating what might come next, she warned them straight away that she could not afford to pay for repairs, and offered to work off the debt instead. The two men looked at the attractive young woman standing in front of them, and kindly refused. 'Do you think we'd put you on the road gang? There wouldn't be any work done—the men would be watching you all day,' one of them told her. Wendy laughs now at the compliment and her own naivety. 'He let me off,' she says.

After months of fertilising, weeding and applying multiple chemical sprays to kill the plagues of beetles, caterpillars and grasshoppers that tried to eat her crop, Wendy finally harvested her first tobacco leaves. But her work was only half done. The leaves then had to be cured in a wood-fired kiln. Every tobacco farm had at least one of these small sheds so they could cure their own crop—a process that required considerable skill and constant attention over a period of days.

As they were picked, Wendy tied the leaves into bunches and hung them from poles. Once the kiln had been brought up to a certain temperature, the poles were suspended across beams in the kiln, carefully spaced so the hot air could penetrate the bunches evenly. The temperature then had to be raised gradually over several days, and kept steady until the webs of the leaves were dry. 'It took about a week to cure a kiln of tobacco, and you had to get up through the night to check the thermometer. As well as doing that, you still had to get up every morning to pick the next crop. It was hard work but I was young—I could do anything then,' Wendy says.

After the drying came the grading. 'You had to have a bit of wet weather before you could grade the leaves because they had to be moist and a bit elastic. In dry weather they were brittle and if you touched them, they would crackle up into pieces,' she explains. While waiting for the autumn break and the right weather conditions, Wendy would go apple picking to earn extra money.

The following August, Wendy travelled to Fremantle for her first tobacco auction. Many of the other 150 or so Western Australian growers went too, looking forward to a few days in the city and maybe even some shopping if the two-day sale went well. The year before a quarter of the bales offered up were passed in because of poor quality and had to be returned to the growers or destroyed, so there was more than the usual level of anxiety. As it turned out, the auction went well with more than 300 tonnes of tobacco sold for a gross total of £332,222. About £600 of that went to Wendy, who bought some new clothes and shared most of the rest with her family.

8

TALL TIMBER DANCING

A year before Wendy planted her first tobacco crop, Giuseppe Bonini stepped off a migrant ship from Italy. Home was a small farm just outside Castelnuovo di Garfagnana in the Tuscan province of Lucca. Dominated by a castle that dates back almost one thousand years, Castelnuovo became a thriving market town because of its location at the junction of two rivers, not far from major trading routes leading up into the Apennine mountains in northern Italy. It is a place that has seen many wars over the centuries, with rich families from Pisa, Florence and Urbino fighting for control, including the notorious Medicis. For a few years it was even part of the French Empire after Napoleon Bonaparte marched in with his army in the early 1800s.

Joe, as Guiseppe became known, was only seven or eight years old when the Germans took their turn at dominating the local population during World War II. Even though the Italians were officially on the same side, he remembers it being a period of great deprivation and fear. Quite a few local men chose to head into the mountains and join the Italian resistance movement, which was very active in the valley where Joe grew up. To discourage them the Nazis introduced a policy of reprisal, killing ten Italian villagers for every German killed by the partisans. At one stage, Joe's mother was so frightened they would be next that she took her son into a nearby forest and hid.

The tensions and hardships became worse towards the end of the war as the Americans started to advance and the Germans chose the valley as the place to make their stand. In December 1944, it became the centre of what they called Operation Winter Storm. The day after Christmas, a combined Axis force of more than 9000 German and Italian soldiers attacked an infantry division of the United States army that was twice the size, backed by local partisan fighters. Despite the odds, after fierce fighting the Axis troops gained the upper hand and the Allies were forced to retreat. 'They were bombing everything,' Joe explains in halting English. 'You don't know if you die or live.'

One morning, he and his mother were alone when a small group of the notorious German Waffen-SS arrived in search of food. His mother warned him to be quiet as she and Joe hid inside the house. Imitating the sound of gunshots, he describes one of the Germans taking aim at the chicken run with a machine gun. The men bagged up the family's few remaining, precious chickens and left. 'That was all we had,' Joe says, explaining that by then food was extremely scarce. 'After that we had to live on chestnuts.'

As it became clear that his prospects would be limited in a country still ravaged by war, Joe decided to take advantage of an Australian immigration scheme offering assisted passage to young men over the age of eighteen who were prepared to work in allocated jobs. Accompanied by some friends from the same town, in 1952 Joe left the port of Geneva aboard the *Castel Bianco*, which was carrying a thousand or so young men. After the ship docked at Fremantle, they were 'fumigated' and loaded onto buses lined up on the docks to take them to the migrant accommodation camp at Northam, about a hundred kilometres north-east of Perth.

Capable of holding up to 4000 people a time, the camp was home to Joe and his mates for about five months. He remembers it being full, the occupants mostly men with diverse backgrounds from across Europe. They were given decent meals and were well looked after, but Joe was anxious to find work and start earning money. Initially, he was among a few men selected to spend weekdays on Rottnest Island, helping to clean up what had been a military base during the war. 'Monday morning we would go out and Friday night we would come back to camp,' Joe says.

Eventually, many of his friends went to Wittenoom to work in the asbestos mines. The mines were offering good money, but in hindsight Joe is very grateful he didn't go, too, because of the health concerns that have since emerged around asbestos. Instead, Joe was sent to work in a timber mill at Walpole, in the state's south-west. The tiny township had only been gazetted about twenty years before, and there wasn't much in the way of facilities or community. 'No life there,' Joe says simply.

Just eighteen years of age, Joe missed his family and friends terribly. He was one of three Italians working in the mill, but he didn't know the others and was trying to make do on his own for the first time in his life. 'I used to cry every night, up in the bush there. There was nobody,' he says. The situation was not helped by the food. It's hard to imagine now, but in the Australia of those days olive oil could only be purchased in small bottles from the chemist, who sold it for medicinal purposes. Even in larger towns, continental groceries such as pasta were hard to come by.

At Walpole there was no hope of being able to source such exotic fare. A staple part of their diet was meat brought in for the mill workers on the back of a truck, covered with damp hessian bags. Joe soaked it in vinegar before he cooked it, to kill the maggots. Not surprisingly, before too long Joe decided to move on. He bought a motorbike and went in search of some

Italian friends who were working in a timber mill at Yornup, about 150 kilometres away, just the other side of Manjimup.

Wendy first set eyes on Joe at a dance. It was hard to look away. Always an impeccable dresser, the handsome young man knew how to move and was sharply turned out in a well-cut suit and a pair of blue suede shoes. 'We always went to dances, the whole family,' says Wendy. 'And he was dancing around with one of my sisters, and I said to Mum, "Ooo . . . I'd like to dance with him," and Mum said, "Well, when he brings Jan back he'll ask you," but he didn't.'

Wendy had to wait until the next event, at a little hall built by the employees at Oregioni's sawmill, a few minutes' drive north of Manjimup. A popular venue with the Italian mill workers, the dance usually featured a small band with drums, piano accordion and saxophone. Everyone brought a plate of supper to share, and Mrs Oregioni always provided a big pot of Italian-style brewed coffee.

Joe came to the dance with some friends, once again wearing his blue suede shoes. When Elvis Presley released his hit song about the fancy footwear a few years later, it took Wendy right back to that first breathless evening dancing with her future husband because, just like the lyrics in the song, she was constantly stepping on his feet. 'I could do the barn dance and the Veleta and things like that, but I couldn't do the modern Latin American dances,' she confesses. 'He taught me those—the tango, the samba, the cha-cha.'

Wendy was only sixteen when she first met Joe, and it didn't take long for the relationship to become serious even though there were more things working against it than their youth. They came from cultures that were completely different in almost every way—language, food and religion. Joe knew very little English and Wendy didn't speak Italian. Joe was Roman Catholic and Wendy was Protestant in an era when this was seen as an impossible obstacle by both churches.

Despite the obvious differences, Joe and Wendy fell in love. Within six weeks of their first meeting, Joe asked Ted for permission to marry his daughter. Ted wasn't impressed. It wasn't because Joe was Italian or Catholic. Apart from Lorna, all of Wendy's elder sisters married people then known as New Australians. 'Mum used to call us the League of Nations when we got together at Christmas,' Wendy says. In fact, she recalls many marriages between people from different countries at Manjimup during the 1950s. 'I don't remember it being a problem. The main problem was that there was a big lack of women, so there wasn't one woman in Manjimup that wasn't married.'

Recalling the matchmaking efforts of a father with a large number of daughters and very little money, she says: 'I was supposed to marry a rich farmer. Dad used to bring all these bachelors home that had big farms. Of course, they were all about Dad's age and that was hilarious. Mum would say, "You're not bringing that old man here again, are you, Ted?" And he'd say, "Well, one of the girls might take a fancy to him." And then Iris married a Dutchman, and Doreen married a Dutchman, and Jan married an Estonian. That left me and Faith.

'So Dad came home this day and he said, "I've met just the boy for one of you girls. I've talked to his mother and she'd be very happy for her son to marry one of you, and she will provide everything for the wedding. Mother, you'll have a new hat, and one of you will have a nice brick house to live in, right in Manjimup." This boy was younger than me because he'd gone to school with John. He was Macedonian and he would have been about fourteen, this boy, but Macedonians arrange marriages, and his mother was trying to arrange this with Dad.'

Faith settled the issue straight away. 'He looks like a toad,' she told her father.

'Well, you kiss him and he might turn into a prince,' teased her brother Peter.

Ted eventually gave up on the idea. When Joe came along, he was obviously concerned that he had very little to offer Wendy in the way of financial security, but he was more worried that his daughter was too young and might change her mind. 'Wait until she's twenty-one,' Ted told the unsuitable suitor.

So Joe waited—for five whole years. 'I gave her a chance to think about it,' he says, with a definite twinkle in his eyes.

Having warned Joe about all her shortcomings as a potential wife, Wendy pressed Joe about why on earth he wanted to marry her. 'I can't live without you,' he told her.

'Well, okay,' replied Wendy. So they became engaged and spent the next five years getting to know each other. They went dancing every weekend and spent as much time together as work and the distance between them allowed. Even during the week, Joe would make the thirty-minute trip from Yornup to visit Wendy at home, sometimes for just an hour before turning around and going back again so he could get up early and go to work in the morning. Meanwhile, they both saved hard and finally had enough money to pay a deposit for a small farm at Northcliffe.

Joe and Wendy eventually married on a wintry day in August 1959. There was little money to spare so it was a modest affair. Wendy bought a short-sleeved wedding dress on special, and had a local dressmaker add a beautiful lace top with long sleeves. Then she made her own bouquet by stitching fresh flowers, small pieces of fern and ribbon onto a piece of cardboard. Her sister Faith agreed to be bridesmaid and had her own dress made for the occasion.

Things didn't go exactly according to plan, as weddings rarely do. Wendy's brother John was supposed to be best man but he was an aspiring professional footballer and rang to say he had just been selected for the first time to play in a big game for East Perth. Iris's husband, Gerard, stepped in at the last minute.

Then Wendy and Joe discovered the priest who was supposed to perform the ceremony had fallen sick. Ted and Doris had sold the farm at Manjimup in the mid 1950s, and bought a better one near Pemberton. The wedding was due to be held in the town's Catholic church but when the wedding party arrived the priest was too ill. Determined that the wedding should go ahead that day, everyone trooped down the road to the Anglican church. Joe didn't mind and the young priest who had recently taken up duties was delighted to do the honours. It would be his first wedding.

Afterwards, the reception was held at the Turners' house. It was mainly family, but that was large enough. Eldest sister Lorna and her husband, Keith, had moved to Australia a few years before and bought a farm not too far away, and most of the other siblings were there, too, some of them married and with their own children. 'Then we went off to Northcliffe. No honeymoon,' says Wendy matter-of-factly. There was a tobacco crop in the ground which needed checking, so going away wasn't an option.

With help from the rest of the family, Joe and Wendy spruced up their first home so it was ready to move into. Built from asbestos as part of a land settlement scheme for soldiers returning from World War II, it was relatively new, with two bedrooms, a lounge and a kitchen, a spacious hallway and a verandah across the front. 'The walls were painted primrose in the kitchen, with a white ceiling, and the cupboards were different colours—charcoal, pink and pale grey. And there was beautiful lino on the floor,' Wendy says.

The kitchen may have looked nice, but Joe was not at all pleased with how Wendy put it to use, at least initially. Having spent most of her teenage years working outside, she had never done much cooking, and what she did cook tended to be very English in style. 'Italians don't cook in dripping, but for the English it was all cooked in fat. You didn't waste butter in those days, and we didn't use oil. I used to fry up chops and eggs and tomatoes for my brothers and they were happy, so that's what I served to Joe for my first meal. Good job it was on a tin plate. It went straight out the door, with the salt and pepper pot behind it.'

Fortunately for the ongoing harmony of the marriage, Wendy's sense of humour prevailed and she laughed about the incident, and then encouraged Joe to teach her how to cook things that he liked. Recognising the potential to make money supplying the large number of Italian migrants who had settled in the area, a Perth businessman was sending a truck down every week with continental groceries such as dried pasta and olive oil. So they managed to buy some spaghetti and Wendy finely chopped some beef. Unfortunately, when the time came to make the meat sauce, it was a case of the blind leading the blind. Joe wasn't much of a cook, either. 'He's standing over me, and he says, "Put more salt in, you haven't got enough salt," so I put more salt in, but he wants more salt, so I put even more salt in, and then we couldn't eat it. Even the dog wouldn't eat it because there was so much salt. We had to have bread and cheese.'

Wendy persevered, learning by trial and error, and then Joe's parents came out from Italy. Joe's mother soon taught her how to cook pasta, and even rabbit, baked slowly with olives and tomatoes. She also tried to teach Wendy how to speak Italian, with limited success. 'I knew some Macedonian after living with the Macedonian family for six years, and when Italian came along I used to mix the two together. I confused myself and everybody else. I could understand what they were talking about, the subject, but I didn't know exactly what they were saying.' One day Wendy muddled the word for meat, *carne*, with the word for dog, *cane*. Instead of saying she was going to fry the meat, she said she was going to fry the dog. Joe's mum couldn't stop laughing.

Despite the laughter on that occasion, not being able to speak Italian proved to be a real issue between Wendy and her in-laws. Joe and Wendy had saved money to help them migrate, but after a short time they wanted to go home. They found the Australian bush far too different. 'If we had been living in Perth, it might have been better,' Wendy says. 'But we were four hundred kilometres away in the bush. People don't know what that's like until they get here.'

They didn't have much, and there was certainly the occasional heated argument or two, but there was also plenty of laughter in the Bonini household in those early years on the farm near Northcliffe. The tiny community is tucked away right at the bottom of the state in an area of extraordinary natural beauty, with towering forests of giant jarrah and karri trees, and the dramatic unspoilt coastline of what is now D'Entrecasteaux National Park.

The town itself only came into existence in the 1920s during the development of a land settlement scheme to establish dairy farms, which proved to be a dismal failure. The blocks were small and many of the new settlers struggled, either with poor quality soils that couldn't grow enough pasture or the effort involved in clearing the forest. By the mid 1930s, most people had walked away. Very little of Joe and Wendy's farm had been cleared, but there was enough ground to grow tobacco and hopefully make a reasonable living. The farm already had its own kilns and drying shed, and they put in a dam. Neither of them were afraid of hard physical work, and they already had experience.

Before too long, Wendy raised the idea of them starting a family. In stark contrast to a prediction by one of her sisters that she would be barefoot and pregnant for the rest of her life after marrying a Catholic, Wendy discovered that Joe didn't want any children at all. More than a little shocked by the surprise revelation, she headed to the bedroom and started packing her suitcase. 'Where are you going?' Joe asked. 'I'm leaving,' she replied. 'Well, I'll come with you,' Joe insisted. The humour of the situation didn't escape Wendy, and the argument soon blew over.

Joe and Wendy celebrated the birth of their first child the day before Christmas 1960. The event was not without its funny moments, too. The plan was that Wendy would go and stay with Doris just before the baby was due, because the farm was so isolated. In what was meant to be the last week of her pregnancy, Wendy went to see her doctor for a final check-up and he told her not to worry, the baby would be some time yet. At about four o'clock the following morning, she woke up with a stomach-ache. With complete faith in the wisdom of the doctor, she put it down to eating some bad food.

A few hours later she reassured Joe over breakfast that she would be fine. He was driving to Manjimup to pick up a part for the irrigation pump and was worried about leaving her alone. At the last minute Wendy changed her mind and decided to spend the day with her mother. Joe could drop her off on his way. 'And we were driving along and every few minutes I got these pains. I didn't have a clue,' she admits.

When they arrived at the Turner farm, Wendy told her mother, 'I've got this terrible bellyache, I keep getting these sharp pains.' Doris immediately ordered Joe to head straight for the Pemberton hospital.

'What for?' he asked.

'She's having the baby!' her mother replied.

At the hospital, the doctor told them both that, given it was Wendy's first child, the labour was likely to go on for some time. In those days men were not welcome in the delivery room, so Joe decided to continue on to Manjimup as planned rather than spend hours pacing the corridors. 'He had only just left the hospital and out pops the baby, eight pounds, just like that. He'd gone, and there was no-one to celebrate with,' Wendy says.

Joe's mother liked the name Lorenzo so that is what they christened the baby. From the beginning they called him Laurie because Wendy was concerned that later on his schoolmates might give him a hard time if he had an unusual name. After developing milk fever, Wendy stayed in hospital for two weeks before the day finally came when she and Laurie were allowed to go home.

Six years later the Boninis' second child, Giuliana, was born. By then they had left the farm and moved to Manjimup. The local tobacco-growing industry shut down in the early 1960s because Western Australian growers couldn't compete against much cheaper imports from Africa, and their product fell out of favour with major cigarette manufacturers who claimed it had a high salt content. Some farmers turned to growing potatoes but in those days it was a regulated crop and a licence was required. The Boninis couldn't get a licence and their farm with its tiny acreage of cleared land wasn't really suitable for much else. So Joe found employment at a timber mill and Wendy worked a three-hour shift at the Manjimup hospital, preparing the evening meals.

The Boninis gave up rural life when Giuliana was about three and moved to a newly developed housing area in a south-eastern suburb of Perth, at the foot of the Perth Hills. But farming wasn't quite finished with the family yet.

❖ ❖ ❖

Picking peaches is an art. Knowing when they are ripe to exactly the right degree. Judging the colour, feel, smell and even shape before plucking each delicate fruit from the tree. Handling it gently so it is not bruised. Giuliana had an inkling of these things before she married an orchardist, but after more than twenty-five summers she can almost do it in her sleep. Not that there is much time for that during harvest.

The seasonal rhythms of the orchard became hers in 1988, when she married Garrie Vincenti, a third-generation grower from the Perth Hills. They met at the Last Drop pub in Kalamunda. Giuliana often went there to catch up with friends on a Sunday afternoon, but this was a Thursday night and she had to be talked into it by a work colleague. Her friend soon spotted Garrie and two of his mates, who she knew, and they started talking. 'Garrie's two friends were in the front and he was behind, and he was saying nothing. He was just standing there, while these two were just yapping and yapping, trying to get my attention, but I wasn't paying any attention to them. I was thinking, why is he so quiet?'

They married eighteen months later on Giuliana's twenty-second birthday and moved into a two-storey house overlooking the Vincenti family orchard at Carmel. She may not have been raised on a farm like her mother, but rural life wasn't completely foreign to Giuliana. Growing up she spent most school holidays and long weekends visiting her grandparents on the Turner farm at Pemberton. Ted finished his days in a small farmhouse with Doris, on the edge of the property, which their sons John and Richard took over after he retired. 'When we got there, I would hop on the back of Granddad's old orange Holden ute and we would head off down to his berry patch. He had a little plot amongst the karri forest, and the soils were spectacular. He grew the most amazing raspberries and strawberries,' Giuliana says.

The Vincentis don't grow berries. Instead they have about 18,000 stone-fruit trees to care for, covering sixteen undulating hectares, rimmed by bushland. 'It feels like that many, too, especially when you get to the beginning of a long row in picking season and it's already thirty-two degrees and it's only six o'clock in the morning. You look up the row, and you think, "Oh no. Look at all that." The rows look so long.'

Originally from the same Tuscan province as the Boninis, the Vincentis have been orchardists in the hills overlooking Western Australia's capital for almost ninety years. Garrie's grandparents settled just up the road at Pickering Brook where they grew vegetables as well as fruit. His parents, Tony and Anna, took charge after Tony's mother died and his father moved back to Italy. They bought the Carmel property in the early 1980s with Garrie, and still live there in a separate house at the opposite end of a shared driveway.

Today the Vincentis' orchard is one of the larger operations in the area, well regarded for the quality of its fruit and the management techniques applied to produce it. They also import specialist horticultural equipment from Europe, which they sell to growers across Australia, and Garrie often finds himself in local newspapers commenting on industry issues and encouraging people to buy local produce. The orchard even featured in an episode of Adam Liaw's popular *Destination Flavour* series on SBS television. Standing among their fruit trees, the celebrity chef demonstrated how to make a classic Peach Melba dessert with an Italian twist, which he appropriately renamed Peach Giuliana.

She may now have a fancy dessert named after her, but Giuliana is no prima donna. She works long days on the property, particularly during picking season, which starts in November and ends in about mid March. It's just gone nine o'clock on a hot Monday morning in December and she has already put in three steady hours. Now she is back in the cool, dim light of her kitchen, quickly gathering up morning tea. There is no time or energy left during the week to bake, so Giuliana cooks at the weekend to restock a large deep-freeze with homemade cakes and slices for her family and their employees. 'My husband has always liked his cup of tea in the morning and afternoon. In the beginning I just gave him biscuits, but I like baking and I thought, why not do it for everyone? It gives me a boost and it makes them happy,' she explains.

Her favourite cookbooks are spattered with batter on the pages with the most popular recipes. Given time pressures, they tend to be ones that don't take long to make and have relatively simple ingredients. One-bowl cake mixes that freeze well are her absolute favourites. Today she sliced up a caramel coffee cake and left it on the bench to defrost before heading to the orchard. She is back inside just long enough to make a large portable container of tea and grab the cake, which she puts in a carry bin on the back of the quad bike that serves as the orchard runabout.

A few minutes later Giuliana parks the bike at the top of a gentle rise and walks down to one of two hydraulic picking platforms that have replaced the more traditional ladders in recent years. Tony, Garrie and son, John, are waiting, along with half a dozen hired hands. During spring, when the crop has to be thinned so the trees can produce larger fruit of better quality, there may be as many as twenty additional workers. They are all backpackers from overseas, and mostly young university graduates, earning money while they travel around Australia. They live in dongas on the edge of the orchard, with some of them staying for the whole season because the Vincentis make a point of treating them well and paying them proper rates. 'You make them happy, you have fun with them and you give them something nice to eat and you treat them properly, and they give you their labour back in return,' Giuliana says.

Unless the weather is extremely hot and there is danger of too much fruit being lost, Sundays are rest days, even at the peak of the season in January and February. 'We are all knackered by then and you need a day off,' Giuliana explains. She and Garrie tend to spend it catching up with family. Often that means sharing a meal with Wendy and Joe, who live only fifteen minutes away, in the same house where Giuliana and her brother, Laurie, grew up. The modest suburban family home has seen of hundreds of family parties and social gatherings over the years. In their heyday, Joe and Wendy often entertained as many as fifty people, dancing under the large pergola at the back where they set up coloured lights and a bar to lend a festive air. If they weren't entertaining, they went out to dances every Saturday night until just a few years ago.

Their health doesn't allow much dancing now, but Joe is still drawn to the Latin rhythms he favoured when he first swept Wendy off her feet. He practises them almost every day on the electronic organ. Even though his skills as a dancer hinted at a natural musicality, Joe did not learn how to read music and play a keyboard until he was in his forties. He took it up when he became 'bored something stupid' during recovery from major back surgery. Once a fortnight he went to see a music teacher, who was impressed with his aptitude and urged him to keep practising.

It is the Sunday after the Kalamunda show, and Joe is serenading his wife while she works in the kitchen. He is playing the Cole Porter classic 'Begin the Beguine' to a syncopated beat. Wendy is humming along as she sets a table with the best china and silverware. Giuliana and her family are coming for dinner and she has prepared a roll of lamb, basted in the distinctly Italian flavours of tomato and olives. It is a long way from the charred chops fried in fat that she served Joe on the first night of their marriage. 'I had no idea,' she confesses, pondering again all the differences that could have made their marriage a disaster.

Joe has been listening in. 'What do they say? Love is blind,' he adds sagely. 'We are still going strong after fifty-six years.'

PART III
THE LITTLE TOWN THAT COULD

9

THE ONE NUN STORY

There's trouble at the whorehouse. A notorious bushranger is on the loose, and the ladies of the night are leaning out the single window of their modest establishment making lewd suggestions to the crowd gathered outside. A sign on the building says Madame McGee's Young Ladies Finishing School and Deportment College, but no-one is fooled. Certainly not the local police trooper, who decides it's time to shut the joint down. He's in the process of warning the crowd to move along when the escaped bushranger is spotted making a dash for it. Mounted on a fine bay mare, the trooper takes off in pursuit.

The year is 2015 and it's a fairly typical Saturday night in Harrow, a small town tucked away on the banks of the Glenelg River, in Victoria's West Wimmera. This scene is what happens when people let their imaginations run riot. When they refuse to accept that the place they love most in all the world is in danger of becoming nothing more than an historic curiosity. When people become convinced they can do anything and that no idea is too silly. This is the story of the little town that decided it could reinvent its future and buck the national rural trend of declining populations and closing services. In the process, it changed the lives of two city women who had never heard of the place just a few years before, let alone considered living there.

❖ ❖ ❖

Unlikely as it may sound, it all started with a nun. The good sister provided pastoral care for people across the Catholic parish of Harrow until the mid 1990s when she was transferred out of town and not replaced. Her loss had an unexpected effect on the local publican, Ange Newton, but not because the nun was a big drinker. Ange could sense the implications were much broader than what might happen to her own business.

'I sat down and thought about the impact one woman would have leaving the town, and I added it all up. It was shocking,' she says. 'There would be a car that wouldn't be serviced a couple of times a year at the local garage, and she covered a fairly big area so she would have been buying a decent amount of fuel. She would have been sending a lot of letters so the post office was affected. She was buying groceries at the grocery store, so they were affected, too. The economic impact on the town was not good. And then I started to think, if one nun can have that impact, what if a whole family left, or the garage closed?'

It was a personal epiphany of the non-religious sort for Ange, who is not the type of person to just sit back and accept the inevitable. She was also very aware that the local community was going through some tough times. For 150 years, most properties in the surrounding area had relied on sheep and wool for their income, but in the early 1990s the global demand for wool crashed, taking sheep prices with it and leaving behind a massive stockpile of unwanted fibre. Government and industry organisations decided the quickest way to turn the situation around was to reduce the national flock by 20 million sheep within a year. For farmers who could not find a buyer, that meant shooting their livestock and dumping them in pits. It was a very bleak time even for old hands in the wool industry, who thought they had seen everything.

The warm and vivacious Ange took over the Hermitage Hotel in 1994. She had no previous experience running a pub but she did know Harrow, having grown up in south-western Victoria. The only licensed premises in town, the hotel was barely managing to sell a couple of kegs a week so there was plenty of scope for improvement. After a while, business lifted a little but she was acutely aware that the town relied on the farming sector to survive. 'Our business was okay, but I wasn't sure how the other businesses were coping.'

What happened next stemmed from a combination of fear and stupidity, according to the very modest Ange who is quick to share credit with the broader community. 'I was fearful enough to want to do something about it, but too stupid to know what I was getting myself into,' she says.

Looking around for inspiration, Ange realised that Harrow's greatest asset was its history. Originally known as Upper Glenelg, it was settled in the 1840s, making it one of Victoria's oldest inland towns. Over the centuries, it has been connected with more than a few colourful characters whose stories are part of a rich local folklore, including explorer Major Thomas Mitchell, who trekked through the area in 1836 and named the Glenelg River; undertaker William Burrell, whose real trade was gun-smithing; and two Chinese market gardeners, who grew vegetables on the riverbank. The town is also the burial place of legendary cricketer Johnny Mullagh, a skilful all-rounder who was part of an all-Aboriginal team that in 1868 became the first Australian cricket team to tour England.

Ange considered their stories provided perfect material for a theatrical sound and light show. The evening event would bring to life the town's history, using its old buildings as stage settings, and the community as the cast and support crew. Hopefully, it would attract visitors who would stay for the weekend and spend some money.

The first step in bringing this grand vision to life was convincing the locals it was a good idea. 'So we had a barbecue and got them full, basically. We told them all how special they were and talked them into their roles,' Ange says. Even though most of them thought she'd lost the plot, they liked their publican and didn't want to upset her, so they agreed to lend a hand. At the end of three months, there were about sixty cast and crew. Most of the community had become engaged in making it happen.

From the beginning, the show has been about making the most of local talent and resources. Two musical brothers who had never played for anyone but their families were recruited to form the band. Anyone who could sew helped to make the costumes. Bruce, a local farmer, was an excellent horseman so he became a trooper. A couple of others were sent off to Melbourne to gain technical qualifications as armourers so they could manage the firearms and explosions that are part of the production. And the pub employed ten more casual staff to prepare and serve dinner and drinks. 'It was this total social inclusiveness. People came together and worked for one goal. It was wonderful, and it still is,' says Ange.

The first Harrow By Night Sound and Light Show was staged in October 1996. Ange was a nervous wreck beforehand, anxious that some of the locals who said it would never work might be proved right. Apart from anything else, she and her husband Jeff had $3000 of their own money riding on it, put up to pay for the sound system. 'The stress was terrible, so I'd just go into the shower, turn the water on, and howl my eyes out. I'd be sobbing with fear, but I was too desperate and there was too much to do. I don't know how it worked, but God was watching and it did. We found our niche.'

The show quickly became a phenomena, attracting national media attention and drawing people from across Australia and overseas. At one point, the community was running fifty-two shows a year, with two shows a week from October to December. Tickets sold out three months in advance. 'It was that crazy,' says Ange.

Local businesses began to thrive and community groups benefited, too. 'I call it the octopus plan,' Ange explains, adding in a whisper that she might be a bit of a socialist. Tickets to the event cost $28, and the proceeds were shared. If a community group or local business provided a volunteer, they were paid a dollar for every ticket sold. That basic system still works today, although the frequency of the shows has dropped to five a year.

The nature of the show has changed a little, too. In its early days, people started the evening with a meal at the pub and then climbed on board a bus which took them from site to site while they absorbed a show that was 'reasonably serious', strongly based on historical fact. Now the script is little more than a guideline and people walk the route along the main street as hilarious mayhem unfolds around them.

The evening starts quietly enough. Cast members arrive in character, wandering up to the pub much as they might have done in the 1800s. First to be seen are Bruce and his bay mare Gertie. A veteran of many shows, she stands quietly on the footpath in front of the pub while Bruce rolls a cigarette and chats away to people taking advantage of the warm evening to sit outside for a drink. Dressed as a police trooper, he is sporting knee-high boots, a dark blue jacket with corporal's stripes on each sleeve, and a long, bushy moustache.

Before too long, someone sits down on a wooden bench under a window and begins to play a set of Irish uilleann bagpipes. Gentle Celtic melodies are still wafting across the street when Dr Potts arrives, sporting a long tail coat and top hat. The town judge is there, too, with his wife on his arm, and a strange leggy-looking chap with long black hair, gloomy features and popping eyes. In costume and make-up he is hard to recognise as full-time portrait painter Ron 'Stretch' Penrose, who walked away from sheep farming to set up a studio in the town's old bakery. Tonight he is Bill the Undertaker. Everyone is seated in an undercover dining area at the back of the pub by the time the harlots arrive and the real fun begins. They help to serve the crowd their dinner on enamelled tin plates, in between an old-fashioned sing-along and dancing.

These are the scenes that met Marnie Baker's eyes in 2011 when she and her husband, Nathan O'Brien, travelled from their home in eastern Melbourne to decide whether Harrow was their future. They had never heard of the Sound and Light Show, and were a bit startled when they walked into the pub for dinner. 'There were all these people in period costume. They were everywhere,' Marnie says. 'The next thing you know there's explosions going off. I can't remember what I had in my hands but that went flying.'

In her surprise, she turned to one of the locals. 'Oh my God, what was that?'

Hand on hip, he replied, 'Don't worry, luv. You're not in Frankston now!'

❖ ❖ ❖

What followed that evening proved the masterstroke in another textbook example of the Harrow community working together with single-minded determination to salvage its future. After thirty-five years running the Harrow garage, its owners, Bernie and Pauline Kelly, were planning to close the doors, bringing to an end a business that was the town's only source of fuel and mechanical services. They had been trying to sell, without success, for some time because Bernie was ill and needed to retire. He could not keep the garage going any longer.

If one nun leaving could upset the balance of things, the whole town knew that losing the garage would be a disaster.

RIGHT: Elaine on a visit to the Harfull farm before she was married.

LEFT: Elaine (right) and her sister Reay with their father, Bruce Schwennesen, in 1928.

RIGHT: The photo Elaine signed and gave to Lyall shortly after they met.

BELOW: Elaine and Lyall leaving the church on their wedding day in April 1946.

BELOW: Elaine and Lyall's home at Mil Lel, c 1946.

ABOVE: Elaine outside the dairy, with Valerie, Elizabeth and Snowy, 1962.

LEFT: Elaine's newly decorated dining room, c 1955.

BELOW: Elaine's parents, Vida and Bruce Schwennesen, inspecting the pigs with Valerie during a visit to the farm, c 1958.

RIGHT: Elaine with her grandson, Thomas.

LEFT: Elaine and Lyall with their children, (from left) Valerie, Roger, Fiona and Elizabeth.

BELOW: A birthday party at Gilmores for Byron (pictured with the cake), including Grace's sons, Norman (back row, left) and Trevor (back row, fourth from left), and Elaine's children Roger and Valerie (back row, right). PHOTOGRAPH COURTESY OF GRACE GILMORE.

LEFT: Grace Gilmore wearing her military service medals, 2015.
PHOTOGRAPH BY FRANK MONGER.

RIGHT: Grace and Ray, 1945.
PHOTOGRAPH COURTESY OF GRACE GILMORE.

LEFT: Grace in uniform, 1944.
PHOTOGRAPH COURTESY OF GRACE GILMORE.

ABOVE: Road to Harrow.

LEFT: Trooper Bruce and his horse Gertie, during the Harrow Sound and Light Show.

BELOW: The old gaol at Harrow, with the seventeenth anniversary memorial in front, and McClure's Kalang Cottage behind.

LEFT: Jesse and baby Bailey, 2013.

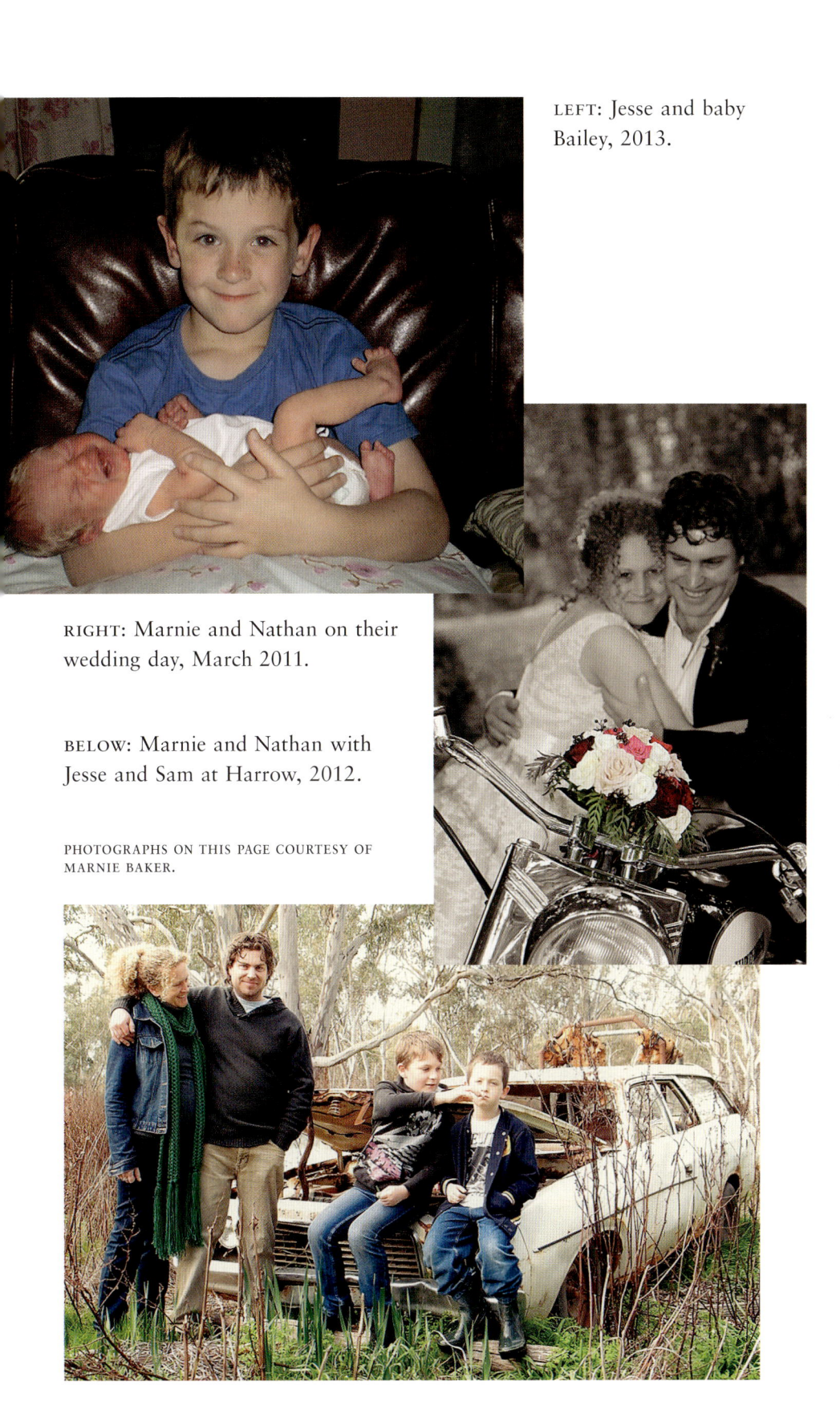

RIGHT: Marnie and Nathan on their wedding day, March 2011.

BELOW: Marnie and Nathan with Jesse and Sam at Harrow, 2012.

PHOTOGRAPHS ON THIS PAGE COURTESY OF MARNIE BAKER.

ABOVE: Geoff and Jean Simpson with their children, Sherryn (left) and Danielle.

LEFT: Mark and Sherryn, c 2007.

BELOW: Sherryn with her dog, Polo.

PHOTOGRAPHS ON THIS PAGE COURTESY OF SHERRYN SIMPSON.

Sherryn and her daughter, Rhianna, on the farm at Connewirricoo.

RIGHT: The Turner family pictured a month before leaving England, January 1949.

LEFT: Wendy, aged 15.

BELOW: Doris in 1934, aged 21.

PHOTOGRAPHS ON THIS PAGE COURTESY OF WENDY BONINI.

ABOVE: Wendy and Joe on their wedding day, August 1959.
PHOTOGRAPH COURTESY OF WENDY BONINI.

RIGHT: Wendy and her daughter, Giuliana.

LEFT: The Vincenti orchard at Carmel.

ABOVE: Daljit on her fruit block near Loxton.

BELOW: Daljit with her husband, Paul, and their children Monica, Tim and KJ. PHOTOGRAPH COURTESY OF DALJIT SANGHERA

ABOVE: The extended family gathered together for Monica's wedding.

LEFT: Daljit (third from right) in a high school sports team.

RIGHT: Daljit (right) with her sisters.

PHOTOGRAPHS ON THIS PAGE COURTESY OF DALJIT SANGHERA.

LEFT: Bunginderry station.

RIGHT: Annabel helping to build the 'fence of hope'.

ABOVE: Annabel sitting in front of her studio.

RIGHT: Sarah Durack. PHOTOGRAPH COURTESY OF WENDY AND JOHN TULLY.

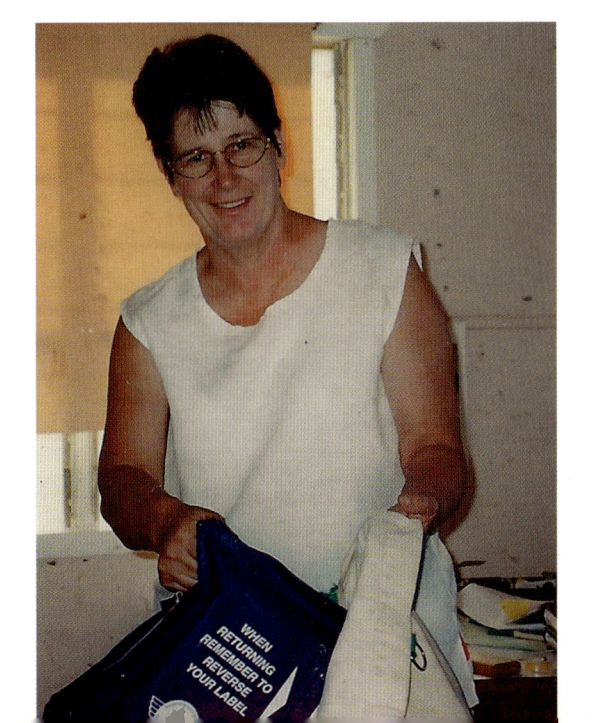

LEFT: Wendy Tully packing her last School of the Air satchel after 18 years. PHOTOGRAPH COURTESY OF WENDY AND JOHN TULLY.

ABOVE: Annabel and her brother, John.
BELOW: Annabel and Stephen, with their children at Bunginderry, 2008.

The Harrow Progress and Development Group called a town meeting to discuss the situation and more than seventy people turned up, representing just about every family in the district. 'It was very clear that all of us desperately wanted to sort something out. We wanted to help the Kellys because we loved them, but more importantly we didn't want the garage to close. If we accepted that, what would be next?' poses Ange.

The meeting in June 2011 formed a small committee to tackle the problem head-on. They considered options such as the community retaining the petrol bowsers with a visiting mechanic providing a part-time service, but what they really had their heart set on was finding a buyer. Top of the agenda was a publicity campaign, starting with stories in Wimmera newspapers and a dedicated Facebook page. Ange used her media contacts and approached *The Weekly Times*, a rural newspaper that has been the 'Bible of the Bush' in Victoria for almost 150 years.

A city girl through and through, Marnie Baker did not usually read it, but one of her friends did. That friend spotted the quirky story about Harrow and its quest to find someone to take over the garage, preferably a mechanic or a young family who could move into the three-bedroom home that came with the business. She pointed out the story to Marnie who was immediately struck by the community spirit it portrayed. In an odd way, it reminded her of the inner-city area where she grew up.

Marnie spent most of her childhood living in Richmond. Her mother, Judi, worked as a senior secretary for future Australian prime minister Bob Hawke when he was president of the Australian Council of Trade Unions in the 1970s. A carpenter by trade, her father, Phil, built sets and props for Channel Nine and the Playbox Theatre Company, before later working for a general builder. Her parents divorced when Marnie was about seven, and she and her younger sister,

Amie, mostly lived with their father because Judi had to travel so much.

Their home was a large single-storey terrace house in a street with only two residential properties. The rest of the buildings were small-scale factories and warehouses, remnants of Richmond's long and proud industrial history. Nearby was Bryant & May's sprawling factory complex, which employed hundreds of people to make Redhead matches right up until the 1980s. The inner-city suburb was also home to Pelaco, a clothing company famous for its men's shirts; the neon sign put up on top of their building in 1939 remains a Melbourne landmark. Rosella tomato sauce was made in Richmond, too, as well as Paragon shoes and Wertheim pianos.

Right next door to the Bakers was a Popsy factory, which supplied popcorn to cinemas. They didn't need to go to the movies to smell it, or eat it. The aroma of hot popcorn embraced their house, and every year on their birthdays the workers gave Marnie and Amie bags of it bigger than they were. If they forgot the house key to let themselves in after school, they would hang out with the employees until their father came home, gobbling their way through their favourite treat.

When Marnie was growing up in the late 1970s and early 1980s, Richmond was known for a low standard of living and considerable unemployment, but what it lacked in wealth, it made up for in a sense of community and a rich folklore that Marnie loved. Around the corner were the stables where Squizzy Taylor kept his horses. A colourful figure in Melbourne's criminal underworld until he was shot and killed in 1927, the notorious gangster made his money from armed robbery, protection rackets, prostitution, gambling, and selling drugs and illegal alcohol. But in Richmond where he lived, to some he was a folk hero. 'Round there he's a bit like Ned Kelly,' Marnie says.

In his spare time, Phil played in a pub band that started out as the Modern Throwbacks and ended up Guilty as Charged. Their style was hard rock, with a punk edge, according to Marnie, who says her father definitely enjoyed his music more than carpentry. The band's main gig was playing at the Sydenham Hotel. The girls had a spot behind the bar, near the loud speakers, where they would curl up in their sleeping bags. Their dad would wave at them from the stage, and the bartenders made them raspberry and lemonade drinks, which the children called Red Neds. 'The only problem was that we would come out of there and couldn't hear anything because the music was so loud.'

Phil gave up playing in the band before his daughters became teenagers. 'As we got older he realised some of that scene became inappropriate. Looking back on it, Dad was good at monitoring how to raise two girls and changing when he had to,' Marnie says.

When she was fourteen, her father moved closer to Camberwell where she and her sister went to high school. They also acquired a baby half-sister when their mother gave birth to a daughter, Katie. Judi was working nightshift at the time, so Marnie played a significant role caring for the baby while pushing through her final years of secondary education. On the same day she received the offer for a place at university, she accepted a full-time job at the Arnott's biscuit factory in Burwood. 'I needed to work, so I took the job,' she says.

Over the next ten years Marnie worked her way up from factory hand, to personal assistant to the production and distribution managers. The plant employed about 600 people, making national favourites like Tim Tams, Iced Vovos and Monte Carlos before, quite contentiously, it was closed down in 2002. 'I really liked the work and it was hands on. I had to drive forklifts and help load trucks, and in the end I had the job of going out and testing new machinery and making recommendations. They wanted me to get a business degree, but I was already doing everything I would do if I got one, so I didn't see the point. And I didn't want to stay there forever,' Marnie says.

Instead, she took a completely different tack. She had been gardening and growing vegetables at her mother's house where there was plenty of space. It seemed to make more sense to do something that she genuinely enjoyed, so Marnie studied horticulture while juggling part-time work at Arnott's. Then she spent two years working full-time in plant nurseries. She loved her new career, but she was being paid a lot less than she had earned at the factory and by then she was a single mum, with two young sons to support. Sam was only two years old and Jesse was just three months old when Marnie and their father split up. The next few years were a financial and logistical struggle. Needing to earn as much as she could while working flexible hours, she took up casual work house cleaning and gardening.

Then in 2008, Marnie met Nathan on the last day of the Golden Plains music festival at Meredith. At the time, Nathan was a stagehand working on the award-winning HBO television series *The Pacific*. Part of the blockbuster American production was filmed in the You Yangs ranges near Geelong, not far from his hometown of Torquay. A qualified mechanic, Nathan took on the short-term position because he was looking for a change after ten years of being employed in a garage. 'We started talking early one evening about music and life,' Marnie says. 'It was the easiest conversation I have ever had and six hours later the festival was over, it was time to pack the tents and we exchanged phone numbers.'

Given she was a little older and had two children, Marnie didn't really expect to hear from Nathan again, but he called within a few days and made plans to visit. She was very nervous. 'I was worried that I mightn't find him as attractive in the light of day,' she jokes. 'I remember opening the front door and thinking, "Phew!" and then "Woohoo!" He was gorgeous.' Sam and Jesse liked him, too, and despite her early reservations Marnie was thrilled to see that Nathan returned the children's affection. After eight months of dating as a family, and long nightly telephone conversations, Nathan found work in Melbourne as a warehouse manager and moved in.

In March 2011, three years after meeting, they were married in a simple ceremony at romantic Woolrich Retreat in the Dandenong Ranges. Woolrich boasts an acclaimed garden that is more than a century old. It was the perfect setting for Marnie to walk down the aisle, on the arm of her very proud father. Her best friend, Melissa, was matron of honour and Nate's best friend, Adam, was best man. Standing right there with them were Sam, who carried the rings, and Jesse, who was a page boy. Marnie's favourite part of the ceremony came when the celebrant acknowledged that it was all about bringing them together as a family, not just a couple. 'He recognised the boys and Nathan's love of them, and the wonderful role he plays in their childhood,' she says.

A few months later, Marnie and Nathan were trying to settle into married life in suburban Bayswater when the story about the Harrow garage appeared in *The Weekly Times*. They had often talked about moving to the bush one day, but thought of it more as a retirement plan. Yet the idea of Harrow and the potential life it might offer their boys kept niggling away at them. They started to think very seriously about what they valued from their own childhoods and how they could give their sons the same experiences and opportunities.

The more they considered it, the more they realised the answers did not lie in Melbourne. They felt disconnected from the community in which they lived, and they did not like having to worry constantly about the boys' safety. Marnie recalls: 'They had friends in the area, but to go and visit them

I had to drop them off because to get there on their bikes they had to cross a lot of main roads. It may sound a little bit paranoid, but there were a lot of car accidents. We were on a dog-leg in the road and in the eight years I lived in that house, there were seven car crashes on the corner, and I had two cars stolen from the driveway.'

Then there was the methadone clinic which operated nearby. Heroin addicts often sat in the street drinking. 'Someone told me that's how you get the methadone to work. It gives you a bit of a buzz if you do it that way. It only happened once a week, but there seemed to be at least five or six people with their little toddlers or babies, calling their kids swear words. Sometimes the blokes would lie on the ground because they had fallen asleep.'

Marnie did not like her boys confronting these things at such a young age, and being forced to explain what was going on when they asked. 'I felt like it was important that I was able to provide my kids with a life in which they could learn about things as they became age-appropriate,' she says. 'I'm not trying to be negative but there were things I couldn't control. I can control what they watch on TV and the food I have in my house. While kids should have a clear view of the world, I don't think they should be afraid. You need to enjoy your childhood while you can. We had a chance to buy the house that we were in because it was owned by a friend of ours so we could have got it straight from them rather than through a real estate agent, but we sat down and talked. We realised that we didn't want to buy it, and we had always talked about living in the country.'

So Marnie and Nathan decided to hop in the car and drive to Harrow for a quick look. The trip took five and a half hours each way and they stayed for barely ninety minutes, but it was enough for them to know the idea of moving to Harrow was worth exploring. For a start, the landscape made just the right first impression. Marnie had never been to the area before but she knew the Wimmera was mostly flat, when she much preferred hills and mountains. Approaching Harrow from Balmoral, she was surprised to see rolling green hills. 'It was August, and the sun was shining, and it was beautiful and lush. It was just one of those perfect fairytale things,' Marnie says.

The town itself made a strong impression, too. Winding their way through towering gum trees, the O'Brien family crossed the Glenelg River and followed a road lined with what looked like an old-fashioned timber paling fence (it's actually made of concrete) into the main street. To their city eyes, it appeared that someone cared. Marnie remembers noticing there were even liners in the public rubbish bins. 'I know that might sound strange, but I wasn't used to that. Usually bins are all funky, and there are things falling all over the ground.'

Pulling up in the centre of town, they paid a visit to the Harrow Discovery Centre, where they were fascinated by its award-winning displays about Johnny Mullagh and one of the largest collections in the world relating to legendary Australian cricketer Donald Bradman. The volunteer in charge introduced himself as 'Pop' and made them feel very welcome. 'He didn't know why we were there—we were just passing tourists, but he was a barrel of laughs,' Marnie says.

Afterwards they walked back along the street to the garage. Bernie was away, but Pauline knew they were coming. When they arrived, the place was deserted so they went across the road to the pub to make enquiries. The friendly barmaid turned out to be Pauline's daughter-in-law. She told them Pauline would be back soon and offered them a drink while they waited. They had no sooner picked up their glasses when the missing garage owner showed up.

'We better finish our drinks first,' Marnie said.

'No, you'll be fine, take them with you,' the barmaid replied.

'Down the street?' Marnie queried.

'Yeah, don't worry about it.'

Shaking their heads at how laid-back and accommodating everyone seemed to be, the O'Briens set off to inspect what might soon become their business. They loved the fact the garage had been rebuilt in 1995 using corrugated iron to complement the heritage feel of the town, complete with an antique petrol pump. Interested in history, they were also drawn to the transport museum set up alongside the workshop, with its fascinating collection of vintage cars and motoring ephemera. If they took on the garage, they would be running this, too.

Tour completed, the O'Briens adjourned to the local cafe for lunch. Watching a group of children playing across the road, Jesse and Sam asked if they could join in. Marnie's city instincts were to decline because she didn't know them. 'And Nathan just sort of looked at me,' she says. Realising she was worrying too much, Marnie gave in. As she watched the boys laugh and run about with their new friends, she realised they were experiencing the same sense of freedom she had enjoyed as a child. Marnie knew the boys appreciated it, too, when they returned from their play session and asked a question she had never heard them ask before after any of their holidays or visits to family and friends who lived in other places. 'Mum, can we move here?'

With that ringing endorsement, Nathan and Marnie tackled the next step—arranging finance to buy the business. They had been working hard and saving for years. Based on their discussions with Pauline, they believed there was enough in the bank to secure an adequate loan. Reality came crashing around them when they got back to Melbourne. According to the banks, the garage was subject to higher interest rates and tougher loan conditions because it was in a rural area. 'So that totally put a spanner in the works. You can't get blood out of a stone,' Marnie sighs.

But Marnie and Nathan had not reckoned on the people of Harrow. Determined not to let the O'Briens slip through their fingers, someone in the community suggested a three-year leasing arrangement to give them time to find their feet. Nathan and Marnie were still waiting to hear back from the Kellys about whether they would accept the offer when a local farmer by the name of Wayne rang up to make sure they were still interested. 'He talked to me for ages,' Marnie recalls. 'He's out in the paddock and the dogs are barking, and he's singin' me the virtues of Harrow.'

Wayne told them he was coming to Melbourne to continue his campaign in person, but before he could make good the promise, the Kellys phoned to say they were willing to consider the idea of a lease. With the main obstacles out of the way, Marnie and Nathan sat down with their boys to make sure they realised what the move would mean if it went ahead. 'Both of us had really good, well-paying jobs. We would have to give those up, pull the kids out of school, and I would have to leave my mum and dad behind. That was really big. I had dinner with Dad once a week, and Mum twice a week. We are very close with them,' Marnie says.

The boys weren't fazed. They thought the garage was cool, and were rapt with the possibilities of all the country adventures awaiting them. They would miss their friends, but they could talk on the phone, and maybe their mates could even come and stay during the holidays. With their children on side, Marnie and Nathan decided they should go back to Harrow one more time to make absolutely sure they were doing the right thing.

Informed of their plans, Wayne leapt into action. Thinking strategically about what it might take to clinch the sale, he invited ten or so other couples to join the O'Briens for dinner at the pub. They included people about the same age, families who had moved to the area and loved it, the persuasive Ange Newton and a handful of local business operators. The logistics weren't easy because there was a Sound and Light Show that night, and half of them were involved in the performance, but the publican set aside a big table in a separate room near all the action so the volunteers could come and go. 'It was like speed dating. We moved from couple to couple around the table,' says Marnie.

Worried how Nathan might be coping, given he tends to be on the quiet side, Marnie looked over at one stage to see him firmly settled at the end of the table, talking to a bloke who had grown up near Geelong. They were bonding over their mutual love of the Geelong football team, the Cats, and were well on the way to becoming firm friends. 'He was happy as Larry,' says Marnie.

Strolling back to their accommodation sometime around midnight, Nathan and Marnie reflected on what had been a wonderful night. Stretched out before them in the light of a gibbous moon was the now quiet main street, with its old buildings sitting dark and solid, reinforcing a sense of permanency. 'What do you think?' Marnie said, turning to her husband.

'I'm not sure, what do you think?'

'I'll be straight with you. I just want to do this. I love this place. I want to give it a go. What's the worst thing that could happen?'

Nathan grinned at her in the moonlight. 'I'm glad you said that because I really want to give it a go, too!'

It took almost five months for the O'Briens to reorganise their life and make the move. Deciding to wait until after Christmas, they spent months sorting out the paperwork, meeting with banks and lawyers, packing up the Melbourne house and saying farewell to family and friends. Finally, in early March 2012, they set off for Harrow with all their possessions. When they arrived at about seven o'clock in the evening, they found a quiche warming in the oven—a thoughtful gesture by Pauline who knew that nothing would be open in town if they needed something to eat.

After a tiring day, the family slept peacefully in their new home, only to wake up the next morning to find they had no water. During the night, the pump attached to their rainwater tank had become disconnected and all the water had drained into the garden. Marnie and Nathan had no idea what to do, so they rang Pauline. As it turned out, the town had a central water supply and the house was attached to it, so all they had to do was flip a switch. It took them days and quite a few unpleasant cups of coffee to find out that the town water wasn't meant for drinking. It was untreated and officially designated unfit for human consumption.

It was the first of many both small and large revelations about life in the country for Marnie and Nathan. 'There's always something where you think, "Well, that's never happened before. What do I do now?" I know stuff happens in the city, too, but if there was a problem I'd just head down the street to my favourite cafe for a coffee,' Marnie jokes.

Meanwhile, some of the issues she thought might be a challenge have never come to pass. 'While I'm social, I'm actually a bit of an introvert and I was worried that everyone would constantly be coming to the house, but they are not like that at all. If you want someone to visit, they will come and visit, and it's not taken for granted. If I'm out and about, I can just say, "I'm going home now, I'll see you later," and no-one thinks it's rude. It's a different dynamic, which makes you more honest and, funnily enough, it's a lot less stressful. In the country, people take it that what you mean is what you say, and they take me for who I am.'

Lubricating almost every situation is a willingness to laugh at themselves that Marnie really values. 'Maybe that's the thing that makes the difference. Everyone here is really humorous,' she says. 'Sometimes people can take it the wrong way. I've been told every blonde joke under the sun, and if I wanted to get offended I could, but if you look at the intention behind it, you can laugh with them.'

Then there are the endearing moments that Marnie likens to scenes from the ever-popular television series *The Vicar of Dibley*. Set in a small English village with its own eccentric way of doing things, every episode includes a parish council meeting where the foibles of each member make for some peculiar discussions and challenging experiences for the astounded vicar.

One of Marnie's favourite examples relates to the Harrow Promotion and Development Group. After promising herself not to volunteer for any committees in the first year of living in the town, she was appointed treasurer. For several meetings, most of the time was taken up discussing a plaque commemorating the Sound and Light Show. For a start, it was being organised to mark seventeen years. Not a nice conventionally round or significant anniversary milestone, like ten years or even twenty-five, but seventeen. 'It's such a strange number,' Marnie thought to herself.

Deciding not to say anything, she tried to focus on the debate about where the plaque should be placed. The idea was to fix it to a rock, but there seemed to be a problem with every site proposed. Eventually, everyone agreed that the ideal place would be next to the old gaol. The only remaining conundrum was that such a move would require approval from the town's historical society, and they weren't due to meet for quite a while. The group didn't want to wait so there was a lengthy discussion about whether they should just go ahead and do it anyway.

As the debate drew to a close, Marnie heard three members of the committee start a whispered conversation, so she asked them what they were discussing. 'We are just having a meeting of the historical society,' one of them replied. Taking in Marnie's incredulous expression, they explained that they were also committee members of the historical society. One of them was even president.

'Why didn't you say anything before?' Marnie asked.

'Well, we didn't want to have a meeting while you were having a meeting,' was the apologetic reply.

Marnie burst out laughing. Unfazed, the historical society committee members huddled together for an impromptu vote, while everyone else in the room tried not to pay attention. Approval for the rock to be placed near the gaol was given, and the promotion group duly informed.

'Bunch of crazies, they are,' Marnie says with great affection, wrapping up the tale.

10

NEW LIFE AND ALMOST DEATH

Marnie is sitting on the front verandah of the three-bedroom house that came with the garage, keeping an eye on the business while Nathan is in Melbourne taking a diesel mechanic's course. The modest weatherboard home is right next door so it's easy enough to walk over if a car pulls up at the fuel pumps. Playing at her feet is Bailey, the newest addition to the O'Brien family and a symbol in more ways than one of what Harrow has come to mean to them. 'We had only been here a few weeks and I got pregnant,' Marnie says. 'I always tell people it's because there's no television, and funnily enough it actually was.'

Her first child, Sam, was born in a Melbourne hospital after about twenty hours of labour; however, Jesse arrived in the world so fast that he was delivered at home. Marnie experienced some pain before her waters broke at about one o'clock in the morning, but no contractions, so when she rang the hospital they advised her to wait a few hours before coming in. Not long after that she had just two contractions, and there he was. Marnie was worried about the same thing happening again, so she went to see Bernie Close who manages the Harrow Bush Nursing Centre.

A remarkable service with a history that stretches back more than a hundred years, the centre not only provides health care to the district but in many ways is the heart and soul of the community. It started with a single nurse, Mabel Price, who was recruited from England in 1913 by the Victorian Bush Nursing Association. Trained in Sheffield and London, she was also a qualified midwife. Harrow must have seemed like another planet to her and she didn't stay long. When World War I broke out, she resigned to return to England. Nurse Price was replaced, and the service continued until 1924, managed and paid for by the local community through annual subscriptions and fundraising. Visiting doctors continued to serve the town after the first centre closed, but there was no resident full-time health care again until 1953, when the Bush Nursing Centre was re-established and it's been operating ever since.

Today's service is a far cry from one nurse equipped with two leather saddlebags packed with what amounted to little more than a basic first-aid kit. Based in a modern brick building just across the street from the garage, it's still managed by the community as a not-for-profit operation, but it employs a team of nurses who are trained to the level of paramedics so they can respond quickly to medical emergencies. Effectively, it means that people in the Harrow district have immediate access to a level of emergency support rarely found in small communities, and comparable in response time to many resource-stretched city services. Marnie has no doubt at all that she owes the centre and its nurses her life.

When Bernie heard about Marnie's last delivery, she spent some time teaching her and Nathan what was involved in home birth should they be caught out again next time. They both felt much better with the extra preparation, and knowing there was support just across the road if needed.

Marnie's pregnancy progressed smoothly until she experienced a bout of severe pain a couple of weeks before the baby was due. She saw her doctor in Hamilton and everything seemed to be okay. A week later she was lying on the couch at about ten o'clock in the evening when an excruciating pain tore through her belly. 'It was terrible and I knew straight away it was a really bad thing,' she says. Within moments there was a lot of blood. Marnie was haemorrhaging.

Nathan was having a quiet drink with friends at the pub, but fortunately for Marnie two of her girlfriends from Melbourne were staying at the time. They leapt into action. Bec distracted Sam and Jesse with computer games while Melissa ran to get Nathan, and Marnie rang 000. She also called the dependable Bernie. The qualified midwife had kept an eye on her throughout her pregnancy, and gave Marnie her personal phone number just in case something happened when she wasn't on duty.

Bernie lives on a farm out of town, but she was there within ten minutes and so was another nurse, Jan. Marnie remembers lying on the floor with half the contents of her linen cupboard pressed between her legs as they tried to staunch the flow of blood, and Melissa standing alongside holding an IV fluid bag of Hartmann's solution. For some reason her friend was standing on one leg. Later, she learnt that in the drama of sprinting across the road to the pub, Melissa had snapped her Achilles tendon. 'I remember looking at her leg and her calf was like a tennis ball,' Marnie says.

Quickly assessing the situation, Bernie decided to call in the emergency helicopter. It takes at least an hour for an ambulance to reach Harrow by road and she wasn't sure they had that long. As a designated Remote Area Nurse with specialist emergency training, Bernie and the other nurses at Harrow have greater authority to initiate certain types of treatment than a general nurse. But she couldn't provide Marnie with the blood transfusions that she needed to stay alive, and then there was the baby to consider.

Fate seemed against them. There were bushfires in the area and the smoke made it impossible for the helicopter to land safely. The closest it could reach was Coleraine, about 50 kilometres to the south. There was no choice but to wait for the ambulance and then drive to Coleraine. When the ambulance arrived it only had one crew, the driver, so Bernie climbed into the back and held Marnie's hand all the way. 'I'm going to be honest with you,' Bernie told her before they left. 'Your baby's fine but I am really worried about you. But I'm here for you, Marnie.'

By the time they reached Coleraine, Marnie was in a great deal of pain and extremely anxious about getting into the helicopter. The helicopter crew were worried, too. If she gave birth mid-flight, they could not guarantee her safety. It was only twenty minutes further by road to the Hamilton Base Hospital so they decided to drive on. The helicopter's medical team could administer blood products, so they grabbed what they needed and one of them climbed aboard the ambulance with Bernie.

At the hospital, doctors told Marnie her placenta had separated from the uterus. The ambulance trip turned out to be a blessing. Because of the bumpy road conditions, the baby had moved and his head settled in the right place to stem the bleeding.

Bailey was born, safe and well, the next morning. After a few days luxuriating in a private room with a balcony view, Marnie was fine, too. Looking back at the ordeal, she says she wasn't scared because she had Bernie. 'It was actually a wonderful experience in an odd way. I knew the bush nurses would look after me and my baby, and I was surrounded by people who loved me, but I don't think I would be here today if it was not for that group of ladies over there,' she says, nodding towards the centre.

Asked for her take on the incident, Bernie agrees. 'She is alive, and her baby is alive, because of the Bush Nursing Centre,' she says with conviction.

❖ ❖ ❖

Bailey's birth isn't the only medical emergency the O'Briens have faced as a family since moving to Harrow. In 2015, Jesse was playing with an overhead sprinkler at the cricket ground when it swung round and hit him in the head.

It was a scorching March day, a last gasp of summer. Everyone was gathered for a barbecue at Johnny Mullagh Park where cricket has been played for more than 140 years. Within minutes of arriving, Sam and Jesse noticed other children running around under the giant travelling sprinkler that helps keep the grounds a lush green, and went racing off to join them. Marnie and Nathan yelled at them to come back, but they were already too far away to hear, so they continued unloading the car. Besides it was 40 degrees, and the cooling sprays of water looked more than a little tempting.

Marnie was chatting to a friend when she noticed Jesse copy another boy and swing off one of the sprinkler's arms. Worried they might break it, she decided it was time to call a halt. 'Hoi, get off that thing,' she shouted, walking towards them. Jesse heard and jumped off. Knowing he was in trouble, he turned to look at her, and the rotating arm hit him in the temple. He was conscious but there was a lot of blood.

Knowing it would take an ambulance more than an hour to arrive, Marnie and Nathan decided to drive their son to the emergency department at Edenhope Hospital about thirty kilometres away. He was there when he started to have a seizure. The doctor intubated him, pushing a flexible plastic tube through his mouth and into his windpipe so they could keep him breathing, and ordered the emergency helicopter.

Jesse was airlifted to the Royal Children's Hospital in Melbourne. After a week, he seemed to be recovering nicely, so the medical team decided it was time to send him home. Then he went into respiratory arrest. They revived him and kept him at the hospital, carefully monitoring his condition. After a couple of weeks, Marnie was concerned that Jesse's breathing still seemed troubled, especially when he lay down to sleep. He sounded a bit like Darth Vader but the doctors thought it was a side-effect of the head trauma and told her not to worry.

Back in Harrow and unhappy with Jesse's progress, Marnie decided to seek a second opinion. She ended up taking him to several different doctors who all told her the same thing; her son was recovering and although it was going to take some time, he would be fine. However, the nurses at the Bush Nursing Centre were concerned, too, so they pulled some strings to secure a quick appointment with an ear, nose and throat surgeon based in Hamilton. She examined Jesse and told his mother, 'You need to take him back to Melbourne today.'

Instructing her to go home and prepare for the trip, the surgeon contacted Jesse's specialist at the Royal Children's Hospital and explained what she had found. 'Two hours later we got the call to go to Melbourne, but by then it was seven o'clock at night and it's a long drive. No-one explained exactly how serious it was so I told them we would come tomorrow.'

When Marnie delivered Jesse to the hospital's emergency department the next day, the medical team explained that he would need a tracheostomy. The surgical procedure involves making an opening in the trachea, below the larynx, and inserting a tube. The aim in this case was to remove mucus which had been accumulating in Jesse's throat. Apparently his windpipe had been damaged during intubation. 'There is a section of his windpipe that is smaller than normal, so when they intubated him, they tore it,' Marnie explains. As a result, it had become inflamed and his throat was secreting more mucus than usual to smooth the damage. The problem was missed during an earlier examination with a scope because it wasn't inserted far enough. Now, he was down to just 20 per cent of his normal airway, threatening his life.

Jesse was immediately given steroids to reduce the inflammation, however by the time he went into surgery he was in a coma. The surgeon was extremely concerned, and Marnie and Nathan were terrified. But a few hours later they walked into his room and found him sitting up in bed, talking. As it turned out, the surgeons didn't need to go ahead with the tracheostomy. 'The head surgeon called him their Easter miracle,' Marnie says. 'He had responded to the steroids and his throat had opened up.'

After weeks taking steroids, Jesse gradually recovered. The treatment temporarily caused his face to bloat and his weight to balloon, to the point where quite a few people back in Harrow didn't recognise him. Marnie was worried what other children might say when he returned to school, but she was blown away by their response. 'He walked back in and not one kid said anything about the change,' she says.

While it would have been much easier to access the ongoing specialist treatment Jesse needed if they had still been living in Melbourne, the community response to their situation was a powerful reminder of why they moved to the country. With the garage to run, Nathan couldn't always be with Jesse in hospital, and it was an extremely anxious time for him. People dropped in to see if there was anything they could do, delivering casseroles and apple pies, and inundating him with dinner invitations. 'They even filled up our wood shed,' Marnie says. 'And when Jesse was in hospital, pretty much every child at the school wrote him a card, and the town bought him a big bouquet with teddy bears and chocolate.'

For Marnie and Nathan, the hardest thing about living in Harrow is not being close to their families. The nurturing and support they receive from the community helps counteract that. 'People care and it means so much,' she says. After just a few years the whole family has a strong sense of belonging. Marnie has even become involved in the Sound and Light Show. She's part of the cast and responsible for scheduling the year's program, although she's still trying to live down the year she locked in one performance for AFL grand final day—a no go, if you want anyone to turn up, including the cast!

She loves being involved in the amateur theatricals, and so do Sam and Jesse who are now cast regulars, shadowing Stretch Penrose as apprentice undertakers. 'There is something very intimate and personal about it. You really feel like you are part of something. It's not just a bunch of actors putting on a show for you,' Marnie says, considering why the event is still drawing crowds almost twenty years on.

Nathan even gave being part of the cast a try, before deciding it was not for him. Instead, he has signed up as a Country Fire Authority volunteer, joined committees for several local events. He loves the relaxing lifestyle in Harrow, and knowing the whole town, although it has an unexpected downside.

Nathan had only ever been to two funerals before he moved to Harrow. In the first two years of living in the town, he attended three. 'In Melbourne you might see your mechanic when the car needs servicing but here it's different,' Marnie explains. 'Even if people are not customers, you see them all the time. You get to know them. It's lovely but it's also maybe a little more heartbreaking.'

While admitting that she liked her privacy in the city, Marnie says in Harrow it just feels right to get involved in the community and be part of other people's lives. 'Moving here, you have to make a choice about the way you live. You shouldn't come just because the rent is cheap. You are not just choosing a house, you are choosing a lifestyle,' she says.

When she stops to think about it, Marnie is still surprised at how friendly and welcoming everyone has been since the very first day they visited Harrow. 'I did spend the first six months thinking it was too good to be true. I keep waiting for the other shoe to drop. It's going to be huge when it happens,' she jokes.

11

A BEAUT BLOKE

The success of the Sound and Light Show shifted something in the psyche of Harrow. Now it's almost as if no idea is too crazy or unachievable to be considered by the town. So when Ange came up with another concept, there may have been more eye-rolling, but the community quickly got on board to expand the idea and make it work.

It started with a conversation over the bar at the pub, just after the annual bachelor and spinster ball. A tradition in many rural areas, most B&S events are all about young people from the bush getting together for a social weekend, which usually involves camping out in swags, music and dancing, and lots of alcohol. Known as the Tussock Jumpers Ball, the Harrow version has been going for more than thirty years and has a reputation for being well run and more orderly than most. It's held every January in the park on the edge of town, and usually attracts about 700 people, with many of them driving long distances to attend. Run by community groups as a fundraiser, it can generate as much as $15,000 in a single weekend.

This particular year some local lads retreated to the pub, all forlorn, as utes and cars carried away the last of the visitors, including all the single women they had met. One of the young men leant on the bar and whined to the publican, 'Oh Ange, we need some girls to stay.' Ange went to bed that night trying to think of a solution.

Like many small country towns, there was a distinct shortage of single, young women in Harrow. Encouraged by their parents, most of them had left the area to go to university and pursue careers in larger rural towns or cities. The young men might go away to agricultural college, too, but they often came back to the family farm, or they just stayed in the area and took up jobs in the rural services sector such as shearing. 'We had so many gorgeous young men, lovely boys, and no women,' Ange says.

What really worried her were the deeper social issues at play. She could detect signs of serious loneliness among the pub's single male patrons, and was concerned about the potential for that to lead to depression and even worse. The media was increasingly reporting that young rural males were particularly at risk when it came to suicide. Ange did not want to see that happen to any of the boys she knew. 'They needed to have fun in life,' she says. 'And I was acutely aware that if these young blokes didn't find partners, they might leave, and I didn't want that either. In small communities, you need succession plans, so I thought that we really needed to do something.'

After mulling over the problem, Ange decided the best approach would be to invite eligible girls to visit Harrow for a weekend of organised activities. The program should harness good old-fashioned country hospitality and give them a concentrated taste of life in rural Australia, as well as the opportunity to meet some local bachelors. Thinking about how to promote the concept so that it conveyed what was on offer, she resorted to the sort of 'boy speak' she heard in the pub, and came up with Beaut Blokes. She took the name and the idea to the blokes themselves and they fleshed out the bones.

It was a simple idea with a simple aim, but the attention to detail in the planning and execution behind the first

Beaut Blokes gathering in June 2003 was masterful. Using promotional skills honed in marketing the Sound and Light Show, the community began to spread the word. An interview on a Geelong radio station proved particularly powerful, and before they knew it applications from interested women were flooding it.

Eighty single women aged between twenty and forty paid $175 each to attend, matching the eighty single men who signed up, too. The girls were billeted with local families, who gave them a home-cooked roast meal on the Friday night. Each home provided accommodation for at least two girls, so they had someone on hand who was sharing the experience, and the families were paid for helping out. Beaut blokes and their families were not allowed to host the girls, with them all meeting for the first time at an organised event on the first evening. 'It was so squeaky clean it was ridiculous,' Ange says with a grin. 'We wanted to show the girls the best time, and we wanted them to trust us to look after them. This was about nice girls meeting nice boys.'

Ange is quick to point out that the men involved were not lost causes. 'There is a misconception that country boys don't know much about women, but that's not true at all. They were not having trouble getting and keeping girls, it's just that there were no girls to get,' she says.

Before they were allowed to take part, the men had to sign a simple pledge: 'A Beaut Bloke must be single, love his mum, be kind to his sister and who's [sic] heart is in rural Australia.' The statement was a reminder of what the weekend represented, and their responsibility for making sure the women were treated with respect. 'It was very simple stuff. You wouldn't want your daughter coming to our town and finding the men are a bunch of hooligans,' Ange says.

When the weekend came, there was so much media interest that a press conference was called at the pub. 'It just went viral. There was national coverage,' she says. 'We begged them to be kind and careful with us because we didn't know anything about the media, and they were brilliant. They could have turned it into something really horrible but they didn't.'

❖ ❖ ❖

The first time Sherryn Simpson heard about Beaut Blokes was during a phone call from her cousin. Louisa had seen one of the television news stories, and thought it sounded like a fabulous idea, so she made enquiries. Meanwhile, in Harrow, Ange was already organising a second event in response to the extraordinary interest the media coverage was stirring up.

Louisa was keen to attend but Sherryn couldn't think of anything worse. The only girl in her family, Louisa looked on Sherryn almost as a sister and they were close, but they had a very different approach when it came to finding potential partners. Her cousin loved dressing up and going out to night clubs to meet boys. Sherryn always thought that she would meet the right man in a casual way, maybe when she was having dinner or a drink with friends. She did not want to go to the very public Harrow matchmaking event. She knew how it would end. Louisa would find a bloke and she would be left on her own to struggle through the weekend, a long way from home, with a heap of strangers. The problem was Louisa had already bought two tickets. 'You're going,' she told her.

Come the designated weekend in August, Sherryn packed her bag, still wondering how on earth she had been talked into something she was certain would prove a dating disaster. The two girls drove out of the city on Friday evening, finding their way to the farm where they were staying about fifteen kilometres from Harrow. Wanting to make them feel welcome, their host had even placed chocolates on their pillows. Then she offered to drive them into town for the initial meet-and-greet at the pub, where every girl would be partnered up with a boy, not as a matchmaking exercise but to help break the ice. During the evening, the boy would introduce the girl to other blokes, and the girl would take responsibility for introducing the boy to the other girls, even though she didn't know most of them.

As they were driving to the pub, Sherryn was calculating potential escape routes. What if her cousin hooked up with someone straight away, leaving her on her own? How could she get back to the farm if the evening turned into a catastrophe?

When they arrived at the pub, their host decided to introduce the two girls to a few of the blokes to get them started. One of them was her nephew, Mark McClure. Sherryn and Mark had very little opportunity to chat before everyone was called to attention so the girls could be given their assigned partner. 'It was my worst nightmare,' says Sherryn, who at the time was studying to be a school teacher. 'Put me in front of five hundred kids and I can sing a song and dance a jig, but put me in front of half a dozen adults and I just freak out. The process happened in front of everyone. We all stood in this room and they called out the girl, and then the boy. Everyone was looking at you.'

The already uncomfortable situation just got worse when Sherryn's name was called. She steeled herself and stepped forward. Then her partner's name was called. Nothing happened. The name was called again. No response. Sherryn was mortified. She could feel the eyes of the crowd looking at her, and she was convinced they were all thinking, 'What a loser!' Embarrassed by the no-show, the organiser moved on to the next girl, and Sherryn was left standing to one side. She later learnt that the bloke who was meant to partner her was a keen footballer and decided not to attend because he had an important game the next day.

For Mark, it was the most exciting development of the night. He would later tell Sherryn that the moment he saw her, he knew she was the girl for him. He was delighted her partner failed to turn up because it gave him the chance to step in. 'I'm not certain what happened to the girl Mark was meant to be partnering, but he obviously managed a very big handball of some sort,' jokes Sherryn.

'My aunty told me to look after her, so I looked after her, and I'm still looking after her,' Mark explains later with his trademark dry humour, before going on to admit, more seriously: 'It was a pretty funny feeling, the first time, meeting a girl that you are keen on, and all your mates are there watching.'

The evening progressed, with Sherryn and her cousin settling into a corner with Mark and his best mate, Shane. Sherryn recalls they were all chatting happily but before long, Louisa and Shane started kissing. 'It was really awkward because they are right there, and I'm thinking, "Is Mark expecting me to do this?" To me, it was all just about surviving the weekend at that point. I knew that I liked him. I thought he was a nice enough bloke and we were having a good laugh, but I probably didn't take enough risks that way. I only ever had a small group of friends, and when it came to love, I was very cautious.'

When the pub closed, Sherryn and Mark were among a dozen or so of the meet-and-greet group that went back to Shane's house for the rest of the night. Known locally as The Castle, it was the place where his mates regularly stayed at weekends rather than driving home after having a bit to drink.

The following morning the boys decided to forgo the next part of the formal program, which involved introducing the girls to typical farm work, such as milking cows or shearing a sheep. Instead they took them mud bashing.

It was a terrifying experience for Sherryn. 'We all got into utes, and went driving through the paddocks in the mud, then they'd stop and have a beer. I'm a bit of a safety freak and flying around sideways in cars doesn't strike me as being terribly safe. They were having a wow of a time but I spent most of it clinging to the door.' Telling the others, not very convincingly, that she was having fun, she was actually scared and just wanted to go home.

On the Saturday afternoon, they reached the part of the program that the Melbourne girl and sports fan knew she would enjoy—attending a football game. But Sherryn's relief was cut short when Mark decided that on the way to the game they would call in to the family farm so she could meet his parents. He didn't seem at all concerned that she was still wearing the clothes she had gone out in the night before and there'd been no chance to freshen up. 'What a horrible way to meet them,' she says.

Sherryn was still in 'survival mode' at the time, with no sense that the weekend might lead to something serious. 'I was just trying to make it to the next bit,' she admits. But she did enjoy the football match. Known as the Southern Roos, the Harrow-Balmoral football club has a healthy following and a stellar track record in the Horsham district league. Like most country communities, Harrow takes its football seriously, and a big proportion of the population usually turns out to watch the game, especially when they are playing at their home ground a short distance north of the town.

A Collingwood supporter, Sherryn grew up going to the team's training sessions and AFL games in Melbourne. She also watched the occasional suburban game with her father and found they lacked atmosphere compared with the big league. 'But the atmosphere at Harrow was awesome. They were all yelling and cheering. Everyone was into it,' Sherryn says.

She was also extremely impressed with the netball games happening on courts right next to the oval. As in many country areas, football and netball competitions go hand in hand in the Horsham league. The matches are played at the same time, usually on the same site, making an all-inclusive great day out for the whole family. 'The level of competition was really exciting,' Sherryn recalls. 'It was full on and I really enjoyed it.'

After the game Sherryn and Louisa returned to their host farm and prepared for the final big event of the weekend—a black-tie dinner at the RSL hall. Sherryn dressed up for the occasion, choosing a short, fitted dress of red silk, which coincidentally matched perfectly with Mark's black suit and red shirt. More relaxed than she had been all weekend, she started having fun. 'We just danced and sang and had a great time,' she says. 'I was enjoying his company, and I realised that maybe there could be something there.'

In a strange reversal of the expected ending to the weekend, the next day Sherryn found herself standing outside the pub and waving goodbye to Mark as he left town. 'Mark ended up leaving before us because he had to go to a machinery sale,' she says, pointing out that she should have taken notice of this as a sign of things to come. She had no idea that as he drove away Mark was feeling anxious that he might never see her again, even though they had swapped phone numbers. 'Later, he told me that it was the worst moment of his life,' Sherryn says.

12

LESSONS FOR THE TEACHER

The first time Jean Simpson set eyes on Sherryn, she politely told the nurse that the baby couldn't possibly be hers. With brown hair and a dark complexion, she looked nothing like her older sister, who came into the world with blonde hair, blue eyes and peachy white skin. But Sherryn was definitely her daughter, and the initial shock soon wore off.

Sherryn was born at St Vincent's Private Hospital in March 1977. Originally from Birmingham in England, her mother came to Australia as a child in the 1950s, as part of the assisted immigration program that became known as the Ten Pound Pom scheme. 'The story goes that her family's house caught fire, and my pop had always loved the ocean and the sun. It was either rebuild their lives there, or move to Australia and make a clean start, so they moved here,' Sherryn explains. The family settled in the seaside Melbourne suburb of St Kilda.

Meanwhile, her father, Geoff Simpson, was growing up in the outer eastern suburb of Canterbury, which was still very rural in the 1950s, with open farmland where he and his brothers went rabbit hunting. The family had roots in the area going back to the 1800s. His great-grandfather, James Britnell, owned extensive holdings at Box Hill but family stories have it that he gambled his fortune away. 'We could have been rich!' says Sherryn.

As a young man in the 1960s, Geoff played in a band influenced by The Beatles. One of the band members, John, was dating Jean, and he started dating her sister, Paula. 'They obviously figured out at some stage that they needed to swap,' Sherryn says. John and Paula ended up marrying, too.

Her parents' engagement raised a few eyebrows. Geoff was from a staunchly Catholic family and Jean was Anglican, at a time when the difference mattered to many, including his mother who Sherryn suspects never really approved. They married in St Dominic's Catholic Church at East Camberwell, after a series of compulsory meetings with the priest. 'Mum always says she was really lucky because they had a priest ahead of his time, who was not interested in converting her or anything like that. It was more about making sure they had thought about the big questions before they decided love conquers all. So she was really grateful to him and more than happy for us all to be baptised and raised Catholic.'

After their wedding, Sherryn's parents settled in Blackburn, close to where Geoff had grown up. 'Mum called it rural living, but it was really suburbia. We lived in a house in a little cul-de-sac and then when I was eleven we moved around the corner to a bigger house.' By then they were a family of six and needed considerably more space.

Three years after Sherryn was born, along came Kieran, and then two years after that Rachel. The oldest by two years was Danielle, who Sherryn describes as one of the most important people in her life. For a start, she credits her big sister with teaching her how to laugh. 'To this day, as grumpy as I can get, she is still able to make me smile.'

Although she does not have the classical features people associate with the condition, Danielle was born with Down syndrome. 'She was pretty sick as a baby, so it was hard work for Mum and Dad, but Mum's parents, Nan and Pop, spent a lot of time helping,' Sherryn explains. She has very fond memories of both grandparents and it is clear that family is important to Sherryn, and that her parents have been an enormous influence. Both instilled a strong work ethic in their daughter. Geoff not only held down a full-time job in the information technology sector, he drove taxis at night to bring in extra money. Apart from a few years following the birth of her youngest two children, Jean worked full-time, too, as a primary school teacher, juggling home, family and school duties.

'We were always raised with a working-class view of ourselves. We weren't well off but we weren't poor by any means because we had a terrific set of parents and family around us, and Mum and Dad worked hard to make sure we had everything they felt we needed,' Sherryn says. 'Mum might slice a chicken breast into four so we all had a schnitzel, but we always had home-cooked meals. Even though they were simple we all sat around the table together. You knew when dinner was getting close because Mum would call out, "Wash your hands," and Dad would be sitting there yelling, "If you're not here in five seconds, there will be no dinner for you." So we would all rush in and sit down.'

The first time Sherryn became conscious they might not have much money was in her first year at high school. After the winter holiday break, her new classmates came back with tans and exciting stories about going overseas, while the Simpsons had spent a few days visiting Pop on Mornington Peninsula.

'Where did you go?' her classmates asked her.

'Oh, we went to Rosebud,' Sherryn replied.

'What country's that in?'

All four Simpson children started their education at St Thomas the Apostle, a small Catholic primary school just a few blocks from home. Danielle ended up moving to Wesley College, because they offered her better support, and in year five, Sherryn found herself travelling twelve kilometres west every day to attend Glenferrie Primary School, where her mother worked. 'Mum had a run-in with one of my teachers,' she explained. 'Later on it came out that the teacher had said not to worry about spending too much money on my high school education because I probably wasn't going to be more than a secretary.' As both a teacher and a mother, Jean was outraged.

As it turned out, the move opened the door to a critical breakthrough in Sherryn's education. She wasn't particularly fond of school, occasionally tricking her nan into letting her stay home by faking a terrible cough. But in year six at Glenferrie she encountered a teacher who captured her interest in learning, and continues to inspire her. 'He was able to make connections for me,' she explains.

Sherryn was a talented swimmer. She trained eight times a week and dreamt of one day swimming butterfly for Australia. She loved the excitement of race meets, the way her body felt as she was powering through the water, and the quiet solace of swimming laps or diving under the surface where she felt totally free. One day in class, she was asked to calculate fifty times four as part of a lesson in multiplication. 'I wasn't that interested and I was battling to figure it out,' she says.

'But you're a swimmer. How big's your pool?' the teacher asked her.

'Fifty metres.'

'And if you swam four laps, how far have you swum?'

'Two hundred metres.'

'And there's how you figure it out.'

Sherryn was ecstatic. 'Oh, my gosh. I can do maths!'

❖ ❖ ❖

After primary school, Sherryn went back into the Catholic education system for two years, waiting for the right time to apply for entry to the highly regarded MacRobertson Girls' High School. Linked to the first Victorian state secondary school, it is named after Melbourne 'Chocolate King' Sir MacPherson Robertson, who donated £40,000 to build a new school, as part of a gift he made to the state in 1934 to celebrate its centenary. Students are selected to make sure there is a broad socio-economic and cultural mix, and it's not easy to get in, but Jean went there, and she was keen for her daughters to share the experience.

From the time she started at the school in year ten, Sherryn absolutely loved it. 'I never looked back,' she says. 'There were none of the social barriers I experienced at the other high school, and I was always going to do better at a girls' school. I found boys quite intimidating when I was growing up, although I didn't mind taking them on in a race in a pool.'

At MacRobertson, enjoying learning wasn't considered 'nerdy'. The school not only challenged her academically, but she became fast friends with a small group of girls who remain close to this day. The school was situated in the city centre, near Albert Park Lake. To get there Sherryn had to catch a train and then a tram, travelling for about forty-five minutes each way. 'We were all on the same train line, and we would all catch the 7.15 a.m. train from Blackburn. The third carriage from the front, back door. That was our spot.'

They got to know other regular passengers, too, despite never finding out their proper names. 'We had the man who worked for Telstra, known as the Telstra Man, and then the man who supported Collingwood, the Collingwood Man. We had all these commuters who, for the four years I was at MacRob, were there for our whole journey,' she says. 'One of my friends loved a good argument, and in our idealistic world we were quite politically driven so we would have these whole-carriage debates. It was awesome, and we met people because they would listen to our conversations and they would be laughing with us, or at us. At the end of year twelve, we had a little party with everyone on our last trip.'

Keen on science, Sherryn set herself the goal of becoming a veterinary surgeon. Her final exam results proved good enough and she was accepted into a Sydney University, then MacRobertson encouraged her to apply for an exchange program. It involved working as a matron for a year at an exclusive boarding school in England. Sherryn thought it would be an exciting opportunity to travel, meet new people and experience different cultures. When she and her best friend were both accepted, they delayed university studies and set off.

Only seventeen, Sherryn was matron of the school's largest boarding house, with sixty girls ranging in age from just six to twelve. She found the work interesting but sometimes heartbreaking, especially when dealing with her youngest charges. After the initial excitement of starting school wore off, some of them came to her at night, crying and wanting to go home. 'Sometimes I just wanted to go home, too!' she admits.

Set between London and Oxford, the school attracted children from the English aristocracy and even royal family connections. For most, going to boarding school at such a young age was a family tradition and they accepted it. 'I don't think they found it as confronting as an Australian child might,' Sherryn says.

During term time, Sherryn's job involved supervising the girls outside their studies, including making sure they did their homework and keeping an eye on them at night. She had her own bedroom, and access to a communal staff room. Her door was always open, even when she wasn't officially on duty, and girls would often come knocking. At weekends, she might take them for a walk into town, or out to play games if they were becoming bored or restless. And then in between terms, she and her best friend would travel around Europe, first on an organised tour and then, as their confidence grew, backpacking independently.

A bit older and wiser, a little more worldly and definitely more confident, Sherryn returned home in 1996 and found that her priorities had changed. She didn't want to go to Sydney, she wanted to stay in Melbourne with her family, so she settled on a science degree at Melbourne University, majoring in psychology and zoology. Four years later, degree in hand, Sherryn still didn't know what she wanted to do with her life. In the short-term, more travel appealed so she signed up with Camp America, a program that recruits Australians to work at summer camps in the United States. She ended up in St Louis, Missouri, working as a general counsellor in a program for inner-city youth deemed to be at risk.

What was meant to be a three-month job turned into three years. Every October she came home for four months, and then she would return, avoiding winter in both places. She became part of the management team, running different areas of the camp and supervising activities to help develop the participants' leadership skills. By the time she finished, Sherryn knew that she wanted to work with children, but she still wasn't entirely sure how.

Part of her dilemma was that Jean did not want her to be a teacher. She was adamant that her children should strive to do something else because teachers worked long hours for too little money. Considering her options, Sherryn decided to join the Victorian police force and become a community officer. That particular section of the force involved going into schools and working with youth who had been identified at risk, to try and help them turn their lives around before it was too late. 'It was pretty similar to what I had been doing in the States, but in a uniform.'

Her plans came undone when it was discovered she was too short-sighted to meet police requirements. Not to be deterred, Sherryn had laser surgery to correct her vision. Her grandmother had set aside money for each of her grandchildren that became available when they turned twenty-one, and Sherryn could not think of a better use. The surgery went well, but she had to wait another twelve months for her eyes to adjust before she was allowed to continue the application process. In the meantime, a job came up at her mother's school, Burwood Heights, working in the after-school care program and as a teacher's aide.

After six months had passed, the idea of joining the police force no longer appealed. It meant a year of training and then two years of probationary service in the general police force before she could get back to working with young people. Meanwhile, she was already doing what she loved. Then one day the principal called Sherryn into her office. 'Have you ever thought about teaching?' she asked. Sherryn explained it had always been off the table, because of her mother's opposition. 'It's something you really should think about,' the principal reiterated, recognising her potential.

While she was pondering her future, she met Mark, and their relationship became serious. Sherryn realised that joining the police force might cause dilemmas in the future, because there was no guarantee where she would be assigned. Mark was a farmer, working on the family property with his parents. Relocation was not an option for him. If they ended up together, she would be moving to Harrow. 'That was a huge deciding factor, too, and I don't regret it,' she says.

Mind made up, she enrolled for a post-graduate degree in teaching. It took two years, because she wanted to broaden her qualifications so she could teach from primary school to year twelve. It would give her more career options in a rural area because she would have the choice of working in both primary and secondary schools. In the meantime, she continued to work part-time at Burwood Heights. If she needed any convincing she had made the right choice, by the time she graduated in 2005 the community officer program had been cancelled.

Now a fully qualified teacher, Sherryn decided to spend her first year working at the school that had supported her through her studies. Mark was disappointed because it meant living apart for another year, but she felt obliged because the school had been so accommodating.

Sherryn soon discovered that she loved being a teacher. Even though Burwood Heights was classified in the lowest socio-economic ranking in Victoria, it had a good reputation and a solid group of dedicated staff. The students included a large number of migrants and refugees from diverse cultural backgrounds, and Sherryn found plenty of scope to use some of the non-conventional approaches to teaching that she had picked up while working in the United States. Outside the classroom, she and another young teacher started the school's first netball club. They took responsibility for everything from administration and applying for grants to buy team uniforms, to coaching. After two years, there were seven teams and the school had claimed two premierships.

In an extraordinary bonus and a very rare twist, Jean and Sherryn ended up sharing a double classroom. Separated by fold-back doors that were hardly ever shut, they each taught combined classes of years one and two. 'She was Mrs Simpson down one end . . . and I was Miss Simpson up the other. It was awesome!' says Sherryn.

The new graduate loved that she could turn to her mother for professional advice and mentoring. Jean had the ability to quickly assess the progress of each child and then work out the best next step. 'She was very pedantic about keeping the classroom tidy, and she wasn't afraid to raise her voice if she had to, but you knew she was a good teacher because of the number of kids who would come back to see her years later,' Sherryn says.

'I always thought the benefit was mine because I could go to Mum when I was stuck. I felt I was always asking her questions. But she reckons for her it was awesome, too, because it was rejuvenating. As much as I would look up to her end of the classroom to see what she was doing, she would look at my end to see what spin I was taking.'

13

CONNEWIRRICOO

It is Monday lunchtime and the door leading into Mark and Sherryn's farmhouse kitchen is coping with a fair bit of traffic. A couple of neighbours have dropped in, and so has a bloke from Sydney who organised a cross-country motorbike event that has seen Harrow packed with visitors over the weekend. The Harrow Vinduro is only in its seventh year, but it's already recognised as the biggest event of its kind in the Southern Hemisphere, and is attracting interest from overseas. Another example of Harrow not doing anything by halves.

Mark is busy making extra ham, cheese and tomato toasted sandwiches for the unexpected guests, completely unfazed by the growing numbers around the wooden kitchen table. Sherryn is trying to settle their sixteen-month-old daughter, Rhianna. Grizzly from lack of sleep, she is temporarily diverted by all the people in the room, and the challenge of picking bits out of her own sandwich. Sitting opposite is Mark's father, Malcolm, eating a lunch prepared by his wife, Susan, before she headed overseas on a farm tour of China. She organised his meals for every day she was away and put them in the deep-freeze.

Behind Malcolm hangs an old map, showing the original blocks created when the area was subdivided from pastoral holdings to encourage more intensive farming. Among those marked is the original 130 hectares taken up by his great-grandfather in about 1870. The McClure family have been farming at Connewirricoo, about 15 kilometres west of Harrow, for five generations. Adam McClure pushed his way through the stringybark scrub to reach his selection when he was only twenty years of age. Six years later he married Bessie Gash and they raised eleven children in a small house with a shingle roof that he built with his own hands, from timber that he cut off the property. Known as Kalang Cottage, today it stands just off the main street, having been moved there in 1988 and restored by the historical society.

Adam witnessed Harrow's growth as more settlers arrived in the area. In its heyday the town boasted two pubs, three blacksmiths shops and three saddlers, but it was already in decline by the time he was in his mid-eighties. Reminiscing on the occasion of his sixtieth wedding anniversary, Adam told a local newspaper reporter that the greatest hardships in the early years had come from flooding creeks and rivers. There were no bridges and when they rode away from home in the wetter months, they often did not know if they would be able to get back again. He almost drowned on one occasion, trying to swim an inexperienced horse across the Glenelg River. The horse plunged into the fast-flowing water and repeatedly went under before Adam managed to guide it to the opposite bank some distance downstream. 'Only the hand of providence saved me on that occasion,' he said.

Mark hasn't seen rain like that in a while, at least not at a time of the year when it is most useful. At about the time Sherryn moved to Harrow, the district was feeling the effects of the worst drought in living memory. To help pay the bills, Mark was working long days off farm, carting water and doing some contract earthmoving. With grain, cattle and sheep prices all looking good at the moment, times are not too bad now, but in the last year or two the vital spring rains that this country relies on to finish off winter cereal crops, sustain pastures and top up dams have been light on.

The McClure farm has always run livestock, but in Adam's day it was known for growing quality wheat, too. In 1902, he was awarded a silver medallion as winner of the Australian championship for grain at the Royal Melbourne Show. He counted the medal among his most prized possessions. Malcolm and Mark still grow some oats for grazing, but these days sheep take priority in an operation that focuses on producing prime lambs for meat. The family runs about 1100 hectares in three sections quite a few kilometres apart, including a property that his mother inherited, and 263 hectares that Mark bought on the other side of the Glenelg River not long before Sherryn moved to Harrow.

'I bought something today,' he told her one night on the phone.

'Oh great, what did you buy?' she replied, thinking it might be a motorbike or a car.

'I bought a farm,' he replied in his understated way.

'What!'

The property included a large weatherboard house which became their first home. Set at the end of a 1.5-kilometre drive, it was badly in need of renovation and full of mice but they could both see its potential and had great plans for it. 'Mark, being a bloke, put in a bed, a couch and a television and he was ready,' Sherryn says. Then she moved in with all her possessions, including boxes and boxes of books, and her beloved German shepherd, Polo. The two of them spent hours exploring the farm while Mark was away working, discovering old bits of machinery and going for runs along the driveway.

Sherryn loved her new home, although she wasn't so keen on the large number of huntsman spiders that were also in residence. Mark would tease her about them. He loved to wait until she had climbed into bed at night and started to relax.

'So you haven't seen the legs sticking out on the windowsill?' he'd ask quite innocently, then he'd laugh when she screamed and ordered him to remove it. 'He thought it was hilarious,' she says.

On weekdays, Sherryn drove to Balmoral, where she had secured a job teaching at the local primary school. Going to the job interview highlighted one of the first sacrifices she would be making in her new life. 'I was due there about nine-thirty so I got up, got myself dressed and psyched up, and headed off,' she says. 'I got there early and I thought I could really go a mocha. That was my standard drink in Melbourne. I'd buy a mocha and a muffin on the way to work and off I went. I thought it would get me nice and relaxed and it would be great. So I went into the cafe and I said, "Can you make me a mocha?" And the woman there said, "Sure, no worries." And then she went out the back.'

Sherryn was a bit concerned that she couldn't hear the distinctive sound of a coffee machine kicking into action, but the woman soon returned and handed over a takeaway cup with a lid on it. Heading outside, Sherryn got into her car and took her first sip. It was so awful that she held it in her mouth, unable to swallow. 'It was instant coffee with Milo,' she says, making an appalled face at the memory. 'Not only did I burn my tongue, but I ended up spitting it out.'

The mocha experience was not enough to put Sherryn off her country move, although it did set her thinking. By then she was completely committed to Mark and thought she had a fair idea of what she was getting into. She and Mark had lived together for six weeks while she taught at a school in Horsham as part of her training, and it seemed to work. 'I was ready to come out here and have a go. I was twenty-eight, and I think I was ready in my life as well,' she adds.

They had been going out together for four years, starting with the very next weekend after Beaut Blokes. On that occasion, Mark and his mate Shane drove all the way to Melbourne, staying in a dodgy hotel in St Kilda. They arranged to give Sherryn and Louisa a call as soon as they arrived in the city, so the girls could meet up with them. 'We're standing outside the car shop,' Mark told Sherryn, who still laughs when she recalls the moment. 'This is Melbourne. You need to give us more!' she replied, uncertain which one of the city's large number of car dealers he might be referring too.

The weekend went well, but at the end of it Sherryn still felt uncertain about the relationship. 'My cousin and his friend were hot and heavy, so how much was Mark wanting to be here with me? Or was he just here to keep his mate company? I didn't know.' The defining moment came a few months later, after Louisa and Shane split up. When her cousin phoned to break the news, Sherryn was convinced the next call would be from Mark, splitting up with her, too.

Sure enough, ten minutes later the phone rang. It was Shane wanting to know if she had any idea what he had done wrong. Ten minutes after that uncomfortable conversation ended, Mark rang. 'Right. This is it. This is the moment,' she thought to herself.

'So, Louisa and Shane have broken up,' he said.

'Yup,' replied an anxious Sherryn.

'You're not going to break up with me, are ya?'

'I wasn't planning on it. Were you gonna break up with me?'

'Nuh.'

'Okay. So we'll just keep going then?' she queried hopefully, sighing with relief when he agreed.

❖ ❖ ❖

As their first year together unfolded, Sherryn and Mark saw each other every month or so, either in Melbourne or Harrow. After eight months, Mark decided to really test their relationship. He took her to the Quambatook Tractor Pull. A massive event that has been running for forty years, it draws thousands to the small Mallee town every Easter, to watch modified tractors tow sledges along a purpose-built track. Competitors and tractor aficionados come from all over Australia, revelling in the smell of diesel and the deafening roars of engines straining to pull enormous weights.

Mark and his father are members of the Rusty Rattlers, a small club based at Apsley for people interested in preserving old tractors and engines, and Mark has a fair collection of old tractors tucked away in a large shed. His pride and joy is a 1938 Caterpillar bulldozer that he restored with a friend and takes to shows. Not so long ago he bought an old front-end loader, too, and put a new engine in it. A qualified boilermaker and steel fabricator, Mark modifies and builds farm equipment for people as an extra source of income outside the busy seeding and harvest periods. A couple of years ago, he and Malcolm spent a month engineering their own air-seeder to sow crops. More recently he was working on an invention to dig out blue-gum stumps. He spends hours sitting at the kitchen table with pencil and paper, drawing up designs, or using the computer to search for components and spare parts.

Going to the Quambatook Tractor Pull is Mark's idea of the perfect day out. Sherryn packed a book. 'That was my tester,' Mark says. He figured if she kept going out with him after that, she was a keeper. 'She reminds me of it, though. Fairly often,' he adds, after a pause.

Mark still hasn't convinced Sherryn to have a go at driving a tractor. He does contract seeding, spraying and harvesting work to bring in extra money. Before Rhianna came along, if she wasn't teaching Sherryn would sometimes take him lunch and join him on the tractor for a few laps of the paddock. But she reckons if she learns to drive a tractor herself, she will end up with another job. 'And I don't need to come home to another one,' she says.

Her first hands-on task on the farm was tying steel droppers onto a fence. She would head out by herself at weekends, taking the sheep dogs for a run. Since then, Susan has shown her how to raise orphaned lambs and she cooks for the shearers, too, treating it as an excuse to try out new recipes. 'I was told right at the beginning that you have to treat your shearers like royalty,' she repeats dutifully.

While she was teaching full-time at Balmoral, it was difficult to do too much on the property, but Sherryn enjoys working with sheep, particularly lamb marking. 'I get to pick up all the lambs and give them a cuddle,' she says. The task involves castrating them and docking their tails, so they probably appreciate the pat, but her first experience highlighted that her predecessors weren't always involved in this aspect of animal husbandry.

Excited at the prospect of lending a hand, she headed out to the yards only to be dismissed by Mark's grandfather. 'There are enough of us here. You probably need to go and see to the smoko,' he told her.

Sherryn was so shocked that she went straight back to the house, tears in her eyes. 'He didn't do it in a rude way,' she says. 'It was a blow to my ego more than anything, but I was just dismissed.'

Susan did her best to reassure her. 'They didn't mean it,' she told her. 'It's just that they're used to working as a crew.'

Sherryn reacted strongly to the incident because it reinforced niggling concerns that life in the country might be more traditional than she was prepared to accept. Since becoming politically aware as teenagers, Sherryn and her school friends had always considered themselves feminists. They wanted to be independent and treated as equals, both in the workplace and in relationships. It's one of the reasons why she refuses to take on all the cooking in the household, although she ends up doing most of the evening meals because Mark works until late almost every day.

When she first moved in, Sherryn discovered that while Mark could cook, he tended to have a pretty narrow repertoire. Home-killed beef or lamb was the staple diet, with fried potatoes and onions. 'If I cooked I got to eat some vegetables or a bit of salad, and I introduced him to chicken,' she says. Apart from broadening their diet, making the evening meal has also become more convenient since she changed jobs, teaching part-time four mornings a week at St Malachy's Catholic primary school in Edenhope. 'Rhianna eats at 5.30 so if I'm cooking for her, I cook for all of us,' Sherryn says.

Lunch has been a greater point of contention, especially since she and Mark moved into the house at the heart of the farm enterprise. Mark grew up there with his younger brother Tim, and their parents were still in residence until 2011 when Malcolm and Susan decided it was time to make room for the next generation. Susan always prepared lunch for the men and Mark thought Sherryn might keep up the practice, at least during school holidays. Sherryn didn't see why she should, just because she was home. After all, she was meant to be on holidays and it was something he was more than capable of doing himself.

Living away from the main farm during the first few years created a greater sense of separation between work and home life. She and Mark would have breakfast together in the morning and then set off. Having grown up in a suburban household where both parents went out to work, it was a more familiar routine. Sherryn also struggles with the rural psyche regarding where the house sits in terms of farm priorities and individual responsibilities. 'Mum and Dad would come back to the same space, and they shared the housework, whereas Mark thinks that if he's tidied the shed, that's his job done.

The house paddock and the house, that's my job,' she says. 'The same with finances. The house is not really factored in. If it needs repairs, well, maybe that can happen next year after we have bought what the farm needs.'

Wrapped up in this tricky area of conversation is her awareness that it's been hard for Susan and Malcolm to walk away from the house that was their family home for so many years. Apart from some painting, she and Mark tried not to make too many changes when they first moved in. Meanwhile, without being asked to, Malcolm respectfully knocks on the back door he once opened multiple times a day without a second thought. Sherryn finds the whole situation confusing. 'I know they moved out for the right reasons, but I still don't really understand, and because of that I guess I still don't feel like it's entirely our house,' she admits.

Brought up by parents who believe in hard work, she says part of Mark's appeal is that he has the same values. The flip side is that it can be a struggle to convince him to take a day off and just sit and relax. On a farm, public holidays and weekends have very little meaning when there are animals to look after and crops to harvest. Sherryn came to understand this leading up to her first Queen's Birthday weekend at Harrow. A keen gardener, her father always pruned his roses then so they bloomed in time for the Melbourne Cup. 'So that was my thing, too. It was always my rose cutting and report writing weekend,' Sherryn says.

Mark had other ideas. Crutching was starting and she would have to cook for the shearers. 'I can't cook. It's a public holiday!' she protested in dismay.

Even Good Fridays often pass Mark by. 'Aren't you meant to be at school?' he has asked her on more than one occasion. And then there is the holiday most sacrosanct of all in Victoria—Melbourne Cup Day. When Sherryn moved to Harrow, she was horrified to discover that while a lot of people stopped to listen to the famous horse race, no-one had the day off. It wasn't a designated public holiday in the area because the local council had the option to reassign it to coincide with a major local event instead. In the West Wimmera, they settled on the Hamilton Sheepvention—a field day about all things sheep and wool, held in June.

Now that he is no longer playing football, Mark works most of the weekend, too. Sherryn was recruited by the local netball team as soon as they heard she was moving to the area, and she has been heavily involved as a player, coach or umpire ever since. That can chew up most of her Saturdays during the season, as well as Thursday nights for practice.

One of her greatest challenges has been adjusting to the fact that no matter what community activity she is involved in, she is going to be mixing socially with the children she teaches and their parents, and that whenever she leaves the farm, it is inevitable she will meet someone she knows. By comparison, city life was anonymous so it was easy to separate her persona as a teacher from her personal life.

'Someone explained to me that being a teacher in front of a classroom is a performance. When you step out of the classroom, you go back to being whoever you are, but down here you step out and you are still with the kids and the parents,' she says. 'In Melbourne, it was very easy to keep things separate. My school had three hundred students and I knew them all, and I only lived ten kilometres from the school, but I would never see any of the kids at the weekend and only very occasionally would I see a parent.'

In Harrow or Edenhope, she bumps into students from St Malachy's all the time—in the supermarket, at the pub where everyone goes for pizza on Sunday nights, walking down the street. 'They are my peers on the netball court, or when we are serving in the netball club canteen, and I am still trying to figure out how to deal with that. When I stand in front of them at school, I am their teacher, that is my personality and my role play, but I don't know how to do that when I am also their equal on the netball court, or when we are serving in the canteen, and they have done it a hundred times more than me. I don't mind having kids explain to me how to do things, but how do they feel?'

She is conscious that even off-duty she represents St Malachy's and needs to behave appropriately, and she often finds herself modifying her conversation. 'We have friends with kids at the school and when we go out and see them and they ask how work's been, do I say it's been a fantastic week or do I admit it's been terrible? I'm still figuring it out to be honest, and it might take a while.'

Despite these dilemmas, Sherryn has taken on the Harrow spirit of volunteering and joined more than a few committees, although she has stepped back a little since Rhianna was born. 'It would stick out like a sore thumb if you didn't do anything,' she admits. Mark has served as president of the B&S ball organising committee for more than ten years. He is captain of the local rural fire brigade, secretary of a new committee trying to start up a mud bash event, and on a committee for the Connewirricoo community centre. He volunteers so much that he was named the West Wimmera Shire Citizen of the Year on Australia Day in 2015.

Sherryn helps him with Tussock Jumpers Ball and the annual billy cart races known as the Mullagh Championship, and is on the committee managing the Johnny Mullagh park. They are both on a committee planning celebrations to commemorate the 150th anniversary of the Aboriginal cricket team tour to England, in 2018. Obvious advocates for how they met, they have helped behind the scenes with Beaut Blokes, Sherryn organising the catering for the black-tie dinner as a fundraiser for the netball club, and Mark serving behind the bar. They even hosted a few girls for the last event back in 2012. There haven't been too many in recent years because the district started running out of single men. After her own experiences, Sherryn wouldn't hesitate to encourage others to give it a go if there are more events in the future. She believes that even if people don't find their soulmates, they will have a good time and make some great friends. 'It can be life changing,' she says. And not just for the participants.

14

THE RIPPLE EFFECT

Meeting Mark at Beaut Blokes created an extraordinary ripple effect. When their first January together came around, Mark insisted that Sherryn visit for the B&S ball. Once again, it sounded like her worst nightmare, but he was president of the organising committee and it meant a great deal to him. To help her cope, Sherryn roped in her sister Rachel and another friend. When they arrived, Mark was so sick with tonsillitis that he was confined to bed.

Not wanting to disappoint her companions after driving all the way from Melbourne with expectations of spending the weekend partying, Sherryn went without him. Deciding to make the most of it and have fun, the girls adopted a time-honoured B&S tradition, and pretended to be someone else. 'We met these two guys and my friend and I told them we were gynaecologists, and they told us they were multi-millionaires in the seed sprayer business,' Sherryn admits. 'Rubbish was flying but they completely believed us, and we believed them.'

Sherryn has never been allowed to forget it because her sister married one of them. Now settled on a farm near Natimuk, Rachel and Dale have three young children and Rachel is working as a business development adviser at the Horsham City Council. In fact, Rachel ended up moving to the Wimmera about a year before Sherryn did.

Their parents weren't far behind. Jean and Geoff sold their house in Blackburn and moved to Horsham. 'Dad has always loved the country. Mum was terrified but for the first thirty years of their married life Dad had agreed to live where she wanted, so she decided to suck it up,' Sherryn says. The added bonus is that they are closer to their two youngest daughters and most of their grandchildren.

Among those grandchildren is Rhianna. It took two years and ten attempts using in-vitro fertilisation techniques, plus a lot of physical and emotional stress, and a considerable amount of money, before she was conceived. It's one of the reasons Sherryn and Mark haven't married yet. They want to do it properly, and much of their savings went towards the treatments.

Apart from immediate family, only Sherryn's boss and a couple of close friends knew they were attempting to have a baby. That made it difficult when someone asked when they intended to start a family, but Sherryn didn't think she could cope with well-meaning people constantly inquiring how it was going and dealing with their reaction every time the procedure failed. 'I spent enough time feeling sad and sorry for myself,' she says.

'As part of the deal, we had to go and see a psychologist, who warned us it was going to be a rollercoaster, but I don't think there is anything that could have prepared us for what was involved. Just the emotional want of it, and then the crushing defeat of it. You tell yourself not to get as excited the next time because it probably won't happen, but you can't help yourself. No matter how much you try to keep a lid on it, you get excited again, and we went through that nine times.'

Sherryn and Mark used a clinic in Ballarat for the treatment—a six-hour return trip for what was often a fifteen-minute consultation. After all the initial form filling, tests and consultations, Sherryn began taking fertility drugs to stimulate egg production. The eggs were harvested from her womb while she was under anaesthetic and then placed in a culture dish with thousands of Mark's sperm. Twelve embryos formed, giving the couple twelve opportunities.

Monitoring to decide the best timing to transfer each embryo involved Sherryn having frequent blood tests. The Bush Nursing Centre at Harrow couldn't guarantee same-day results, which is what her doctors required, so she drove to Horsham. She would set off early to be at the clinic as soon as it opened at eight o'clock and then rush to work after the test.

Sherryn felt like her body was in training, making progress with each embryo transfer, but after nine failed attempts she was physically and emotionally exhausted. 'I got to the point where I couldn't do it anymore, so I took four months off, which probably wasn't a bad thing. I had a great summer, and that spread into autumn, and then it was winter.' She told Mark: 'If we're going to have another go, I'm feeling pretty good so let's give it a crack.'

They only had three embryos left and realised there was a limit to how many more attempts they could make. 'We talked about drawing a line in the sand. At what point did we just admit defeat and accept that it is just the two of us. Mark was adamant it would all be fine, and he didn't want to look at fostering or adoption.' So Sherryn headed back to the clinic for the tenth attempt.

Blood tests soon confirmed she was pregnant, but the couple didn't allow themselves to hope that this time might be different until the pregnancy passed the critical twelve-week point. A month before the baby was due, Sherryn finished work. The same day she travelled to Ballarat with Mark for a routine check-up. The baby was in perfect health but Sherryn's glucose levels had started to rise at about week thirty and her doctor was now so concerned that he wanted to admit her to the Ballarat hospital immediately and induce delivery. Mark and Sherryn were still in shock when they were told the delivery would have to be delayed a few days because the hospital was full. 'Crikey! We almost had a kid. Were you ready for that? I wasn't ready,' she confessed to Mark during the drive back to Connewirricoo.

Sherryn went into hospital the following Sunday. She ended up having a caesarean and Rhianna came into the world on St Patrick's Day. There was no pressure on hospital beds then, so she stayed for a week. Mark was there, too, which gave him a wonderful opportunity to bond with his new daughter. 'Those extra three days were great, because no-one knew we were there and we had that time to ourselves,' she says.

Now a toddler, when she isn't being cared for by one of her grandmothers, Rhianna loves being outside with her father. They often head off in the ute together to feed the sheep. A chip off the old block, she likes tractors and spending time in the shed, too. On her visits to Melbourne every two months or so, Sherryn occasionally looks at her brother's child who is growing up in the city and wonders if Rhianna is missing out. 'Then I come back here, and we spend four hours roaming around outside, and she is digging and splashing and skipping and jumping, and using her imagination.'

Sometimes Sherryn thinks of the city and the variety of choice it offers—Melbourne's kaleidoscope of restaurants serving food from all over the world, being able to swim in heated pools year-round, going to the zoo or Luna Park. She has been known to drive to Horsham just to be around more people. What she misses most is waking up on a day with no commitments and knowing there are limitless options about how to spend her time. But she has found that she likes the open spaces, too.

Interestingly, she recalls that way back in high school, she and her best friend, Katherine, shared dreams of owning farms one day during an exercise in English which involved going through a rural newspaper where they saw advertisements for farms, kelpies and utes. Sherryn sends a text to Katherine every now and then with a photo of the beautiful view of rolling hillsides from the farmhouse. 'Just watching the sunset over my paddocks!' she teases. Now a lawyer, living in Canberra, and the mother of three boys, Katherine will reply, 'Just eating at a fine food restaurant!'

Sherryn doesn't mind. After the mocha experience, she has come up with a solution. She and Mark have bought the old bakery in Harrow's main street and are steadily restoring it. They have plans to one day open a coffee shop, so Sherryn can make her own.

Part IV
RESILIENT SPIRIT

15

A LONG WAY FROM HOME

The first rosy light, undershot with gold, is colouring the dawn sky as Daljit Sanghera pulls away from her house. Following a short sandy driveway lined with grapevines, she turns her vehicle towards the main highway. Within minutes she is passing through dark clusters of citrus orchards, over Gurra Gurra Creek and onto the salt-washed floodplains of the mighty River Murray. A broad expanse of sky evolves into muted pinks and greys, soft as the downy feathers of a fledgling galah, as she crosses the bridge into Berri and doubles back towards the senior citizens' club.

While most of the town still sleeps, the modern brick hall is a hive of activity. It is Saturday and stallholders for the weekly Riverland Farmers' Market are setting up in the car park. Country music spills from the door of a large white van, providing the perfect soundtrack as they put up gazebos and unfold portable tables to showcase their produce.

Daljit bypasses the stalls and drives around to the back of the hall where she unloads a stack of plastic boxes. Tucked inside are dozens of samosas, spinach rolls and pakoras made the day before in her compact home kitchen. She carries them through the back door and into the main auditorium where other stallholders are already preparing for a brisk morning's trade. Most of them come weekly and set up in the same spot each time.

Daljit is in the far corner from the hall kitchen, alongside Frances, whose display cabinet of continental cakes and desserts is a market favourite. First-generation Australian with Italian parents, Frances is a neighbour on the land, too, living just down the road from Daljit. 'This woman here, I tell you. My husband always says, "I don't know how she does it." Three kids, and the block, and then to do this,' says Frances watching Daljit unpack.

Across the aisle, Kaylene Letton is poking gentle fun at her husband, John. Supposedly retired, his bowls club held their season wind-up the night before and apparently he was slow getting up this morning so they are running a bit late. Their poultry farm at Paringa has been in operation for about fifty years and they have been regulars at the market since it was founded almost ten years ago. Customers love their fresh eggs and they are cheaper than can be found at the local supermarket. 'We have people come up from Adelaide on a regular basis and take eggs back for the family. We even have one lady who is taking eggs back for a whole street,' Kaylene says.

Behind the Lettons is another stall reflecting the family heritage of its trader. Anita has spent most of the week baking the traditional German biscuits and cakes that her mother taught her how to make. 'I've written the recipes down but the thing is to watch how they are made,' she says. What was an enjoyable pastime turned into a useful money earner when people tasted Anita's gingerbread biscuits. Based on a family Christmas favourite, they are flavoured with a special blend of nine spices. Anita is not saying what the blend contains, except that there is no ginger!

Trying to avoid the temptation of eating too many sugary treats, Daljit is more interested in the persimmons she has spotted on a stall just inside the front door. Customers haven't started arriving yet so she takes time to quiz the trader. It's very early in the season to see persimmons and as a fruit grower with her own orchard she is curious about the variety. Daljit knows that produce which ripens either early or late in the season tends to attract better prices and she is always on the lookout for opportunities to improve the profitability of her small farm. She has already planted 300 Fuyu persimmons to help diversify her income. This variety has the curiously catchy name of Ichikikijiro. She is offered a piece to try and it proves to be sweet and crisp like an apple, completely different to the old astringent variety which used to be found as a decorative tree in many Australian backyards.

Pleased with the discovery, Daljit heads back to her stall. The market hasn't officially started trading but her first customer has appeared. It's Phil from the dried fruit stand. He loves her samosas and usually has one for breakfast whenever she is there. Daljit tells him they are not quite hot enough yet, but he has already picked up his cup of locally roasted coffee and he's ready now.

By eight o'clock shoppers are starting to fill the hall with the sound of friendly greetings, chatter and muted laughter. A group of friends who meet up at the market every Saturday has settled at a large table just in front of Daljit's stall to have breakfast together. A few of them opt for her spinach rolls after they discover there are problems in the kitchen. None of the power points are working and the staff can't open the till to give people change.

Everything is working again by the time someone sits down at the hall piano and starts to play 'If You Were the Only Girl in the World'. In a segue that jumps more than half a century, the old-fashioned sing-along classic is swiftly followed by John Lennon's 'Imagine'. No-one seems to notice the odd juxtaposition, or the music either, as the player finishes up without applause, but it turns out she is not the main act. Live music is a regular feature of the market and today the pianist is there to accompany a small choir. There are smiles when they begin their set with the timeless French song about a sleepy monk. The choir has modified the words appropriately, to begin, 'Farmers market, farmers market; here we are, here we are . . .'

❖ ❖ ❖

Generations of Australian children have grown up learning to sing 'Frère Jacques', but Daljit Sanghera was not among them. Her childhood unfolded in a very different place. Daljit was born in 1961 in the small regional city of Nakodar, on the vast alluvial plains of the Punjab, in the far north of India. Set between two rivers in the central north of the state, the town lies at the heart of an area known for its agriculture which takes advantage of rich soils and irrigation to grow crops like wheat, corn, cotton, sugar cane and chickpeas.

Even though they lived in the town, her family were farmers. Her father, Bawa Singh Purewal, and his three brothers shared thirty-two hectares of land not far beyond the outskirts of Nakodar. Tiny by Australian standards, it was considerably more than the usual two hectares or so that most farmers in the region relied on to make a living.

The land was first taken up by Daljit's grandfather, who was forced to move to the area after India gained independence from Britain in 1947. With independence came partition, a process that saw the province of Punjab divided along religious lines. The eastern section, where the majority of the population was either Hindu or Sikh, remained part of India. The western side of the Punjab, which was predominantly Muslim, became part of the new nation of Pakistan.

Tens of thousands died in the civil unrest that erupted between Hindus and Muslims in the period leading up to independence and negotiations to determine where the final boundaries between India and Pakistan would be drawn. In the extraordinary chaos that followed, up to 15 million people were uprooted from their homes, as Sikhs and Hindus who found themselves on the Pakistani side of the border fled to India, and Muslims in eastern Punjab fled to Pakistan.

Before partition, Daljit's grandfather and his four sons had cleared and worked a farm in the west, determined to work hard and improve the prospects for their family. But they were Sikhs so after independence they joined the hundreds of thousands of displaced farmers who walked away from their properties and were allocated replacement land by the Indian government. In an attempt to make the allocations as equitable as possible, a complicated process was set up to take into account not just the area of land that people left behind, but its productivity. Four acres (1.6 hectares) of dry unirrigated land was deemed to be equal to one acre of fertile, irrigated country. With some 500,000 claims for land lodged within a single month and less land to go around than had been left behind, it took a team of almost 7000 civil servants to sort things out.

The Purewals ended up with thirty-two hectares on the outskirts of Nakodar where the four boys and their father worked together to grow rice, corn and wheat and run a few cattle. When Daljit was a child, they still relied on horses and buffalo instead of tractors to pull ploughs and tow carts. 'When my father was young it was very hard work,' she says. 'All by hand. I didn't see but my dad is telling me. When I was growing up, Dad got tractors and machines.'

The entire family set up home in the town, sharing a single house, even as the four sons married and began their own families. Each brother and his wife and children occupied a couple of bedrooms, with a separate outside cooking area where meals were prepared. So Daljit grew up in a typical extended family, with aunties close by to help keep an eye on her and plenty of cousins to play with after school. 'All people lived like that, you wouldn't find any different,' Daljit says. 'It was a good way to live.'

Apart from her parents, Daljit shared her part of the house with an older sister, Narinder, and two younger sisters, Jaswinder and Rajwinder. She has an older brother, Kulwinder, who went to live in Germany when he was eighteen. There was a younger brother, too, but he died during infancy.

Most days she saw little of her father, who was usually away working on the farm and would often stay overnight even though it was only a short walk out of town. Although she saw very little of him during her early years, she says he was kind. Daljit laughs recalling that he had trouble remembering the long formal names of all his children, preferring to call them by affectionate nicknames. Hers was Bubbly.

More particularly, he treated her and her sisters just the same as their brother, which was very unusual in a culture that prizes boys much more highly. Sons were the favoured children who would inherit all of their parents' property and look after them in their old age. Even though India was being led by its first female prime minister, Indira Gandhi, when Daljit was only five, women in her community were expected to focus on cooking and raising children.

Daljit's mother, Mohinder, never worked on the farm, and certainly did not play any role in making decisions about how it was run. However, each morning she would walk out with breakfast for her husband and collect milk produced by the family's small herd of two or three cows. She would return to the farm again with lunch and dinner. The men might make themselves tea when the women were not there but otherwise they would never think of preparing their own food. 'They wouldn't even get a drink of water by themselves,' says Daljit. 'But we are used to it,' she adds matter-of-factly, explaining that for women like her mother, living in rural India, it was very much accepted practice then. 'It's the normal thing,' she says.

Life became easier for her mother when Daljit was about fifteen, and the entire family moved out to the farm. Initially, the brothers and their families again shared the one house, but over time each one built their own home on their own patch of eight hectares, separated by only a hundred metres or so. The families still spent a great deal of time together, and during school holidays the cousins were often joined by more cousins from other places, who came to stay.

Even as adulthood approached, the idea of going out for the evening with a few friends, like most Australian teenagers would do, was never considered, by either the boys or the girls. But the cousins would often go together to see a movie, chaperoned by Daljit's mother and her aunties. Movies made locally, with people speaking Punjabi, were particular favourites. 'But we couldn't go by ourselves,' Daljit stresses. 'Maybe in a big city like Delhi, but where I grew up I didn't see that sort of thing. Just go to school and come home, and that's it.' Looking at the much freer lives her own children have experienced growing up in Australia, Daljit has no regrets. 'My childhood was really good,' she says. Revealingly, she adds: 'I loved my life. I have no trouble. Before I get married I couldn't understand people with depression, or these sorts of problems.'

Daljit's mother may have been content focusing on the traditional role of raising her family, but the Purewals made sure their daughters had a good education. Bawa only went to school for a couple of years and struggled with reading and writing, but Mohinder completed at least seven years of primary education before her family, like the Purewals, was also forced to move from Pakistan to India because of partition. At one stage she was even asked to teach, but it was very unusual for women to become teachers at that time, so her parents refused permission.

By contrast, Daljit went to a government-run girls' only primary school, where all of her teachers were women. Daljit loved school. She did well at her lessons, although she was expected to work hard and there was too much homework. 'In India, if you don't do the homework at that time, then next day you go to the teacher and get hit with a stick. Even in school holidays they gave us lots of homework to do, so we would try and finish it as quickly as possible and then the rest of the time we can play.'

After school, Daljit usually met up with cousins and neighbours' children in the street outside their homes, to play hopscotch or jump skipping ropes. 'That was really good fun. I still remember that,' she says. They did not have a lot of toys, so they used their imaginations, and boys and girls all played together. Sometimes Daljit even had a turn at marbles, which was usually the boys' preserve.

After eight years of primary school, she moved on to a larger government-run high school in Nakodar for the next two years of her education. She enjoyed her lessons, although she struggled with science until a few months of special tuition set her on the right track and it became a favourite subject. She was good at sport, too, imagining as a child that one day she might become a sports teacher. 'Then I would go to school and teach, and then when I come home I would have a servant to cook for me and clean for me.' She laughs now at the idea of having servants.

Her favourite sports were volleyball and *kabaddi*. An ancient Indian contact sport with numerous variations, *kabaddi* sounds a little bit like a grown-up, formal version of 'catchy' or tag. The traditional Punjabi game is usually played on a circular pitch about twenty metres wide, with a line through the middle, but other versions have rectangular fields and the number of players on the field at any given time can vary, too.

In the game that Daljit played, two teams of seven face each other, with one team designated as 'raiders'. The teams stand on either side of the line, and one at a time a raider crosses over and attempts to touch a player of the opposing team. Once they have touched someone, the raider must flee back to their side of the line before the player they have touched catches them and prevents them from returning. The catching can involve some pretty aggressive rugby-like tackling and wrestling on the ground, even in the women's version. 'You have to be quick and strong,' says Daljit.

After she finished high school, Daljit studied politics, history, English and Punjabi at a college in Nakodar to gain a Bachelor of Arts. With high education and literacy rates among girls in the Jalandhar area compared with many other parts of India, Daljit doesn't look on it as anything particularly special or unusual. Most of her friends did the same thing, and her younger sister has a masters degree in political science. Daljit did not get that far. She was only into her second year of a masters degree in the Punjabi language, which she was studying by correspondence, when her parents decided it was time for her to marry.

16

TRUSTING YOUR LUCK

Despite attempts by reality television, it is impossible for most Australians to imagine marrying someone with whom you have never even held a proper conversation. For Daljit, and all the other young women she knew in her town in the 1980s, it was completely normal. In fact, none of her cousins or friends married for love. Growing up, Daljit had always known and accepted that the day would come when her parents would set about choosing her husband. She trusted that they would do their best to find someone who had the means to provide for her and offer her a good life. 'All the parents, they try to do their best. They are looking for a boy that can look after you, and has good income,' she explains.

On the man's side, the parents want a girl who is well educated. It is a bonus if she can speak English. Daljit could not, but she had a university degree and was obviously smart. For Daljit's parents it wasn't important that her prospective husband be well educated. Traditionally, a Punjabi father would have been keen for his daughter to marry another farmer who owned, or was due to inherit, a decent parcel of land. With the vagaries of farming, the more land the better, because it increased the likelihood of a more reliable income.

However, by the time Daljit was approaching marriageable age, most parents in her community were no longer keen on farmers as prospective husbands. It was too hard a life, with far less security than could be offered by someone earning a regular salary. Or better still, an Indian man in good health, living overseas in a country where the chance of a better life was much greater. The United States, Canada and Australia were favoured options, so when a man they knew in a neighbouring town mentioned that he knew a family looking for a wife for their son in Australia, Daljit's parents were very interested.

This is normally how things begin. A 'middle man', who knows both sets of parents, hears that they are each looking for partners for their children, and if he thinks it might be a good match, he then approaches them with the suggestion. For the girls that Daljit grew up with, the search usually started when they were in their early twenties, about to finish their university degree. The middle man may know the girl and that she is approaching marriageable age, and start the process. He usually gathers information about both parties and their families and shares it with the parents. If the parents are open to the suggestion, then a meeting is set up so they can talk. If that meeting goes well, another meeting is arranged, with the prospective couple in the room, too.

That is what happened with Daljit and Paul Sanghera. They met for the first time sitting in a room at her house, under the watchful eyes of their parents. 'We didn't talk, just look at each other,' Daljit explains. Her first impression was that he looked nice. 'That's it. I didn't ask anything. We just trust our luck,' she says with a laugh. When she was told he lived in Australia and that she would be living there, too, Daljit was excited at the prospect. The idea that she would be a long way from her family didn't bother her. It all seemed a big adventure.

A week later they were married. There were no other meetings, with or without parents. No dating. Not even a phone conversation. According to Daljit this was perfectly normal, and besides, there was limited time because Paul needed to return to Australia. They even skipped the traditional Mehendi ceremony, which is usually performed a day or two before a Sikh wedding to paint the bride's hands, feet, arms and legs with intricate designs in henna.

Instead, Daljit and her mother threw themselves into organising the catering for the reception and a shopping expedition to buy new clothes. High on the list was a traditional Punjabi suit, or *salwar kameez*, made up of a long blouse or tunic and loose-fitting pants, and a long gold-embroidered scarf, or *chunni*, to cover her head. There was no time to order a custom-made outfit, but Daljit found something suitable in a local shop, in the traditional bridal colour of joyous red.

Daljit says she remembers every moment of her wedding, although the main ceremony took a lengthy three hours or so. Her sisters gathered early at her parents' house to help her get ready. Soon after came the guests, mainly family and a few close friends who lived nearby. Then came the groom's party, who were formally welcomed by Daljit's family with garlands of flowers. Everyone sat down to breakfast before the actual ceremony began. Led by a local priest, it was held at Daljit's home rather than in the *gurdwara* where the family worshipped.

The newlyweds lived together as husband and wife for about six weeks before Paul returned to Australia. He went alone because the paperwork approving Daljit's migration was not finalised—that would take another six months. His parents also lived in Australia, so in the meantime Daljit stayed with Paul's grandparents. The older couple treated her well and it gave her time to adjust to her new family and get to know their way of doing things.

When Daljit finally stepped onto the plane for Australia in October 1986, she was very excited. Paul had flown back to collect her, so they boarded the flight together in New Delhi. He was sitting by her side when it landed at

Melbourne's Tullamarine airport on a sunny spring day. 'I am not imagining—I have no idea how it would look,' Daljit says of her expectations about Australia. 'But when I come into the airport and look, it was absolutely different things. It looks very nice but different.' Paul's parents were there to greet them, and drive them back to what would be Daljit's first home in Australia—a suburban house in Epping, about twenty kilometres north of the city centre. To Daljit, all the houses and streets looked the same. 'For the first few weeks I couldn't find it,' she admits.

Paul had a job working a twelve-hour nightshift in a fabric factory at Thomastown about ten minutes' drive away. The first night he had to work, Daljit was extremely anxious about being left alone.

'You can take me with you, I can sleep in the car,' she suggested.

'No, you can't do that,' he told her and went to work.

Sometime later a neighbour knocked on the door. Not knowing who it was, Daljit hid. 'I was that scared I quickly run from the lounge room to the bedroom. I just hide myself there in the bedroom. I can't forget this thing. Oh, my God, I don't know why I was so scared.'

It is easy to understand that Daljit might have felt overwhelmed. She was in a new country, with a husband she was still getting to know. It was just the two of them living in the house, when she had spent her entire life surrounded by a large, extended family, and she was worried about leaving the house on her own because she might get lost. She couldn't ask for directions or make friends easily with the neighbours because she didn't speak English. And she was more than seven months pregnant.

Becoming a mother was a joyous experience for Daljit. In many ways, having a baby to look after gave her new life in Australia a stronger focus, and her mother-in-law was there to help when needed. However, the birth was not easy. She was in labour for three days in the Preston hospital before the doctors decided a caesarean section was necessary, and Monica was delivered. Her husband spent as much time with Daljit as he could before and after the birth, but when he wasn't there to help interpret she couldn't communicate with the nurses, and she felt even more isolated after being placed in a room on her own to recover. 'I found it very hard experience,' Daljit says. 'The nurse would come and I don't know what she is asking me. I understand a little bit, but I can't tell her what I want. That was a very hard time for me.'

It was made even more difficult by the hospital food, although this did provide one of the funnier moments that Daljit enjoys recounting about her early days in Australia and how much she had to learn. At home, she would usually have an Indian type of flat bread for breakfast, with yoghurt or dhal. In the hospital, they brought her a small box of cornflakes. Having no idea how to eat them, she just opened the box and picked them out one by one, chomping on the dry flakes like potato chips. 'I be honest, I didn't know,' she says, laughing at the idea now. 'I can't forget that one.'

Relief came in the form of her mother-in-law, bearing homemade food. She helped later on, too, looking after the baby while Daljit packed shoes in a nearby factory. 'Everyone else was working and I wanted to go to work as well,' she says. It not only brought in extra money, but mixing with the other workers gave her an opportunity to practise her English. 'That's where I started learning, slowly, slowly.'

Daljit only worked in the shoe factory for a year or so before giving the job up to have her second child, Tim. She admits he was spoilt as a baby because he was a boy, but she says Monica was spoilt, too, because she was the first child born into her husband's family since his youngest sister about twenty-three years before. 'Everybody was excited when she came because long time since the last child, and she was a good girl as well,' Daljit says. The children were four and two years of age when Paul decided he'd had enough of nightshifts and factory work. It was time to follow in his father's footsteps and become a fruit grower.

17

TO THE RIVERLAND

Approximately halfway between Loxton and Berri in South Australia's Riverland, the small rural community of Bookpurnong is part of an area that early settlers nicknamed 'the waybacks' because it was so far from anywhere. Officially, it is named after a station that once covered hundreds of square kilometres, extending as far as the Victorian border. The run was one of several large pastoral leases taken up by the enterprising Chambers brothers, John and James, during the late 1840s when there was a rush to occupy new grazing land with frontage on the River Murray.

The river not only provided precious water for livestock, there were visions of it becoming a major transport route that would open up the riches of inland Australia and make the wealth of property owners and traders along its banks. By the 1850s, the first paddlesteamers were carrying produce to market, and bringing in passengers and supplies. But it was tough country where pastoralists struggled to make a living because of drought, sheep-eating dingoes and plagues of grass-eating rabbits. By the 1880s, Bookpurnong was a millstone around the neck of leading South Australian sheep breeder and parliamentarian Alexander Murray, who was glad to quit the station even though he walked away with nothing.

The pastoralists' days may have been done, but another pair of enterprising brothers were about to create a completely new future for people like the Sangheras. Canadians George and William Chaffey were pioneering experts in irrigation who came to Australia in the late 1880s after hearing about the potential of the Murray Valley. Although their initial focus was Mildura, disagreements among Victorian politicians stalled their plans so they turned their attention over the border and worked with the South Australian government to establish Renmark. It became the first irrigation settlement in Australia.

The Chaffey brothers' business collapsed within a decade, but the idea persisted of developing irrigation settlements for intensive horticulture. New schemes and towns sprung up along the River Murray's banks, drawing thousands of migrants seeking a better life. Inspiration even came, in part, from the Punjab, with South Australian newspapers carrying reports in the late 1880s about the extensive irrigation systems found there as a sign of what might be possible closer to home. By then the Punjab already had 6000 kilometres of irrigation canals and 9000 kilometres of auxiliary channels irrigating almost 800,000 hectares of land.

Among the men employed by the Chaffeys was Walter Muspratt, who was born in the Punjab and came to Australia in 1891 to work as a civil engineer at Mildura and Renmark. He later took up a fruit block at Renmark, and was engaged by the government to teach soldier-settlers about fruit growing under irrigation after World War I. In fact, from the earliest years, the Riverland drew settlers from India, mainly British soldiers looking for somewhere warmer to live than England after retiring from active service. Families of English descent were even encouraged to invest in fruit blocks by the Punjab's district superintendent of police who toured the Riverland by paddlesteamer in 1892.

Others who took up the challenge were retired cavalry officer Colonel Charles Morant, a distant relative of the infamous Breaker Morant, who lived in a house called Bangalore at Renmark; the Wylies, who boasted generations of military men that served in India, including a governor of Bengal and a military secretary to the viceroy of India; Hubert and Monty Woodward, whose father was a judicial commissioner in the Punjab; and Frank Cunningham, whose three great-uncles served with the East India Company. One of them, Captain Joseph Cunningham, published the first history of the Sikhs written by a foreigner, which remains generally well regarded for its cultural insights and sympathetic approach more than 160 years later.

It's unlikely that Paul Sanghera's father, Piara, knew of these historic connections when he arrived in the Riverland to pick oranges sometime around 1960. At the suggestion of some Australian friends, he was looking for seasonal work in between cutting sugar cane in Queensland. His own father had cut cane, too, returning to India after earning enough money to keep his family for a year or two, and then coming back again when it had run out.

Piara preferred working in the orchards and he liked the area so he bought a fruit block at Waikerie and brought out his family. Daljit is not sure of the details, but she thinks they may well have been among the first Indians to settle in the Riverland in modern times. He mentioned the place to friends and soon other Indians, many of them Sikhs from the Punjab, came too. Today there are more than 200 Sikh families in the region which even has its own *gurdwara* at Glossop.

Like his father before him, Paul decided to buy a fruit block. He settled on about sixteen hectares established around 1960 when five fruit growers had pooled their resources to create their own mini-irrigation scheme. They bought eighty hectares of farmland that had once been part of Bookpurnong station, subdivided it, and set up a shared central pumping system. Later on, Paul expanded his holdings with another twelve hectares of grapevines about sixteen kilometres away.

Daljit was quite happy to move from the city to the country. As she points out, it made little difference because she spent most of her life at home. 'I stay home there, I stay home here—it's all the same,' she says. At least the block had a spacious modern house, with plenty of room for a growing family and Paul's parents to live there, too. But she found the heat very trying, especially during the first summer when she was out in the orchard picking oranges while her mother-in-law cared for the children.

In those first years, Paul did not employ any labour. He and Daljit picked all the fruit by hand, even the grapes, and pruned all the trees and vines, working long days so they could pay off the money they borrowed to buy the property. In the beginning, Daljit had no idea what to do but Paul taught her the basics of picking and pruning. 'When we moved here, I didn't know anything, and all the varieties looked the same to me. Picking oranges is nothing hard, but at the start I didn't know what to prune,' she says.

Encouraging her efforts was Daphne, a neighbour who became a cherished friend. Not long after the Sangheras moved in, she showed up at the back door with flowers and her phone number, encouraging Daljit to call if she ever needed anything. 'That was a really nice feeling. It made a difference,' Daljit says. 'She was a bit older but I feel like I could talk to her about anything. With her there was no need to do the formalities. She was by herself and she come sometimes to my place when she feel lonely.' Daphne passed away some years ago. 'I miss her,' Daljit finishes simply.

Daljit also made friends among the local Sikh community. She doesn't remember there being that many Indian families in the area when they arrived, but Paul's family had friends on fruit blocks nearby. They also gave Paul some tips on the more complex aspects of managing the block, like controlling the myriad pest and diseases that attacked their fruit trees and vines. Daljit wasn't part of this exchange. Normally when the families got together, the men would sit in one place and 'talk their own things', and the women were in another room. It just wasn't usual for Punjabi women to play any sort of role in running a farm. Daljit was pushing boundaries enough by helping outside in the orchard. She even learnt to drive the tractor, and she gained a truck licence so she could deliver fruit to the wholesaler at Loxton during the busy picking season.

Meanwhile, her more traditional role as a wife and mother expanded. 'We thought one girl, one boy, we will have one more,' Daljit says. Karamjoyt, known as KJ, was born in 1996, ten years after Monica and eight after Tim. With the benefit of hindsight, Daljit looks at the gap as a blessing. It meant KJ was by her mother's side every day through the years of grief, depression and intense struggle coming her way. 'We didn't know that at the time, but I think the gap was a good thing. I didn't know, but God know,' Daljit reflects.

18

WHEN GIVING UP IS NOT AN OPTION

Daljit was only forty when her husband died from an illness in December 2002. She does not like to talk about this painful part of her life, but his death changed everything. Except the rows and rows of grapes and fruit trees waiting outside the back door that needed irrigating, and the three children who required her love and attention.

News of Paul's death spread quickly, and her house was soon full of relatives, friends from the Riverland's Sikh community and concerned neighbours dropping in to see if there was anything they could do. Her mother and sisters flew from Canada, her mother staying for six months to help however she could. As the days passed Daljit came to a decision that surprised many. It certainly went against the traditions of her culture and upbringing. After considering the options available to her, she resolved to keep the fruit block and run it herself.

Her parents were not convinced it was the right choice. They wanted her to sell up and move to Canada, where her mother and sisters would be on hand. Even though she had visited the block several times and spent six months there supporting her daughter after Paul's death, Mohinder looked on Bookpurnong as an isolated wilderness on the other side of the world, where Daljit would be facing unknown dangers and taking on a responsibility tackled only by men. 'My grandma is very Indian, very traditional, and she still says to this day, "Paul left my daughter in the jungles of Australia!",' Monica explains wryly.

While moving to Canada may have seemed the easiest option, for Daljit the choice was not that simple. For a start, her children had all been born in Australia and grown up in the Riverland. Monica was sixteen when her father died, Tim was fourteen and KJ was only six. The Riverland was their home.

Then there were the fifteen years Daljit and her husband had put into the block to improve it and pay off the mortgage. After all that hard work, she could not just walk away. There was also the very practical realisation that, given it was debt free, the enterprise was her best hope of earning a living to support herself and her children, especially if she could manage most of the work herself. 'If I didn't do the block work, what else I can do? To look after my kids I have to do something,' she says.

The first twelve months on her own made it very clear to Daljit that there was a great deal she did not know. 'My goodness me, I had no idea,' she admits. Compared with other challenges that lay ahead, organising the grape harvest not many weeks after Paul died was not too complicated—the Sangheras had been using contractors for a few years. They come in with mechanical harvesters for a day or two at a time between late January and early April, as different varieties of grapes ripen.

However, monitoring the crops and learning when and how to apply fertiliser and chemical sprays was a completely different story. It is potentially one of the most complex aspects of managing any horticultural enterprise. The plants are not going to thrive and produce healthy fruit if they don't have access to the right nutrition, especially on the red sands of the Riverland, and crops can easily be wiped out if problems with pest and disease are not diagnosed quickly and the right action taken to control them. 'Things like which chemical to use, when to use, how much chemical to put in the tank, and what time of year to do. I think, how I do that?' Daljit says, listing only a few of the things she didn't know.

Just as big a challenge was learning how to manage the irrigation system on which her trees and vines rely for survival. The property shares a pump with four others, and each grower takes a turn operating it. There are no open irrigation channels in this part of the world; the water is delivered to the blocks through large pipelines. On Daljit's property the pump feeds into a drip irrigation system which trickles water into the root zone of each vine and tree, making sure every drop is used as efficiently as possible. It is a critical step forward from the old days of flood irrigation, given the precious and limited nature of the resource, especially in years when drought affects the entire complex and fragile River Murray system. Daljit had no idea how much water the orchard needed, or what to do if the system broke down.

Most of the machinery kept in the property's big green shed was a mystery to her, too. 'I have no idea. You would say I'm lying but it's true. The chainsaw, anything, even the spray plant. I didn't know how to open the jets and how to clean them.' She laughs at the idea now, but even in the house, simple tasks like changing the tubes in fluorescent lights challenged her at first because she had never done it before. Paul always took care of any maintenance.

Determined to become self-reliant, Daljit applied her commonsense and quick mind to learning how to do most things by herself. More than happy to ask for advice and take it on board, she turned to a combination of willing neighbours and professional expertise. Paul had already engaged a Loxton-based consulting service to check the orchard every month and provide agronomic advice. She kept them on to guide her through fertilising and spraying. 'They show me, so I start slowly, slowly learning,' she says.

She also approached Ken, a worker employed by a neighbour, and offered to pay him to help her. 'He said if something go wrong just leave a note on the car and he'll come over after work. I'm not good learning by reading, I'm just good by seeing, so when he was working I was watching. I think I am a quick learner if I watch how to do things.' Over the next three years, Ken taught her many practical skills, including how to graft trees and fix common problems with the irrigation system.

Later on, Daljit joined the Loxton branch of the Agricultural Bureau of South Australia, an organisation established almost 130 years ago to help farmers share experiences and access the latest scientific information. She started going to their regular gatherings so she could talk to other growers. When she joined she was the only woman in the area running a fruit block on her own, and often she was the only woman attending. She found the men friendly and welcoming, and the talk about what was going on with the season and the other properties extremely helpful. 'It's really good for me,' she says.

Her immediate neighbours proved towers of strength, too. Among them are David and Judy Jaeschke, whose family has been growing fruit at Lock Four since the 1940s. Taking over from his father, David was a large-scale dried apricot producer for many years. His four or so hectares is down to less than half a hectare now, but he has refused to give up the enterprise altogether despite rising production costs and having to compete against cheap imports.

David and Judy have enormous respect for Daljit. 'I met her soon after she moved here and we got on well right from the start. She was just very friendly and welcoming,' Judy says. 'I suppose we got to know each other more after Paul died. I would just come over and say hello, and ask her how she was going, and she would say, "It's okay, it's okay," but it probably wasn't. It was only afterwards that she told us things . . . She is very independent and resourceful. She didn't push herself on us.'

Reluctant to describe himself as her mentor, David says Daljit only asked for help when absolutely necessary. Often it would amount to casual conversations about particular issues or problems. Local growers thought she had guts and were very willing to share their experience. 'I don't think she has taken undue liberties or anything like that at all. She is a very hard worker and she understands things quickly,' he says. 'And it's been a two-way thing, too. There have been times when I've been short of labour during the harvest in the apricot season, and she'll come and help.'

Daljit was very conscious about not becoming a nuisance to her neighbours. 'You can't ask everybody all the time. Even the people that said when you need us ring us, I just do only if I can't work it out. Otherwise people get sick and tired of you, even if they don't say.'

Her challenges were often harder in the early years because of her limited English. Even though she has come a long way, Daljit is reminded regularly how difficult this can make life because in her spare time she acts as an interpreter in Punjabi for the federal government's Centrelink department, helping Indians in the Riverland to access social and welfare services. She knows from personal experience that many Indian women have limited opportunities to practise English because their life is focused in the home. If they do go out or socialise with people outside their family, it tends to be with other people from their community.

As her own English improved, Daljit enrolled in courses to boost her business and farming skills. She went to the local adult education facility for lessons so she could use a computer and accounting software to keep the farm books, rather than doing it all by hand, and she gained the accreditation required in South Australia to handle farm chemicals. In recent years she has also tackled marketing and management subjects, and she is training to join a sustainable farming initiative known as Eco-Citrus. To be part of the initiative, she is learning how to reduce spraying to a minimum and rely more on natural insects, as well as other basic management practices that help care for the environment. For any part of her orchard to become accredited with Eco-Citrus, she has to keep a close record of everything she does.

Daljit enjoys being a student and has gained great satisfaction from every step towards independence. 'When I learn even the small things so I can do myself next time, I feel very good,' she says. Throughout the first few years, she kept a record of everything she did and learnt in the orchard so she could refer to it in future seasons. Along the way, she made many mistakes. Often they were little things, but sometimes the mistakes were big and had serious implications.

There was the season she decided not to spend money buying extra irrigation water for her citrus trees. At the time, water restrictions were in place because of drought, and she was very focused on monitoring the block's financial performance. She was trying to limit her risks and not spend more money than was coming in. But she learnt to her cost that without water at key times, citrus trees don't produce fruit so there was only a small harvest of oranges that year.

Daljit may have been dismayed at what she saw as a costly error in judgement, but it was a testing time for all the Riverland's fruit growers. They were experiencing one of the most difficult periods in the region's history. Environmental experts and industry leaders had been warning for years that the river on which they relied for survival, the very reason their communities existed at all, was in diabolical trouble. Too much water was being taken out for irrigation, and the whole system was in danger of collapse. With a prolonged drought biting hard across most of the vast basin that feeds the River Murray and its tributaries, their dire predictions seemed to be coming true.

Political arguments raged across four states about who was responsible and what might be done as the health of the river became a major national issue, affecting not just the environment, but the social and economic well-being of thousands of people. With the drought at its peak, in 2007 sweeping water restrictions were introduced which resulted in many growers having to make do with just half their annual water allocation. For some, it was the final straw. They gave up irrigation altogether, leaving thousands of trees and vines to die. By 2008, a thousand hectares of mostly orange trees had been pulled up in the Riverland and 200 citrus growers, a full twenty per cent, had left the industry.

The worst of the drought conditions were over by 2010, but by then another major threat to Daljit's survival was looming. That season the average price of grapes grown in Australia's warm climate areas dropped to less than $300 per tonne, compared with more than $470 a few years before. Experts pointed the finger at over-supply, falling export demand and the global financial crisis. The price was so low that growers across the Murray–Darling Basin left 13,000 hectares of grapes rotting on their vines that year. Quite simply, it would cost more to harvest than they would earn.

By 2015, the plight of the industry was making national headlines. Grape prices in the Riverland slumped to as low as $200 per tonne for some varieties, and reports suggested more than eighty per cent of the nation's grape growers were not making enough to cover costs. Keeping her ear to the ground, Daljit learnt of a buyer prepared to pay $210 per tonne for her Chardonnay grapes at a time when rumours were suggesting the price might fall as low as $180, and took the offer.

Throughout this ongoing tsunami of events beyond her control, Daljit kept going. At least six days a week she pulled herself out of bed, put aside her personal sorrows and the stress of what was going on around her, and went to work.

Keeping a watchful eye on her mother, and doing whatever she could to lessen the burden, was KJ. Only six when her father died, she found it difficult to come home from school and see her mother upset. Even at a young age she would try to help by preparing the evening meal, or making lunch and taking it out to her mother in the orchard, and she accompanied Daljit everywhere, even to agricultural bureau meetings. 'When I look back, we did do a lot of things together. She liked having the company so every time she went shopping I'd go shopping. If she went to a meeting I'd still go with her, even though I'd just sit there and be bored. I worked at the farmers' market making coffee for seven years so we were there together, too,' KJ says.

Although KJ didn't spend much time working on the fruit block, during the picking season she would sometimes take over delivering bins to the orchard so Daljit could head inside early. Occasionally, she would even pick a bin or two of oranges. One of Daljit's favourite stories is about KJ's endeavours when she was only about ten. Her daughter badly wanted a new pair of expensive Adidas sports shoes, so Daljit told her she could have them if she earned them by working in the orchard. 'She was really young and the pickers get a big surprise. She was picking all day. She filled the bins all by herself. I can't remember if she filled two bins or three, but she got the expensive shoes.'

KJ moved to Adelaide at the age of seventeen, to study marketing at university. Tim went to university, too, and in 2015 was back home for a while, working nightshift at a local winery and helping on the block. He is still making up his mind where his future might lie, but while she will always think of herself as a country girl, KJ can't imagine returning to live in the Riverland. In between studies and part-time work at an

Adelaide cafe, she still comes home though, whenever she can and lends a hand. Daljit says KJ knows the block almost as well as she does. KJ doesn't agree, and she worries that her mother is still working so hard.

At peak times in the season, Daljit might be in the orchard for more than twelve hours a day, pushing herself physically to get everything done, mostly on her own. From June, when she starts pruning vines and picking Navel oranges, the tasks line up and she feels that if she has a few lazy days she will fall behind and the amount of work that needs to be done becomes overwhelming. The pruning doesn't finish until August, and then she needs to deal with weeds. Harvesting Valencia oranges usually starts in November, and spring and early summer is a busy time for spraying, too.

Daljit will wake up as early as 5.30, have a cup of tea and watch a bit of television to ease herself into the day, and then spend eight hours sitting on a tractor. Depending on where she is working, she will pack lunch and take it with her. If she has time, she might help pick some oranges, working alongside the five or six backpackers employed to do this work. Mostly, she just keeps an eye on the large bins they fill, removing the full ones which are collected from the block, and replacing them with empty bins.

During the hot summer months, the grapevines need watering every second day and the irrigation system needs constant checking. Some years, if orchard work allows, Daljit takes an off-farm job in late summer, working in a local winery as a cellar hand to earn extra money. Depending on the weather and how quickly her own grape harvest is over, that essentially left April and May as the only opportunity for a holiday, until she planted persimmons and lemons to diversify her income. The persimmons are usually picked in March and April, and the lemons in May. 'One job finish, the next one ready,' she says.

May is also the time when preparations have to be made for renewing the orchard with fresh plantings, a constant process that helps keep her enterprise viable. It's when trees or vines need to be pulled if they are no longer producing enough fruit or the variety has fallen out of favour and is not attracting enough money. Replacing them is an expensive exercise, and extremely labour intensive. Because most fruit blocks are small and neither trees or vines come into full production for at least a few years, it also means that part of the orchard is not earning anything. Daljit aims to replace no more than about a hectare a year, and she thinks carefully about what to plant. Her strategy is to study market trends for fruit that will offer better returns, and diversify the orchard to reduce risks and generate income in as many months as possible.

In between the never-ending cycle of responsibilities, there is the farmers' market and the extra work Daljit has taken on cooking for community events. She usually attends the market fortnightly, as going every week is just too much on top of everything else. She goes into town and buys the ingredients she needs on a Thursday night, and then spends all day Friday cooking. After the market, she often comes home and sleeps for a couple of hours before heading out to the pump shed to turn the water on at four o'clock, as per the roster agreed with her neighbours.

Daljit admits it's getting harder to work long days in the orchard as she gets older. She will come inside in the evening, eat dinner and then go straight to bed. As the weekend approaches, her body tells her it needs a rest, so she tries to spend one day pottering around doing housework and watching television. For Daljit, time inside is a treat. So is sitting down in the evening to a simple meal of pizza. Much like her experience with cornflakes, she didn't like it at all when she first tried it. 'Now I love pizza. I could eat it every day,' she admits.

❖ ❖ ❖

Looking back on her mother's achievements, Monica realises that as children they never really thought hard enough about what Daljit was going through and what it took to keep the fruit block. 'Your mum's your mum. You never stop and think, but really we should,' she admits. 'She is brave, she is a hard worker, and she is kind. Maternally, she was pretty tough. We didn't hug a lot in our family, I don't know why, but we are better at that now. It was more an attitude of getting on with it. If something happens on the farm, she doesn't panic, she just works through it, and she doesn't cave under pressure.'

Too young to remember moving to the Riverland, Monica says she loved growing up on a farm, but it wasn't easy for her and Tim as the only Indian children attending their primary school in Loxton. 'We definitely had a hard time. You are different so you get picked on,' she says. Reflecting on a quandary faced by many first-generation Australian children with Indian parents, she points out that there was a very strong sense of not completely belonging anywhere. When they visited India, they were not fully accepted because they grew up in Australia, but they were not the same as most of the other children they grew up with, either. 'So we were sort of lost kids,' she says.

For a start, Monica's first language was Punjabi. That is what the family spoke at home, and she only learnt English when she went to kindergarten. 'As kids you pick up languages pretty easily so it wasn't that much of an issue, but now I am older I'm a pretty direct person and I think I got that from Mum. She had limited English so you had to be direct,' Monica adds.

Then there was the lunchbox issue. A seemingly small thing now in a country which embraces food from around the world, it was not the case in the early 1990s at their school playground.

While most of their peers sat down to sandwiches made with white bread, she and Tim often opened their lunchboxes to find Indian snacks. Much to Monica's amusement, the same people who gave her a hard time over it are now buying Daljit's food at the farmers' market.

Although her father tended to be more strict with them than their mother, Monica says he was fun and that she had a great childhood. She was also spoilt by Paul's parents, who lived with them for about six months every year, and spent the rest of the time in India. Her grandmother died of cancer when Monica was twelve. Her grandfather died a year or so after his son, compounding the sense of grief and emptiness in the house.

Monica was sixteen and about to start her final year of high school when Paul died. She coped by throwing herself into her studies. Her parents had always wanted their children to go to university so they had more options in life, and Paul's untimely death did not change Daljit's determination that they should have that opportunity. Inspired by her parents, Monica made up her mind that she would like to run her own business. She settled on becoming a pharmacist as the best way to achieve that ambition.

Despite doing well in her exams, Monica didn't achieve enough points to be accepted into her preferred university course in Adelaide. 'Pharmacy that year was really hard to get into, and I was pretty devastated,' she says. A place was offered to her at Townsville in Queensland, but it was a long way from home. Encouraged by her mother, she accepted the offer anyway and was packing to go when a second-round offer came through from the University of South Australia. The relief was enormous. Monica wasn't worried about leaving her mother because Tim and KJ would be there, and she had never helped much on the farm anyway, but she would be much closer to home if needed.

Like many of her Indian friends, Monica enjoyed the freedom of living away from home in a large city. Relatively speaking, she even let her hair down. 'It was funny little things, like getting a piercing up on my ear,' she confesses. In a move her friends thought was crazy, once she gained her qualifications Monica returned home. 'I wanted to be there for my mum,' she says. So she worked at a pharmacy in the Riverland for two years, before moving to Victoria where she lives now with her husband.

The story of how Monica and Hamon met reflects changing attitudes in the Sikh community, within certain limits. 'There are not as many arranged marriages in our generation but you still need the approval of your family, and it is not looked on well to have boyfriends,' Monica explains. 'My husband and I met through mutual friends and I was so scared someone would tell Mum I had a boyfriend that I told her straight away. My mum is more relaxed about these things compared with some other Punjabi families, but as soon as you say you're seeing someone, it signals you are expecting marriage.' Hamon told his parents, too. They had grown up in England so their attitudes were more relaxed, but he still wanted their blessing.

When it came to the wedding, there was never any question that it would take the form of a traditional Sikh celebration. Daljit even took Monica on a trip back to India to buy a custom-made wedding dress, and the main ceremony was held at the Sikh temple at Glossop, a few kilometres out of Berri. Monica says the whole occasion was much more relaxed than an arranged marriage, because the key players knew each other, but it was still full of deep symbolism, marking the traditional concept of a bride leaving one family to become part of another. Relatives flew in from around the world, joining local friends from outside the Indian community, such as Judy and David.

Happily married and living in suburban Melbourne, Monica realised her ambition to own a pharmacy when she was only twenty-six. Reaching her professional goal so early in life has left her thinking about what might come next. It's not a question she takes lightly, and not just because she is a person who likes to set goals. In September 2014, she was diagnosed with thyroid cancer. 'I went to the doctor for a regular check-up and when I was there he said, "Have you noticed a lump on your neck?" He had a biopsy done and it showed that it was benign,' Monica explains.

When the lump grew to the size of a golf ball, her mother-in-law insisted that she get a second opinion. This time the doctor recommended surgery to remove it. Monica was extremely busy at work because her business partner was on maternity leave, but she reluctantly agreed. 'I was not happy because I thought it was benign,' she says.

When the pathology results came back after surgery, everything changed. The growth was malignant. Monica soon found herself back in surgery, having her entire thyroid gland removed. Then they discovered the cancer had escaped the thyroid so a few months later she had radiation treatment.

Monica says the whole experience has proved very confronting for her mother. 'She doesn't like talking about it. I can understand why, but I am very open about it. For me, it's about raising awareness. If something isn't right, you should get it checked. Being a pharmacist I know it can happen to anyone. I had a patient who was diagnosed with bone cancer and he died three months later. I'm just lucky we found it, and got rid of it. After radiation I had a scan and it was all gone. Now I'm on thyroid medication. I just have to take a tablet and have six-monthly check-ups.'

Strong like her mother, Monica tries not to worry about the cancer returning. 'There is not much you can do. It's out of your control. When the time comes round for my next body scan, I will deal with it then,' she says.

For Monica, the illness has reinforced the importance of family and having someone close by who you can be with and talk to, not just in moments of crisis but to help deal with daily pressures. Looking back at her mother's experience, she realises how hard it must have been for Daljit, with all her own family so far away. 'Now I'm older she asks my opinion, but she didn't have anyone for quite a while,' Monica says.

'I was sixteen when Dad died so I didn't process everything that was going on, but I knew it was a big deal, everything that was happening. She was pretty brave to raise three kids and stay on the farm. A lot of farmers had to sell up with the drought, but she is still there and doing well. We don't give her enough credit, and she doesn't give herself enough credit, either. Even the neighbours think she is amazing, and I think she has probably amazed herself as well.'

KJ says her mum is quietly proud of what she has achieved, including receiving the Zonta Riverland Business Owner of the Year Award in 2010, when she was given an emotional standing ovation during the presentation dinner. 'She knows how well she has done, but she does underplay it. She has run two fruit blocks, raised three kids, and kept going,' she says. Reflecting on how she would describe her mother, KJ adds: 'She is very hardworking. She is always working. Always. She wants to provide well for us so we have the best opportunities in life. Our futures always came first, and she has always provided what we needed.'

❖ ❖ ❖

The Sikh temple at Glossop does not look at all remarkable on the outside. Low profile with a flat roof, it would draw very little attention if it wasn't for the small tower at the front, topped with a white dome. A pair of large wooden doors open into a small foyer. Off to the right is a well-lit hall with a grey linoleum floor, and an open kitchen in the back corner. Ahead is a closed door, leading into the main worship area, known as the *darbar sahib*. Inside, the weekly Saturday service is in full swing, and the amplified sound of drums and a lone voice singing is clearly audible.

Daljit removes her flat black shoes and slips inside. Moving quietly, she finds an empty space among a group of women and children sitting just inside the door, and drops to the floor. In accordance with strict customs of the Sikh church, her hair is covered. Like most of the other women, she is wearing a traditional *salwar kameez*. Her translucent scarf, matching baggy pants and short-sleeved top are a beautiful sea-green trimmed with gold, but the vibrant colour is subdued in the dim lighting of this corner of the room.

The men all sit in a much larger, brighter space that runs off at a right angle to the women's area. Most are wearing Western-style pants and shirts, but every head is covered with the traditional turban that is compulsory for Sikh men. The colours vary from the predominant black to electric blue and peacock green. All the men have beards, some of them flowing to their chests with distinguished streaks of grey. Traditionally, Sikh men do not trim their beards because cutting hair is forbidden, but not all the men in this congregation adhere strictly to the principle.

There are no chairs in a *gurdwara*. Everyone is sitting cross-legged on the floor, which is covered in a 1980s-style neutral beige carpet with a thick sculptured pile. Behind a low wooden balustrade at the front of the hall is a timber throne with an ornate carved canopy and a raised platform covered with a beautiful silk cloth of dazzling yellow. Underneath lies the Sikh holy book, the *Guru Granth Sahib*. More than 1400 pages long, it containing words spoken by the gurus who founded the religion in the form of *shabad* or hymns. The church contains no idols or statues, and there is no incense, just large vases of flowers standing on the floor in front of the throne.

Off to one side, three musicians and singers sit on a low platform. One of them has been playing the *tabla* since Daljit entered the building. As she settles, there is a quiet pause before another musician brings an Indian harmonium to life. The gentle droning ebbs and flows in soothing waves as the priest leading the service begins speaking in Punjabi. The other musicians join in as he moves into a hymn and the congregation starts singing along, following the words as they appear on a large projector screen. They are written in three forms—English, Punjabi written phonetically using the English alphabet, and Gurmukhi, the ancient script traditionally used to write Punjabi. Two young boys are sitting in front of the screen with a laptop, changing the slides as the hymn progresses. At one point they move on too quickly, and one boy nudges the other to go back, but there is a fair amount of repetition to the words and the singing doesn't falter.

At the end of the service, volunteers move among the seated congregation handing out *parshad*. The sweet pudding made of flour, sugar and clarified butter has been sitting in a large silver saucepan on a table near the throne. Everyone accepts a small clump of the soft, warm mixture, holding up cupped hands to receive it, as a sign of humility and respect. The formalities over, people move next door to the dining hall for a shared meal of vegetarian food. Saturday worship always ends this way as an important expression of equality and caring among the community. The food is free and freely given, with no attention paid to gender or social status or even religion.

Daljit finds a place among the women and children who gravitate to three long runners of blue-grey carpet stretching from one end of the space to the other. Light pouring in from large rectangular windows brings out the rich and varied colours of their scarves as they sit side by side, in single file.

While they chat comfortably with each other, half a dozen or so young men move along the rows handing out stainless steel *thali* plates onto which they dollop out large spoonfuls of food. Today volunteers have prepared a simple but delicious mild okra curry, dhal, chapattis and a runny pudding made with sweetened condensed milk.

Daljit doesn't go to the *gurdwara* every weekend. Friends of her husband introduced them to a Christian church in Loxton, and she goes there most Sundays. She feels absolutely no quandary in this unorthodox combination of worship. Monica says it was not necessarily the same for her as a child, adding to her confused sense of identity. 'And it is a bit controversial in our community,' she adds.

For KJ, the situation is different again. 'I feel more Australian than I do Indian, and I feel more comfortable at the Christian church,' she admits. 'I know more people and I understand it better, and the pastor there has always been in our family's life. If Mum has a problem and needs to talk to someone, she would often go to our pastor because he's always there for us. If we ever needed anything, he would always help us out.'

In her own mind, Daljit has a very strong conviction that the religions have more in common than most people realise. Like Christians, Sikhs worship one god. Both religions stress the importance of doing good works—it is not enough just to go to church once a week and follow the rituals. Followers are encouraged to keep God in their hearts and minds at all times, live honestly and work hard, treat everyone equally, be generous to the less fortunate and serve others. 'At the end of the day, all the gods say the same thing—love each other, help each other. I don't know much, but that is what I am thinking. It doesn't matter where you go, you need to trust what they are saying and bring it practically into your life,' Daljit says.

Her faith has certainly given her great strength during the past fourteen years. 'I think God help me a lot. It must be his help, otherwise there is no way I can do this. On my own, I won't make it that far but I'm still here,' she says.

After catching up with a few friends who are very pleased to see her, Daljit heads back to the farm. It's Saturday afternoon and that means it's her turn to start the irrigation pump. Despite the warm weather, she changes into a baggy, long-sleeved checked shirt, reminiscent of the flannelette shirts favoured by many farmers long before hipsters made them fashionable. Paired with tracksuit pants and work boots, she looks very different to the traditional Punjabi woman that walked into the temple at Glossop a few hours earlier.

But this version of Daljit is just as real. It is the Daljit that has emerged from years of hard work and struggle to rebuild her life—a confident, self-reliant woman who faces problems head on and is proud of her achievements. Before her husband died, she'd led a generally happy life and could not really understand what people meant when they talked about being depressed. 'Days with my parents, no problem. Get married, no problem. Come here and start work, no problem. I miss that life. It was easy. Just stay home and spend the money, not make the money,' she says.

'The problems come after he passed away. That was a life change. When people say they don't feel happy, they feel sad, then I know all that. Before I didn't know. Then I feel how sometimes the days come and you can do a lot of work, and sometimes the days come and you don't feel like doing anything. I didn't get the depression but sometimes I worry about things. It was very hard time, but it's gone,' she adds softly.

Daljit says no matter how tough it got, she never considered giving up. 'Giving up was no option,' she says emphatically. She tried not to dwell on what had passed and instead focused on the future. In the process she has not only survived some critical times for the fruit-growing industry in the Riverland but she has improved and expanded her landholdings, buying part of the orchard next door and saving enough money to purchase a unit in Adelaide. Out in the orchard, she proudly points out the orange trees she grafted over to winter Navels and mandarins after Paul died, the lemon trees she planted three years ago and her new patch of persimmons.

Nurturing the orchard, she has also nurtured her own independence. In the beginning she missed not having family close by who could take over the farm, and guide the decisions she made for herself and her children. 'Now I'm really glad that we are independent. We can go anywhere. We are not dependent on anyone,' she says.

Even though it is not the life she would have chosen for her daughter, Mohinder is very proud of her achievements, which means a great deal to Daljit. The two women are exceptionally close. Daljit phones her every morning, for as long as an hour. On Sundays she calls her sisters, and she frequently uses Skype so they can see each other and talk at the same time. A day hardly goes by without speaking to her daughters, too. Looking back on her life so far, Daljit says family remains the single most important thing to her. 'That's what keeps me going,' she says.

Part V
HERE I AM, HERE I STAY

19

CREATIVE COWBOYS

It starts with a dot, or maybe a dash, or even an arrow. Then before you know it there are flowing waves of vines and flowers, swirls and circles filling every corner. Forget the craze for adult colouring books sweeping the world, in the Quilpie Shire Hall supper room people are creating their own images to colour. In just a few hours, sixteen would-be artists have set aside their adult inhibitions and reconnected to their childhood selves, playing with marker pens and crayons and pots of paint.

It may seem like a frivolous way to spend a day, but the gathering has a very serious purpose. Quilpie lies at the heart of a community in the far south-western corner of Queensland that is dealing with what is being described as the worst drought in the state's history—a formidable benchmark for a place with a long record of extreme weather events. By September 2015 more than 80 per cent of Queensland was drought declared, and heading into at least their fourth year of doing it tough.

The ripple effects are far reaching. They spread across every sector, like the fissures that crack open dry mud at the bottom of empty dams and waterholes. Graziers who have been part of the landscape for generations have been forced to sell up, businesses have closed, marriages have crumbled, and lives have been sacrificed to the black dogs of depression and despair.

Annabel Tully is very conscious of the unrelenting pressures that people are facing and the toll they are taking. She knows from personal experience the debilitating effect of serious illness and deep depression. As a mother of five, she understands, too, the overwhelming urge to always put those you love first. So she is here today with a message, clothed in colour and curlicues: 'It is really critical that we look after ourselves, so we are well enough to look after others,' she says.

Settling into the familiar role of teacher, Annabel compares the situation to the safety messages delivered before a plane takes off. 'They tell you that if you have a child seated next to you, in an emergency you need to secure your own oxygen mask before your secure your child's. That always blew me away. As a mother, it made me feel sick in the stomach to think that I would look after myself before them, but airlines don't spend millions of dollars on in-flight training for nothing.'

There are nods around the room. People start to lean forward, listening intently, as Annabel shares her own story and the experiences that led to her running workshops that encourage people to explore their creative sides. She has found solace and satisfaction in discovering her inner artist, and she believes strongly in art as a form of therapy to improve mental health and well-being. The concept was central to a project she proposed as a finalist in the Queensland Rural Women's Awards in 2012. She intended to use the funding that came with the award to set up 'Creative Cowboys', a program offering sessions where people could leave their stresses behind them for an hour or two, and rejuvenate their spirits. As far as she knows, it was the first time a project linking mental health and art had been proposed in the agricultural sector.

Annabel didn't win but she had so much faith in the idea that she decided to run some workshops anyway. She used her own money to get some training in public speaking, and to develop a promotional poster featuring stick figures. The idea was to emphasise that people didn't need to have any recognisable skills or experience at drawing to sign up. It was all about making time to relax and have some fun.

She travelled to small communities around western Queensland, and ran sessions at a gathering organised by the Queensland Rural Regional and Remote Women's Network. Recognising the potential of what Annabel was offering, Anglicare funded some workshops at Longreach where the drought has bitten particularly deep. Today's session has been organised by the Quilpie branch of the Country Women's Association, with some support funding from the local shire and a Queensland regional arts program.

The CWA branch has never done anything like this before. Michelle, the branch president, wasn't too sure what to expect but she felt very strongly that her organisation needed to do something to help the local community. So she rounded up the branch members who have used their celebrated baking skills to sweeten the temptation with a morning tea of homemade scones, cake and sausage rolls. The offering has been laid out on trestle tables set beneath a discreet plaque commemorating the supper room's official opening by colourful National Party politician Wally Rae, a former jackaroo and World War II bomber pilot who was knighted later in life despite his reputation as a bit of a larrikin.

Fierce morning light floods the space where thousands of cups of tea have washed down thousands of scones since Wally did the honours about fifty years ago. It glances off the polished hardwood floor and creates a strong backlight for Annabel as she stands in the centre of the room, a confident figure in a dark blue dress. The workshop participants face her from behind long tables set out in a large u-shape. In front of them are small sheets of white paper and black markers. Basic tools, but Annabel wants to keep it simple while she coaxes people to explore the creative and intuitive parts of their brains.

She starts the session by reading Peter Reynolds's book *The Dot*, about a little girl name Vashti who is convinced that she cannot draw until one day an inspired teacher asks her to make a mark on a piece of paper. The reluctant Vashti draws a dot. Then the teacher asks her to sign it. When Vashti returns to class the next week, her dot is framed and hanging on the wall. Imitating the story, Annabel turns to her audience. 'Make a mark on your paper. Any mark. It doesn't matter what it is. One dot. One line.' Everyone obeys. 'Okay, make another mark.' They comply again. 'Now sign it.' People laugh, but they do it. 'Hold it up,' instructs Annabel, raising her hands as if holding a musical triangle. *'Ting, ting, ting, ting!* I would like to officially open the Quilpie Art Gallery.'

It's a simple but clever ploy that helps people overcome their initial anxiety. Soon everyone is head down, working on more complicated drawings based around repetitive shapes. Annabel urges them on with soft words of encouragement as she walks around the tables, taking time to speak to every participant. A few hours later people are quietly astounded at what they have produced.

Thanking Annabel at the end of the workshop, Michelle confesses that she was a little bit nervous about taking part, but curious too. Despite Annabel living in the area and being well known as an artist, she had never run a Creative Cowboys workshop in Quilpie, and Michelle had not known what to expect. 'I have thoroughly enjoyed it,' she says.

An older woman named Pat has tears in her eyes as she speaks up next. It's clear Annabel's core message has resonated deeply. 'We have to be well, so our families will be well. When you get to the lowest ebb in your life, I have found that the only one who can really help you is your mother. You have to look after yourself,' she says.

Always seeking to do better, Annabel reflects on how the day went as she pulls out of town later that afternoon and heads west towards Bunginderry station, on the eastern edge of what is known as the Channel Country. This vast, ancient landscape takes in a quarter of Queensland's landmass, but is home to fewer than 1400 people. It's a place of fearsome heat and shimmering mirages that famously claimed the lives of explorers Burke and Wills, but made the fortunes of legendary cattle kings like Patsy Durack and Sidney Kidman. A place of wide open skies, mulga and Mitchell grass, salt pans and rich red ochres that inspire Annabel and literally seep into her paintings. And it's the place that became home when she fell in love with a man whose family has been here for five generations and has never been tempted to leave, no matter what life has thrown at them.

❖ ❖ ❖

Annabel grew up in the semi-rural suburb of Brookfield, on Brisbane's western outskirts. A dozen or so kilometres from the heart of the city and a world away from the Channel Country, it is leafy and green, with flowing creeks and rolling hills that ring with the sound of bellbirds. Its towering forests of cedar, pine, eucalypts and silky oak were felled to provide timber to build Brisbane in the mid 1800s, clearing the way for dairy farmers and tropical fruit growers who made a living from small acreages of land.

An easy drive from the city, today many of those farms have been divided into even smaller acreages for people wanting to escape true suburbia and maybe keep a horse or two. The area still has the strong sense of community that Annabel remembers growing up, with the locals getting together every Friday night on the verandah of the member's bar at the showground for a barbecue.

Annabel's parents, Rodney and Ruth Pettigrew, moved to Brookfield after meeting and marrying in Rockhampton in the late 1960s. Originally from Brisbane and a mechanical engineer by trade, Rod ran the local produce store, which sold horse and stock feed as well as fresh fruit and vegetables. One of Annabel's fondest memories is going with her father to the Brisbane wholesale produce market at Rocklea to buy the store's daily supply of green groceries.

A trained nurse from a medical family in Rockhampton, Ruth gave up working after she married and the family came along—first Paul, who was born in Rockhampton in 1969, then Annabel, born in Brisbane in 1972, and eighteen months later, John.

When their daughter was about eight, the Pettigrews relocated from one property to another on the same road so they had more space. Their new home came with eight hectares, an old orchard with a hundred custard apple trees, a large packing shed and a farmhouse that Rod expanded by knocking out a few walls and adding a small extension. 'It was about as rural as you could get in the city,' Annabel says.

The 'rose between two thorns', as she liked to tease her brothers, Annabel was a bit of a tomboy despite her mother's best efforts. The three children had horses and bikes to ride, built cubby houses in the old orchard, and there was a large dam where they swam and had mud fights. The biggest drawcard was a flying fox Paul built over the dam. Her brothers loved it and so did their school friends and the neighbours' children, but Annabel was not allowed to play on it because her mother thought it was too dangerous for a girl. 'You had to climb about twenty metres up this tree, and then you would fly across about twenty metres of scrub before you came out across the dam wall, to a telegraph pole at the other end. Mum used to let the boys do it, but I was never allowed. It used to drive me mad.'

Annabel was particularly close to her younger brother, especially when Paul left home as soon as he finished high school to join the Royal Australian Air Force. She and John were closer in age, too, and more social by nature, while Paul tended to take after his parents, who were quieter and preferred their own company. 'Mum was always there for us when we were at home. She is beautiful, and has always prided herself on being fashionable and well spoken, but she is not a social person,' Annabel explains. 'We never brought lots of friends home. I had a friend down the road who was one of five children, and we would go over there and there would be kids everywhere, and bikes and horses, and it was really fun, or at least that's how I saw it.'

Meanwhile, her father preferred to spend his spare time in the packing shed, which he turned into what Annabel thought of as Santa's workshop. A creative 'nutty professor', Rod tinkered with inventions and made the children all sorts of fun things, such as a small motorbike powered by a two-stroke lawnmower engine. He didn't mind his children playing in the shed, but Annabel knew better than to respond when he called for assistance. 'If you said yes, you would be holding things for hours, so you didn't go anywhere near the workshop,' she says.

For the first five years of her education, Annabel went to a small local state school, and then she moved to St Aidan's Anglican Girls' School at nearby Corinda. 'Education was really important for my parents, and they wanted us to go to private schools,' she says. Although not necessarily the strongest student academically, Annabel loved high school. 'I was more enthusiastic than I was clever. I had lots of leadership roles, probably because of that enthusiasm, and I made some great mates, but then when I finished school I needed to get out.'

Her opportunity to escape came when a school friend told Annabel that her aunty was looking for a governess. The job would involve teaching three young boys for a year, on a station about 600 kilometres west of Brisbane. Thinking that it sounded far more exciting than going straight to university, Annabel asked for an interview. Unfortunately, it fell in schoolies week, when she and her friends joined hundreds of other students on the Gold Coast to celebrate the end of their schooling. 'I had a hoarse voice after a very big party,' she admits. 'And I slicked my hair back, put on lots of bright lipstick and a Liberty shirt, trying to compensate and look presentable.'

Despite her initial reservations about employing an eighteen-year-old to look after her rambunctious sons, Ali Lamond was impressed. 'I'd had a young governess before and it hadn't been truly successful, but my mother said let's just meet her,' Ali recalls. 'The fact that she was willing to come back from schoolies to meet me says something. She was this lovely girl, open, friendly and out there, and beautifully dressed.'

Duly hired, Annabel packed her bags, hopped on a bus and headed west. Having told all their children they would support them no matter what they chose to do in life, as long as they were happy, her parents tried not to worry. Before she left, her father showed her how to change a tyre and replace a fanbelt, practical skills that might prove immensely useful on isolated outback roads. 'Mum was a bit sad, but they always encouraged us to be fiercely independent,' Annabel says.

Ali and Mac Lamond lived at Braemore Park, a 4900-hectare property about forty-five minutes drive from Dirranbandi, south of St George, on mostly dirt roads. Her parents discovered just how treacherous these could be when they bought Annabel a second-hand Subaru station wagon and delivered it. 'It had rained, and it was heavy, black soil country. They slipped and slid all the way in, and they got stuck in a bore drain so we had to go and rescue them. You can just imagine Mum. "Oh, my God, where is my daughter?" But Mum had always wanted me to marry a rich, good-looking sheep farmer,' recounts Annabel. 'I did point out to her that perhaps those three things don't exist in one sentence!'

While marriage wasn't on the cards just yet, the next twelve months did change Annabel's future. She took to teaching and station life like a duck to water, although there were times when the boys tested her to the limit. Beau, then aged ten, and Toby, aged eight, were typical station children, in that they much preferred spending time out on the property than in the school room. Their younger brother, Harley, only five, was not quite old enough to have started his formal education, but Annabel kept an eye on him, too. 'I had done plenty of babysitting and I knew that I loved being with kids, but it was my first time teaching, and they knew it. I remember crying once to Mum, saying it was all too hard because the boys were playing up,' Annabel says.

'Well, just come home,' her mother told her.

'Oh, I couldn't possibly do that. That would be giving up.'

To help lift her daughter's spirits, Ruth took to sending care packages. Annabel was often bemused by the contents and her mother's perception of what might be useful. 'Mum would send a Liberty blouse and toilet paper,' she says, smiling ruefully at the memory.

As governess, it was Annabel's job to take the boys through their lessons, which were set by a distance education program for remote families, run out of Charleville. Known as the School of the Air until 1990, it involved sessions in which Beau and Toby could communicate with fellow students and qualified teachers via two-way HF radio. Then, once a year, they would travel into Charleville for a special week of sports activities, when they would get to meet and play with their virtual classmates.

The Lamonds' schoolroom was on the homestead verandah. Annabel and her two oldest charges spent weekday mornings and early afternoons there, while Harley more often than not sat outside and stirred up ants' nests. Her biggest challenge was keeping Beau and Toby in the schoolroom and focused on their lessons. On one notorious occasion, she discovered them playing on the roof. 'They were free spirits,' Ali admits, but she thought Annabel coped well, most likely because she could draw on her experience of growing up with two brothers. 'She took to it like she takes to life—full on and no looking back. Everyone loved her.'

Once lessons were over, Annabel and the children were free to join in whatever was happening out on the property. 'At lunchtime I'd always say to Mac, "Right, what are you doing after school? Can I come?" And that's how I first learnt to do sheep work,' she says. It also gave her some fabulous tales to share with friends when she went back east during the school holidays. 'I probably had the best of both worlds because I was doing exciting things and everyone else was at university. I would come back with all these crazy stories about being stalked by emus and chased by bloody bulls which they thought were pretty amazing.'

At that time the Lamonds did not employ any stationhands. Ali had grown up on Boobara station, on the Paroo River, north-west of Cunnamulla, and she played an active role helping Mac to run the property. Towards the end of the year Annabel spent with them, sheep and wool prices crashed, so Ali was often left to run the place while Mac was in Brisbane where he took on work as a fencing contractor. Ali was also working part-time at the Dirranbandi hospital as a nurse. A governess who was willing to do more than regular teaching duties was very welcome. 'Annabel liked to get her hands dirty, and nothing fazed her, although it was a bit of a lonely time because there wasn't a lot of other young people around,' says Ali.

Annabel remembers one young man, though. A tall, skinny bloke who worked on the property next door, he would take her into town for a drink at the pub. One night he settled into a session with some mates, and Annabel decided to wait for him outside. Spotting his swag in the back of his ute, she rolled it open and lay down. Sometime later he emerged from the pub, 'full as a tick', and sped off. 'I'm rolling around in the back, thinking "I'm gonna die, I'm gonna die", and then he pulled off the road and tried to jump in. I'm saying, "No, no, no," and he promptly passes out, so I drove home. Didn't I learn that lesson,' she reflects, with a hearty laugh. 'You don't roll someone else's swag open and not expect to get hit on!'

While there may not have been many people her own age in easy range, Annabel didn't mind. She loved the Lamonds, who were naturally social people and made her feel very welcome. 'Ali is this little pocket rocket and her husband, Mac, was this huge burly bloke,' Annabel says, imitating his loud, snorting laugh with obvious affection. 'They were an awesome team, really good for each other, and they were hard working, salt-of-the-earth people who knew how to have fun.'

The Lamonds eventually moved to the Sunshine Coast, where Mac died in 2013, but Ali remains one of Annabel's closest friends. 'She is my second mum. My own mum is beautiful and fantastic, but Ali is a mum for me in this life. She's the one that taught me when you have your back against the wall, it's important to have the home sorted. When the boys are busted, just make sure home is fine, so that when they walk in the door they don't have anything else to worry about. Keep it smooth,' Annabel explains. 'And she is bloody good fun!'

When Annabel left Braemore Park at the end of 1990, she took with her a love of gardening, nurtured by Ali, and a book of handwritten recipes. 'It was all my favourites that she used to cook. It's falling apart now but it's still my bible.'

❖ ❖ ❖

Before her year at Dirranbandi was up, Annabel knew that she wanted to become a teacher and return to the outback.

While she was still at high school, she had spent a fortnight in a city architect's office on work experience. She thought being an architect would satisfy her creative side, but time with the Lamonds reinforced her hankering for adventure and wide open spaces. 'The idea of sitting in a box and designing other boxes made me want to puke,' she says, with typical candour.

Back in Brisbane, Annabel devoted three years to studying to become a primary school and physical education teacher, only to find on graduating that there were no teaching jobs available in her beloved south-west. So she signed up to be the first and only carer in a new program funded by the Country Women's Association. 'On Fridays I would rock in to see Madge from the CWA, in her little house in Charleville. I would have a cup of tea in bone china, and a chat, which I really loved, and she would give me a cheque.'

The role involved Annabel providing respite support for isolated families with preschool aged children. She was placed with families in need by Frontier Services. A national charity run by the Uniting Church to support families in remote areas, it grew out of the extraordinary work by Royal Flying Doctor Service pioneer Reverend John Flynn and the Australian Inland Mission. The childcare program that Annabel helped kick off was later expanded to become the Remote Family Care Service. 'So it was pretty special to be at the beginnings of all of that,' says Annabel.

Newly graduated, and from a caring and supportive family, Annabel often found the work very confronting. 'I went out to some of the most incredible family situations for a little girl from the city. I'd had one year at Dirranbandi, and then a lovely time during university, coming back out for every single holiday I possibly could, but that was my total experience,' she says.

Annabel still gets goosebumps, of the unpleasant kind, when she thinks about one situation in particular. She was sent for two weeks to provide an extra pair of hands for a couple on a station, with a six-year-old child doing preschool by School of the Air. Annabel says that every now and then the woman would 'blank out' and head towards a river about five kilometres from the house, in an apparent attempt to drown herself. 'She was a big woman, and I had to get behind her and stop her from going in the water. Then she snapped out of it and just started bawling. There I was consoling this poor embarrassed, terrified woman.'

Annabel was horrified when she discovered what might have led to the woman's condition. 'She told me that she had experienced ongoing domestic violence,' Annabel says. 'I didn't tell Mum and Dad about it, because Mum would have freaked out and never let me go back, but I knew I was doing good things. That child was taught every single day I was there, and I cooked good meals for them at night. I stayed well clear of the husband and I was never scared when I was there. He was going through a severe stage of remorse about what he had done to this woman he loved, and she was about to go back to hospital.'

It was by far the most confronting situation that Annabel found herself in, but she came across several other families where education was not considered at all important, and the children were left to their own devices while both parents worked. 'It was only six months, but it was probably one of the best things I have done, because it gave me a good grounding in life in remote Australia, and a part of humanity that I hadn't experienced before.'

After six months, Annabel found work as a supply teacher for a cluster of small schools across south-western Queensland, filling in when teachers were sick or away on leave. Her first permanent appointment was to the tiny state school at Windorah. As the only teacher, she was responsible for all twenty students, who covered every grade from year one to seven. 'I was twenty-three and very new in my career. I'd had one term's experience doing no more than a week in each classroom, and here I was. I was pretty sassy to be taking it on,' she admits. 'I had a supervising teacher, who helped me out over the phone, and because I had no idea what I was doing I planned everything. Planned, planned, planned. I spent hours and hours doing preparation.'

Her time at Windorah reinforced her love of teaching and working with children. 'I liked the routine, and the kids were spunky and fun. All different little personalities,' she says. 'And I really loved the light bulb moments when you'd explain something one way and they have a blank look, and then you'd try something completely different and all of a sudden, you can see the light bulb go off.'

When she needed a weekend break and a bit more social life, Annabel would drive four and a half hours, pass the gate to Bunginderry, through Quilpie and on to Charleville, where she had made quite a few friends. During one of those long drives, she spotted a couple of mates pulled over on the side of the road. They were on their way to a B&S ball at the Eromanga pub. Annabel should join them, they said.

❖ ❖ ❖

Eromanga is a tiny dot of a place which claims to be the furthest town from the ocean in Australia. Another 100 kilometres west from Quilpie, it's fast becoming a major tourist destination despite its size and isolation because of the discovery of dinosaur bones in the area, dating back 95 million years. Built in the mid 1880s, the town's iconic pub was once a staging post for Cobb and Co. With the rather grand sounding moniker the Royal Hotel, it is a low-set building of white-washed stone, which to Annabel felt like an underground cave inside. A crowd of about 200 packed its bars and verandah for the event, which drew people from surrounding stations and bush communities.

Saturday night passed by in a blur of partying and catching up with friends, and it wasn't until the Sunday morning that she was introduced to Stephen Tully by one of his distant cousins. They chatted for a while, and then parted company. From that point, their relationship was slow to develop. Annabel only became aware of his interest three years later, when she was living in Charleville and teaching at the School of Distance Education. Stephen would come into town occasionally, and doss down on the floor of the flat she shared with a girl from Quilpie, who he knew well.

Stephen finally made his interest clear after he learnt that Annabel intended to head overseas on a prolonged trip around the world. When she did eventually return to Australia, she did not plan to return to Charleville and he sensed that if he didn't act before she left town, the opportunity to take things further might be lost forever. 'All of a sudden I had this fellow standing right next to me that I couldn't quite kick off. For the next four months, we saw each other every single weekend,' she says.

It started when his weekend visit coincided with the Charleville show. Annabel was volunteering as a steward and he offered to spend the weekend helping her. 'He was always very quiet, and then he started to talk to me. That's when I started to notice him. And then we were walking down the street and he held my hand. And I thought, "Oh my God!" His side of the story is that apparently he had liked me for years but I didn't know anything about it. Whether he wasn't ready or I wasn't ready, whatever it was, I don't know.'

Their first serious date was the annual Quilpie Cup race meeting weekend, when Stephen kissed her under the blue light out the front of the local police station. He had already told his parents he was pretty serious about the Brookfield girl, but she didn't know that at the time. A keen amateur pilot who flew his own plane, his father showed up at the race meeting in a leather aviator hat, with faux fur-lined ear-flaps folded up on top. When a friend spotted John in the crowd, she dug Annabel in the ribs and joked, 'Future father-in-law over there.' It didn't scare her off at all.

Nor did her first encounter of the Tullys en masse at Bunginderry. Because of the twenty-year age gap from oldest to youngest, it was reasonably rare for all nine children to be in residence at the same time. The oldest were away at boarding school and university or starting their careers, leaving a bit more space for the others and a lot less work for their mother Wendy. However, Annabel's first visit to the station coincided with the school holidays and most of the family was home. Big, noisy, and dominated by active and competitive males with large appetites, they were a completely different kettle of fish to the quiet and cruisy Pettigrews.

'I was helping Wendy with dinner, and she used to put all the pots out and you would come in and serve yourself. Trying to be polite, I just sat back nicely and waited. By the time I got there, there wasn't a stitch left and I looked over and here are Stephen and his siblings, head down, wolfing into it,' Annabel describes with great energy. 'I've told this story to the Tullys and they do not get that this isn't normal,' she adds. 'It was pretty overwhelming but I loved it. And you know what? The second night I didn't wait. I was in there, too.'

Some months later, Annabel went ahead with her overseas trip, tearful as her plane flew out of the Brisbane airport. By then she and Stephen were in love and not keen on a long separation. After she spent four months travelling by herself in Africa and Europe, they met up in London. Stephen brought a ring with him, planning to propose when they reached Venice. He figured it was one of the world's most romantic cities and the perfect location, but when it came down to it, he couldn't wait. After two weeks, Stephen popped the question while they were in Ireland, in the market town of Carrickmacross. It was probably just as well, because he wasn't all that taken with Venice when they got there. 'It's a dirty, stinking sewer of a place. Thank God I didn't wait,' he told his highly amused fiancée.

After Stephen flew back to Australia, Annabel travelled on to North America. Her plan was to spend a month in Canada, and then three more months in the United States before flying home. 'But I missed him. I got all pathetic and decided to come home early,' she confesses.

The series of events that happened next served as warnings to Annabel both of the disruptive influence nature often generates in Queensland's south-west, and the practical priorities that can overtake romance when it comes to life on the land. Planning to surprise Stephen with what she thought would be a grand romantic gesture, Annabel changed her bookings without telling him and flew home two months early. Realising that she couldn't just rock up at the station unannounced, given that he lived there with his parents, she rang Wendy and asked for permission to come and stay. Annabel swore her future mother-in-law to absolute secrecy. 'Usually she is a very good matriarch of the family and keeps everyone in the know, but she didn't even tell John,' says Annabel, clearly impressed. Meanwhile, she worked her way across Canada, lying through her teeth every time she and Stephen spoke on the phone.

After landing in Brisbane, Annabel spent a few brief moments with her parents and then headed west. She got as far as Miles on the Darling Downs, only to be caught up in a long line-up of cars and trucks. Floodwaters were rising over the Warrego Highway and the police had set up a checkpoint. 'Right. Last chance to get through. We're shutting the road,' an officer warned.

'Bloody hell,' thought Annabel, who hadn't checked the weather conditions in her excitement about seeing Stephen again. After all the organising, the secrecy and hours of travelling, she was not going to let a flood stop her. 'I was in love, heading west, and I couldn't wait,' she says. It was clear her little car would never make it, but there was a solution. Taking off her shoes, she hitched up her skirt, waded towards one of the trucks and knocked on the door.

'Where are you headed?' she asked the surprised driver.

'West,' he replied, looking down at her.

'Can I come with you?'

'Yep. Sure.'

So Annabel quickly parked her car, grabbed her backpack and climbed aboard. The truck took her as far as Morven, where they parted ways because it was swinging north. A bus was leaving soon for Charleville, but she had run out of options to complete the rest of her journey. It was about lunchtime so she rang Bunginderry, hoping someone would be inside. A surprised John answered the phone.

'Do you think you could come and pick me up in your plane?' Annabel asked him, still hoping that she could keep her impending arrival secret from Stephen.

'Well, I could, but we're in the middle of a cattle muster,' John told her, adding that Stephen might think it odd if he flew off without any explanation during such a major task in the life of the station.

'Alright, put him on,' Annabel sighed, realising that she had no choice.

'Hi, I'm here,' she told Stephen, breathless with excitement. 'I'll be in Charleville in an hour. Can you come and get me?'

There was a long pause. 'I've got cattle in the yards,' he said.

Annabel was astounded and more than a little hurt. 'You can stick your fucking cows. I've just travelled the whole wide world to see you,' she yelled.

'That was my first lesson about life on the land,' she says now, smiling at her own naivety. 'If you have mustered for three days, you do not let the cattle out of the yard for anyone, not even your loved one who has travelled around the world to be with you!'

20

GRASS CASTLE LEGACIES

When it comes to outback Australia, few names are as legendary as Durack. Patrick 'Patsy' Durack was an obstinate, adventurous and visionary Irishman who opened up some of the most isolated pastoral country in the world, establishing vast cattle stations across far south-western Queensland and the Kimberley region of northern Australia.

Patsy emigrated to the colony of New South Wales in 1853 with his parents and siblings. He came from a family of tenant farmers, driven into poverty by a combination of the Potato Famine and greedy English landlords who evicted many thousands of small tenants during the late 1840s and early 1850s so they could increase the profitability of their holdings. It is thought that as many as 1.5 million people died of starvation and disease during this period, fuelling a long-standing hatred of the British. Desperate to escape poverty and hunger, another million or so left Ireland for far-flung colonies such as Australia.

The Duracks headed to the Goulburn district where another branch of the family had settled a few years before. Patsy was only eighteen when his father was killed just two months after they arrived, crushed to death under a wagon loaded with timber after the horse pulling it was spooked by a kangaroo. Young Patsy was driving at the time. Chronicling her family's remarkable story in her best-selling book, *Kings in Grass Castles*, his granddaughter, Mary Durack, wrote that the tragedy turned him from a boy into a man overnight.

As the oldest son, Patsy took responsibility for the family and securing their future. After settling his mothers and sisters at Goulburn, he joined thousands of people from across the globe making for the Victorian goldfields. Unlike most of them, he set himself a clear and modest goal. All he wanted was £1000 so he could buy some land and a few cattle. He reached his target after eighteen months on the Ovens Goldfield, just over the New South Wales border, and returned to buy a property at Mummel.

During his time on the goldfields, Patsy became acquainted with another Irish digger by the name of Patrick Tully. Mary Durack described him as a thoughtful young man with gentle manners, from a farming family that had fought the Irish cause for generations. Patrick landed in Melbourne with his brother Joe and two cousins the same year that the Duracks arrived in Australia. His quest for gold took him to the Ballarat diggings in time for the famous Eureka rebellion in December 1854. He claimed to have helped build the wooden stockade where twenty-two diggers and five troopers died in bloody protest against exorbitant mining licence fees. The family story, as Stephen Tully knows it, is that his great-great-grandfather fortuitously missed out on the action, because he had left the stockade to fetch supplies.

The Duracks and the Tullys became inextricably linked when Patrick married Patsy's favourite sister, Sarah. His right-hand 'man' on the family property at Mummel, she was an excellent horsewoman, known for her pluck and spirit, and her ability to work stock with the 'cunning of an old hand'. According to a family history written by Stephen's great-aunt Fleur Lehane, Sarah was very pretty, with dark hair, grey eyes and a clear Irish complexion. Happy and bright, she loved to dance and was a talented singer like her mother, who also taught her daughters to be fine cooks. Patrick met Sarah through a goldmining friend who married her sister. They became better acquainted when he visited relatives in the Goulburn district, and called in to see Patsy. Sarah convinced him to give up mining, and they married and settled initially on a block at Hume Creek, where they ran a modest mixed farming enterprise.

Thirteen years after they married, the Tullys headed north to Queensland, drawn by the enthusiasm and generosity of Patsy, whose hunger for land swept up most of the extended family in the coming decades, leading some to fortunes and others to ruin. His first attempt to open up new country in south-western Queensland in 1863 ended in disaster, when the 400 cattle and 100 horses he took with him died on the journey from lack of feed and water. He and his party only escaped with their lives because of help received from some local Aboriginal people.

Despite his near-death experience and considerable financial loss, Patsy refused to give up his ambition to build a cattle empire in what everyone thought of as an unforgiving and inhospitable wilderness. He was convinced that he would find permanent water, and that the losses during bad seasons would be far outweighed by the gains in prosperous times. He knew that the land burst into life whenever drenching rain and flooding waters spread through its intricate network of creeks and channels, leaving cattle wallowing belly deep in rich fodder.

Driven by a restless energy and a tendency to work like 'he had the devil on his tail', Patsy returned a few years later when better conditions prevailed, establishing Thylungra station on a tributary of Cooper's Creek. Riding over rough terrain for many days, he and his brother-in-law, John Costello, staked claim to more than 44,000 square kilometres between them, stretching from just west of where Quilpie now stands to the Diamantina River.

Among the holdings was land which Patsy earmarked for Sarah and her family, on the eastern boundary of Thylungra. He kept writing to them, urging them to come up, but Patrick didn't want to be a burden when the seasons were not favourable, and he and Sarah had more than a few family tragedies to deal with, including the death of her sister and three of their own babies in just a few short years. After Sarah's best friend died, and what was promising to be a bumper wheat crop succumbed to rust, the Tullys finally decided it was time to leave their troubles behind them and make a fresh start. They sold their farm, packed their belongings into wagons and bullock drays, and in 1874 headed north with the best of their cattle and horses. They were accompanied on the 1600-kilometre journey by their five surviving children and Sarah's sister, Mary, her husband, Dinny Skeahan, and their three children. Along the way, Sarah gave birth to another son.

After months of travel, they arrived at Thylungra where they stayed for a month, revelling in the luxury of having a roof over their heads and being reunited with family. Then the Tullys moved on to their new property, which became known as Ray station. Ten years old at the time, their daughter Margaret recalled the wind blowing balls of roly-poly burr across the plain as they reached the site in the late afternoon. They were greeted by the excited chatter of a group of Aborigines camped on the bank of the creek where the Tullys built their first timber and daub homestead, thatched with cane grass. Sarah insisted her new home face towards Thylungra so she could see her brothers coming from the front verandah, even though it meant facing the prevailing desert winds and hot afternoon sun. According to Mary Durack, she also told her husband that Ray would remain their home no matter what happened. 'We live and die here, the lot of us,' Sarah said.

Sarah and Patrick remained adamant, even when Patsy's lust for land and the prospect of greater riches pushed the Duracks to leave western Queensland and open up the Kimberley district of Western Australia. The Tullys had made a home in the Channel Country. They would stay and make a go of it. Besides, Sarah was not going to leave the son and daughter buried in the cemetery on Thylungra. Francis, the baby born on the trip north, had died in her arms when he was only two. Despite being a talented healer, her mother was unable to save him and the nearest doctor was in Roma, an impossible 500 kilometres or so away. Her daughter Annie wandered off when she was only three while the family was attending mass and a christening, during a rare visit by a Catholic priest. Sarah had sent the restless child out to play and did not notice her missing until much later. After an exhaustive search that went on for days, they found her body lying in a gully, wildflowers clutched in one hand. Whether it was from guilt or grief, Sarah never got over the terrible loss. Patrick was convinced that she had a breakdown, and relatives talked of her personality changing completely. She rarely smiled and was terrified of letting her children leave her sight. As they became adults, she liked to keep close control of her daughters, and discouraged them from marrying and leaving home.

It was without question a hard life at Ray, coping with isolation and an extreme climate, with few if any luxuries. In the early years, there was no way of communicating with the outside world. Supplies were only delivered to the station twice a year, and the men were often away for months at a time, working cattle, droving them to markets as far as Adelaide, or fetching supplies, leaving the women to manage everything in their absence.

Sarah did not restrict her attention to the home paddock; she was keenly interested in livestock and the business side of the station. Mary Durack says Sarah even persuaded her husband and Patsy to take on sheep, despite their misgivings that they were not suited to the area, and would never produce wool of any quality. Patsy questioned what a woman could possibly know about such things, but Sarah believed the Channel Country would one day grow wool fine enough to dress the pope. Bowing to his wife's suggestion, Patrick bought 500 sheep in the early 1880s. The venture proved so successful that he later gave up cattle altogether. After it passed out of Durack hands, Thylungra went on to become one of the biggest and most respected sheep stations in the world, producing a 1400-bale wool clip from highly regarded Merino bloodlines.

Patrick and Sarah celebrated their sixtieth wedding anniversary before Patrick died in 1922, followed a few months later by his wife. They are both buried in the family cemetery on Ray, which is still in Tully hands. Looking back at what drew his ancestors to settle and then stay in a place so starkly different to their cool, green homeland, Stephen reckons it comes down to their nature, and a fierce determination to escape English authority. Queensland might have been a British colony, but the Channel Country was a long way from the nearest bureaucrat. 'I don't know for sure, but going on what a lot of the Tullys are like, I think they had a feisty attitude and a fierce sense of independence,' he says. 'They knew it was up to them to make a go of it. If they failed, they failed on their own and no-one was going to tell them what to do. Yes, it was hard, it was tough, but it was all about what they could make of it. It was a case of, "Here I am, here I stay. This is it."'

❖ ❖ ❖

Stephen could well be talking about himself. He was only a toddler when he made up his mind that he wanted to follow in the family footsteps. 'There was never any question,' he says.

One of ten children, Stephen spent most of his childhood at Bunginderry, living in the house which is now home to his own family. His parents, John and Wendy, bought the property in 1977, reclaiming another lost link. It was originally taken up by Patsy Durack for one of his sisters, but she died in childbirth and it was resumed into the neighbouring station of Pinkilla, which was purchased by the Tullys in 1905. Bunginderry was later separated again by the Land Commission and offered up for selection, with the Tully family holding it until the 1950s.

John grew up on another family property, Tenham station, further north-west, towards Windorah. His mother, Genevieve, was the daughter of pioneering Brisbane orthopaedic surgeon Dr Authur Meehan. From 'the posh end of town', she had no thoughts of becoming a station wife because her husband, another Patrick, did not plan to spend his life on the land. A barrister of the Supreme Court in Queensland, he served as an associate to Judge Hugh Macrossan and was all set for a glittering legal career until one of his older brothers was lost over the North Sea while flying with the Royal Australian Air Force during World War II.

Rejected for military service because he had only one kidney, Patrick was called home to run Tenham. He and Gen stayed for more than thirty years, raising a family of ten children. 'She had never been out west. She would have lived a grand life and to go out there it would have been a big cultural shock to her,' reflects Wendy, who considers the changing circumstances she had to adapt to in the 1960s much slighter by comparison.

Gen took on teaching all her own children, relying on a correspondence school providing lesson material until a School of the Air was established at Charleville in 1966. No stranger to medical emergencies with her own family, Wendy has been told stories of how Gen had to cope with a stationhand accidentally cutting off his arm with a circular saw, and her husband being operated on at the homestead, after his head was caught in a windmill. The Royal Flying Doctor Service brought in a doctor, who undertook the surgery while the pilot held a light for him to work by. Gen was eight months pregnant at the time.

Wendy was only nineteen when she arrived in the Channel Country. One of five children, she grew up within a couple of hours of Brisbane, on a dairy farm so close to the outskirts of Kingaroy that she could ride her bicycle to school. After finishing her secondary education, she worked in a shop but adventure was calling. When she saw an advertisement seeking 'a companion help' for Tenham, Wendy thought it sounded like a good place to start. 'I was going to travel around Australia, and this was meant to be my first stop,' she says.

John likes to tell people that he picked his future wife out of a line-up. The second eldest of the Tully children, he was given the task of selecting the successful applicant while he was visiting Brisbane on holiday. The employment section of a stock and station agency had placed the advertisement on Gen's behalf and culled the responses to those most suitable. After interviewing the remaining candidates, John thought the quietly spoken but poised lass from the South Burnett would fit the bill admirably. On her part, Wendy thought John seemed kind, even if he was wearing unfashionably wide pants when hip youngsters preferred them narrow. 'He was a bushy. He wasn't modern by any means,' she adds dryly.

Wendy arrived at Tenham in the blistering heat of January 1966. Looking back at those first weeks, she wonders why she stayed. 'I slept in this little room, and it had windows on the western side and one door. And I remember getting out of bed and sleeping in the doorway, and wetting a towel to try and keep cool. Of course, it didn't work.'

As a companion help, Wendy took on domestic duties such as cleaning the house, relieving some of the pressure on Gen who had three remaining children to raise and teach.

The Tullys had just built a new homestead fitted with a lot of modern conveniences, but Wendy still had to contend with red dust that seeped into every room, and creek water that flowed dirty brown from the taps. Then there were the mosquitoes and sandflies that plagued her after it rained. 'I had allergic reactions to them, and I'm a scratcher, so I had sores all over me.'

On the plus side, there was John. Within six months he and Wendy were falling in love, and by New Year they were officially engaged. They were married the following June, and their first child, Tony, arrived twelve months later. Meanwhile, they were living at Tenham, sharing a house with John's parents. The situation was not ideal, so John took up a position managing Alaric, a station north of Quilpie owned by another branch of the Tully family.

When they arrived after getting lost on an ill-defined track that wound across two stations, they discovered an old homestead surrounded by lawns and garden beds, nestled beside a picturesque waterhole lined with large coolabah trees. The rooms were on a grand scale, with embossed ceilings and timber-panelled walls, but the amenities were basic. In a book John wrote about family life, he explains that Wendy had to contend with 32-volt power, a rambunctious diesel generator and a wood stove. To get hot water, a fire was lit under a 44-gallon drum in the backyard.

For Wendy, one of the greatest challenges in their first years at Alaric was the loneliness. There had been a reasonably active social life at Tenham, with John and his brothers and a young stationhand providing company of her own age. In a wet season, they could waterski on Kyabra Creek, and people from nearby stations would often come together for tennis parties, picnic race meetings, sing-alongs around the piano and even movie nights out under the stars. There were very few visitors at Alaric, and most of the time there were no other hired staff.

Quilpie was ninety kilometres away via a dirt road that became treacherous when it rained and completely impassable if the creeks and channels flooded. Sometimes three months would pass between visits to town.

Wendy did not like being left on her own at night, either. 'I was a scaredy cat,' she says, blaming her father, who was frightened of being outside in the dark and instilled the same fear in his daughter. 'But I got over it. John used to take me out and show me the stars and how tranquil it was, and eventually I could walk outside without being scared that something would jump out at me.'

Her feelings of loneliness softened, too, as the family expanded. Wendy and John had five more children in the eight years they lived at Alaric. Tony was followed by Paul, Stephen, Ian, Christine and Greg. As they grew, the children became actively involved in station life, helping with musters and out in the sheep yards, except on school days. There was no need for School of the Air at Alaric, because a provisional school was set up on a neighbour's station about seventeen kilometres away, becoming a social hub for families in the area.

The school reduced Wendy's sense of isolation, but nothing prepared her for the day Paul died. A fearless little boy, he was always active and keen to be involved in whatever was going on. He loved helping in the yards no matter how many times he was knocked over by the cattle and sheep, and would not hesitate to put into action all sorts of schemes and adventures conceived by his older brother, including tackling wild pigs, turning wheelbarrows into boats and climbing the tallest trees.

Paul was only seven when he was electrocuted after falling on powerlines connecting the generator to the house. He had used a ladder, and then his bare feet and hands, to climb the pole supporting the wires, so he could inspect a bird's nest at the top. Wendy discovered him in the almost dark when she went to call everyone in for dinner. John and the stationhand gently lifted him down and attempted resuscitation, but it was too late.

Writing about the tragedy many years later, John described the overnight transformation of a vibrant, happy household full of laughter, into a place that was desolate, bleak and without joy as they battled to deal with the shock and grief. 'It was very hard,' says Wendy. There were no counsellors to consult in those days, but she spent hours talking to one of John's aunties who lived nearby and shared the phone line connecting their homestead to the telephone exchange at Quilpie. People were usually discouraged from talking too long, with the exchange operators interrupting every three minutes to check if they wanted to extend the call. 'I must have been on the phone for half an hour or more, and they didn't come on once,' Wendy says.

She also found solace sitting outside and taking in the landscape, and the tall trees growing around the waterhole. 'It made me feel there was something bigger, that there was a God,' she says. Having the other children to care for helped to ground her enormously, too. She and John had planned on having six children, but Paul's death reminded them of the richness that children brought to their lives, so they stopped counting and welcomed four more.

Bridget, Jonathon, Gerard and Nicholas were born after they moved to Bunginderry. The house was only small given the size of their growing brood, but there was a large, well-equipped shearers' quarters close by. With no school in easy driving range, Wendy engaged a governess to help teach the older children for the first two years with support from School of the Air, but after that she took the task on herself, encouraged by her mother-in-law. 'She taught her own children and she was confident that if she could do it, I could do it,' Wendy says.

Meanwhile, there was the house and the garden to look after. Keeping the garden alive in hot weather was always a challenge, and so was the endless amount of cooking required to feed her voracious sons. She tried hiring someone to help with the house but the first two employees didn't last long, so Wendy found a way to manage. 'I'd do the housework at night and then I could wake up in the morning and everything was done,' she says. On more than a few occasions she worked until one o'clock in the morning. 'Then I would have a bath in that dirty water, and do a cryptic crossword when everyone else was asleep.'

❖ ❖ ❖

When the Tullys bought Bunginderry, the station covered about 22,260 hectares. As time passed and they were rewarded with a few good seasons, they scrimped and saved to buy more land from adjoining holdings, gradually expanding the property to 74,000 hectares. One of the blocks John purchased was part of Pinkilla. Its rambling old homestead became Annabel and Stephen's first home after they married at the beginning of a wet, green January in 1999.

Back in the early 1880s, Pinkilla belonged to an English aristocrat turned drover. Lord Henry Phipps was a son of the third governor of Queensland, the Marquess of Normanby. He sold the place in 1883 and refocused his attentions on a property at Beaudesert just south of Brisbane, but for much of its history since 1904 it has been in Tully hands.

When Annabel and Stephen moved there during what turned out to be a lush, wet summer, the homestead had been empty for some time. It was surrounded by an enormous number of disused outbuildings, all once an essential part of running a large property that employed as many as fifty people. Men's quarters, storehouses, slaughter yards, a pigsty and chook runs all stood empty, but with many of the old fittings like gun racks and flour bins still in place. It was like living in a ghost town. Out in the middle of a clay pan, there was even a concrete cricket pitch where Quilpie used to compete against Pinkilla every year, when the station had enough employees to field its own team.

The newlyweds set to work renovating the house and garden, starting at one end of the old timber homestead and working their way to the other. During the first year, their energies were restricted to weekends because Annabel had a full-time job at the one-teacher school at Eromanga. She would leave Pinkilla at seven o'clock on a Monday morning, and then come home on Friday night. The routine made it difficult to settle into her new life so after a year she turned to casual relief teaching instead.

Extremely happy in Stephen's company, Annabel loved going out on the property to work alongside her husband whenever she could, and she had no trouble coping with the basics of living at Pinkilla. By comparison with generations of women before her, the amenities were more than adequate. The house was connected to mains power, there was plenty of water and even a dial-up internet connection. It was a reasonably easy run into Quilpie on a good dirt road when she needed to travel into town, and mail was delivered twice a week. Once a week she faxed a grocery list to the supermarket in Quilpie and the supplies would come out on the mail run.

'I never really felt physically isolated. It was more about my sense of self. The hardest thing was making friends, stepping into someone else's world where I didn't have any go-to's or back-ups. Family and friends were a long way away, and all of my new friends were Stephen's friends. So Annabel Pettigrew may as well have been wiped off the planet. I was Annabel Tully, Stephen's wife. No-one really knew *me*. I had no identity,' she says.

She remembers asking Stephen when she first moved to Pinkilla how he made friends out here, but it was a question he couldn't answer. He was living in the place where he grew up and his friends were people he had known most of his life. The situation was made easier for Annabel when Stephen's brother Gerard returned to the district with his wife, Jody, and moved onto the property next door. 'Gerard and Jody are beautiful. I really love having her next door, but their house is still an hour and twenty minutes away and I might only see her once a month.'

Getting involved in the Quilpie and District Show Society helped Annabel begin to feel like she was part of the local community. As a child, she had entered competitions in the Brookfield Show for everything from art and cookery to chooks. While she was working at Dirranbandi, someone even convinced her to sign up for the Miss Showgirl competition, still a popular part of country shows in Queensland. 'I don't know why I did it, actually. I was such a naughty party girl,' she says. During the interview process that every entrant must undergo, they asked her how she spent her weekends. 'I go to B&S's and the pub,' she told them. 'They would have just looked at me and gone *pap-pow!*' she says, imitating the game-show buzzer noise that indicates failure.

More mature and a lot wiser, she volunteered as a steward for the Quilpie Show and ended up serving as the show society secretary for five years. The experience gave her the opportunity to meet people and become more comfortable talking with older generations. 'I just didn't know how to do that,' she admits. 'Both sets of my grandparents were dead, and I didn't know how to talk to older men, or even older women, really. My dad is not a conversationalist and I don't have any uncles so I found it quite difficult. Men of the land just talk shop, and I used to be terrified of them, so the show society was really good for me. Everybody comes to the show, from babies in prams to grandparents.'

Another major adjustment after she stopped teaching was going from earning a regular, healthy salary of her own to being financially dependent on Stephen, who was being paid a wage by his parents as well as doing contract work on other properties in the area. 'It is very hard to put your trust completely in another person to provide money for you, when you have been so incredibly independent,' she says. 'Back in those days I wasn't involved in the decision-making or anything like that on the property, which I didn't mind at all, but I found it difficult to go from earning a good wage as a school principal to all of a sudden not making any decisions about our financial situation.'

Annabel and Stephen soon had an awful lot more to worry about. In 2001, their first child, Lachlan, was born. A few weeks before he was due, Annabel travelled to Brisbane so she could be close to her parents and expert medical care. The baby was finally delivered by caesarean section, after a long labour. Then eighteen months later their second child, Sophia, arrived in much more dramatic circumstances.

About a week before her baby was due, Annabel went to see a lactation specialist. She'd experienced some difficulties breastfeeding Lachlan, and wanted to consult an expert to avoid a similar experience with her next child. She could feel a lump in one breast, about the size of a grape, and wondered if it might be a blocked milk duct. After examining her, the specialist was so concerned that she organised for Annabel to go and see a doctor immediately. 'That was on a Friday morning. By Tuesday I'd had the baby and been in for surgery.'

The lump turned out to be breast cancer. The breast surgeon wanted to perform a lumpectomy as a matter of urgency to remove the tumour, and then start chemotherapy, so Sophia was delivered by caesarean section slightly ahead of schedule. There was no time to take in the diagnosis properly, or to have a natural birth with her second child as she had planned. 'We just followed instructions and trusted the doctors,' says Annabel.

The first night after Sophia came into the world, Stephen stayed with them both at the hospital, and then he took charge, with Annabel's mother, Ruth, as back-up. Between the caesarean and the lumpectomy, Annabel could not get out of bed, let alone care for a baby. 'Essentially, Stephen looked after Sophia from day dot. He did a brilliant job,' she says.

After her surgery, Annabel went back to Pinkilla to recuperate. Once her wounds healed, she returned to Brisbane every three weeks for chemotherapy, over a period of about four months. 'I would leave my babies and my husband behind and fly down on a Tuesday and then back on Thursday. Then I'd be in bed for a week, then I'd be okay for a week, and then I'd go back again. It turns out that I have a really low pain threshold. I could handle the nausea, but I was shocking with the pain,' she says. Throughout this period Stephen ran the house and looked after her, and Wendy helped with the children, although Annabel struggles to remember the details. 'Isn't it funny? Obviously I knew that they were alright. I was just so sick, I couldn't look after anyone.'

Ali Lamond remembers being very frightened for her friend when she came to stay on the Sunshine Coast for a few days during her treatment. Ali recalls: 'Her parents had the flu so I went down and collected her, and I brought her home. I was scared that she seemed so vulnerable and so rundown. She sat on the couch and I held her hand, and she took her wig off. That was the weekend that I wondered whether she was going to make it.'

There was no history of breast cancer in her family but Annabel was only twenty-nine and her doctors wanted to do everything possible to make sure the cancer did not return or spread to other parts of her body. 'We are going for a cure here. We are going to jam it as hard and as fast as we can,' they told her. After chemotherapy, they recommended radiation therapy. That meant staying in Brisbane for six weeks and going to the hospital every day so her breast could be treated with targeted exposure to radiation. 'I've still got this big lump with scar tissue from the radium, and it's still sore to touch. It's incredible the way it screws your skin, but there is no way anything could grow back in there,' Annabel says.

Because she was going to be away for such a long period, Annabel took the children with her and Ruth helped look after them. 'We stayed down on the coast near Mum and Dad, and Mum would come over at the ugly hour [five o'clock in the afternoon], when the kids were tired, cranky and hungry. Then I would go and do my bit for the next couple of hours. Sophia didn't bat an eyelid because she was little and her basic needs were being cared for, but it really threw Lachlan. He was at that stage between one and three when separation anxiety is at its peak, and it took him until he was about eight to have any sort of confidence. He would freak whenever I left. While I didn't put it on myself, the guilt is big-time as a mother. You are trying to do your darnedest and you can see it unfolding in front of you, but I didn't know what was going on at the time. I was just trying to keep my head above water. I couldn't do it all. It wasn't until later when I was feeling better and back on track with being a mum that I could see we had some catching up to do.'

The next step in Annabel's treatment was hormone therapy. The aim was to switch off her pituitary gland so that it stopped producing oestrogen. The doctors believed it was contributing to the growth of her cancer, because what are known as hormone receptors were found on her cancer cells. Inhibiting the amount of oestrogen her body was producing would reduce the risk of the cancer returning. Another more drastic option was to remove her ovaries because they produce most of the oestrogen in a young woman's body. Annabel did not want to pursue that alternative because she was only twenty-nine and planning to have more children.

On the plus side, she didn't have to go to Brisbane for the hormone therapy. It involved needles that could be given by nursing staff at the Quilpie hospital. On the negative side, the needles were huge, and she had to have them in her belly once a month for two years. Even worse, they triggered menopause. Annabel was only thirty, and the symptoms were full blown. 'It was pretty foul, but when you have a choice between that and death, you don't really have a choice, do you?'

It was at this point that Annabel rediscovered her creative side, and the healing power of art. She started playing with paint and joined the Quilpie Cultural Society, set up in 1972 to develop the arts, and provide activities and a meeting place for isolated women. The society has been extraordinarily successful, with the town today boasting a vibrant arts culture. 'The girls took me under their wing and encouraged me to be part of their group, which has been really special.'

Annabel began by signing up for some of the society's regular tutorials and designating two days a week to painting. Deciding that she wanted to become a professional artist, after experimenting for a couple of years she committed to her first solo exhibition in 2004, at the Quilpie Museum and Visitor Centre Gallery. Titled *Nostalgia*, it explored the history of the Tully family and their connection to the land, drawing inspiration from old family photos and the landscape around her. 'It was my way of finding the link between my former life and my new life,' she says.

The exhibition was closely followed by winning Queensland's Brian Tucker Award for regional and emerging artists, but her breakthrough moment came the same year when she took part in a 'Living the Landscape' workshop led by Mandy Martin. Then in 2007, Annabel was selected to join Martin in an episode of *Painting Australia*, an ABC television series in which a different professional artist each week challenged three emerging artists to complete a work interpreting the landscape in two days. Martin took Annabel and two other artists out into the Simpson Desert. 'It was a pretty cool experience. She just took me under her wing.'

A professional artist living in New South Wales, Martin has an international reputation for work exploring the Australian landscape and natural environment. She has exhibited in more than a hundred solo exhibitions both in Australia and overseas, and her works are found in many public and private collections, including the National Gallery of Australia and the Guggenheim Museum in New York. 'She uses found ochres and pigments in her landscapes, and she is just amazing. To me, she ticked all the boxes because I like to paint special places, and we have ochre pits here up in the hills. It all just fell into place then.'

Landscapes that capture the Channel Country where she lives, using paints made from ochres gathered on the station, have been Annabel's focus ever since. 'For the past ten years that's what I've done. I haven't painted anything else since, and I never get sick of it,' she says. Annabel quickly found her audience, too, with her work selling strongly at solo and group exhibitions across Queensland, from Brisbane to Longreach. She even established her own gallery at Pinkilla, called Grass Castles. The name was inspired by the famous Patsy Durack quote: '"Cattle kings" ye call us, then we are kings in grass castles that may be blown away upon a puff of wind.' Set up in one of the old worker's cottages, the gallery drew steady traffic because the entrance to the station was off a well-travelled road that connects outback tourists to Longreach and Birdsville, and they only had to travel seven kilometres on a decent gravel track to reach it.

The gallery closed in 2006, when Stephen's parents retired and moved to the farm where Wendy grew up, just out of

Kingaroy. Stephen and Annabel leased Bunginderry from them and decided to move in. 'Pinkilla was a bit closer to town and a great place to live, but Stephen essentially drove away to work every morning, and if you are living in the middle of nowhere you want to be together, and have your kids around you,' Annabel says.

Bunginderry homestead was too far off the road, on a track with too many difficult channel crossings, for Annabel to set up another gallery. Instead, she came up with an even better idea, inspired by the Brushmen of the Bush, a group of artists including Pro Hart and Jack Absalom that gathered regularly at Broken Hill, and the Bundanon artist-in-residence program run at Arthur Boyd's former home on the Shoalhaven River in New South Wales.

The concept involved running artists' camps where people could retreat from the distractions of daily life for a week or two, and work side by side with some guidance and encouragement from specialised tutors. The camps took in up to ten participants at a time, accommodating them in the workers' quarters. Every day they were ferried to different locations on the station, giving them the chance to focus completely on developing their skills while capturing some extraordinary landscapes and connecting to the bush and station life in a much deeper way than is possible for passing tourists. In the evenings they would share a meal with the Tullys and sit around together talking.

'It not only ticked the creative box for me, but Stephen and I love sharing this place with others, so they have an understanding of what life in the bush is really like. We can only do it in a small way, but we are really passionate about getting positive messages back to the city. We wanted to get people in here and staying, not just pulling off the side of the road, camping for the night and then keeping on going like many people do. There were no frills, but they got to live with our staff and be one of us,' Annabel says. 'And I loved being able to go to a place on the station, and there would be ten different people and you would all be looking at the same thing, but there would be ten completely different paintings or photographs at the end of it. Seeing your homeland through someone else's eyes was cool.'

Most years, the Tullys hosted two major camps, one for painters and one for photographers. As Annabel's reputation grew, in between camps a spattering of people came to work one-on-one with her, and there were the occasional smaller groups who would ring up and ask if they could come and do their own thing. Many of the artists who spent time at Bunginderry have since staged their own exhibitions of work inspired by the landscape. In 2011 Annabel even curated a touring exhibition that brought together the work of ten participants, which travelled around regional Queensland with support from the state's Arts Council. 'You do not realise the legacy you have left behind,' one of the artists told Annabel when she decided to wind up the camps in 2015. 'There are so many people that have gone on to do other things, or have connected, because of Bunginderry.'

Annabel's life as an artist wasn't the only thing expanding during their first few years at Bunginderry. In 2005, their third child, Harriet, was born. She was followed fourteen months later by Hugo and then just ten months after that came Eve. Annabel had always wanted six children, but even Stephen said 'That'll do!' when they got to four, so they organised to see a fly-in surgeon about a vasectomy. 'By then slippery little Eve had got through. I remember doing the walk of shame down the Quilpie hospital corridor with Stephen. I was pregnant. I had Hugo on my hip, and I was holding Harriet's hand because she was toddling, and Stephen was holding the other two.'

'What if you lose a child?' the surgeon asked, wanting to make sure that they were certain about the procedure given the couple were still in their thirties.

'How could you ever replace one of these little darlings?' Stephen asked him. 'No, I'm done. Even if Annabel is ever done with me, I'm not having any more kids.'

With Eve's birth, there were three children in the house under three. 'It was like having triplets without sympathy. You just had to chill out and let it go,' reflects Annabel. Stephen was a dab hand at changing nappies, and they employed a governess. 'I've got a damn good husband, and it was always teamwork. If it hadn't been like that, I wouldn't have gone past two!' she says firmly.

21

THE FENCE OF HOPE

It is early August. The sheep were mustered and shorn back in autumn, and the cattle work is done for now. Before the weather starts to warm up, Stephen and Annabel are out on their eastern boundary, building a fence. It is not just any fence. It is a symbol of hope. An act of defiance against a drought that is dragging into its fourth consecutive year. The Tullys can't make it rain, but they can build a fence that they believe will improve their prospects dramatically once it does. 'The fence will fix everything,' Annabel says, only half in jest.

Financially, physically and emotionally, there is a lot riding on this barrier of posts and wire. Across much of central and western Queensland, pastoralists are doing battle with more than drought. Wild dogs are killing their sheep in escalating numbers. Much as the pests are ripping out the throats of the livestock, graziers believe they have ripped billions out of the economy, forcing people to walk away from sheep altogether and threatening the viability of a once-vibrant industry. Australia's favourite rural television program, *Landline*, reported in September 2015 that 8000 wild dogs had been trapped in a single year in the combined local government areas of Barcaldine, Murweh and Blackall in an effort to reduce the problem. At Quilpie the local shire employs two full-time trappers and sets out tonnes of bait in a program that costs the council almost half a million dollars a year. It has helped but graziers are still losing thousands of sheep.

Kangaroos may not be killing and maiming livestock, but graziers are convinced they are also doing untold damage. They strip pastures bare and when grass is scarce they destroy native vegetation, in turn affecting endangered wallaby species that are also desperate for food, and decimating the habitats of smaller ground-dwelling native animals. Parts of Queensland that have received a little rain are struggling to bounce back because the kangaroos are eating fresh vegetation as soon as it emerges. 'There are stations at Longreach that completely destocked, trying to do the right thing and give the country a chance to recover, but there are so many kangaroos it's making no difference,' says Stephen.

A paper put together in 2014 by Queensland's environment department estimated there were more than 27 million red and eastern grey kangaroos and common wallaroos in Queensland, compared with about 12 million in 2010. The government sets quotas for the commercial harvesting of all three species, and also hands out what are called 'damage mitigation permits', allowing landholders to shoot up to a thousand over a twelve-month period. Commercial harvests are controlled through quotas, which allow between ten and twenty per cent of the population to be culled in specific zones. Since 2009, those quotas haven't come close to being filled because export markets for roo meat have collapsed and there are fewer licensed shooters around to do the work.

One of Stephen's neighbours reckons he saw about 5000 kangaroos during the last mustering in a paddock that runs 700 sheep. They are so thick on the ground that after sprinkles of light rain bring up the tiniest amount of green pick on the edge of local roadways, they line up along both sides like a guard of honour. In this part of the world, people avoid driving after dusk because kangaroos are a major hazard, but there are still countless bloated carcases all over the roads. Police further north at Longreach reported in January 2015 that up to forty were found in a stretch of just forty metres, and there is a section of road between Longreach and Barcaldine that's known as 'the killing fields' because there are so many. 'The numbers have never been like this here, ever,' says Stephen.

No farmer likes to see the livestock he has worked hard to raise mutilated or dying of starvation, and Stephen is no different. He is passionate about the need for action to reduce the damage both wild dogs and kangaroos are doing, not just to the rural economy but the environment and social well-being of local communities. As chairman of a macropod working group set up by the Queensland rural advocacy organisation AgForce, he is playing a part in doing something about it. The advisory group is pushing governments to give landholders a greater say in how kangaroos are managed so that some more effective practical solutions can be found.

There is plenty of debate between landowners, government departments and environmentalists about the best approach. Culling kangaroos is an emotive topic, because they are a native animal and an iconic symbol of Australia. Then there are the practical considerations of the costs involved and the difficulty of effectively patrolling vast acreages of land with few roads and access tracks.

Governments are reluctant to install barriers like they did in the late 1800s, when a fence covering more than 5600 kilometres was raised between the Darling Downs and the Great Australian Bight. Often described as the world's longest fence, it was designed to keep dingoes out of the southern states. However, smaller fences, protecting clusters of land covering a few properties, are starting to find favour, and that is what Stephen and Annabel are putting up at Bunginderry.

They have combined forces with Stephen's brother Gerard, who manages Canaway Downs on their northern boundary, and cousin Rod Tully, from Ray station, to secure a grant and build the first cluster fence in the Quilpie district. It will stretch over 320 kilometres and protect 275,000 hectares of land from feral animals such as wild dogs and pigs, as well as roaming mobs of kangaroos. The three properties are contributing more than $650,000 and their own labour, with matching funds towards material costs coming from the South West Natural Resource Management Group. In return the group is closely monitoring the results, to see if scientific and practical lessons can be learnt to help protect other properties and the natural environment. 'What we are trying to do is control the total grazing pressure on the land. We want to get kangaroo numbers down to a sustainable level, and hopefully eradicate dogs and pigs,' says Stephen.

Looking around at the people who hung on after the last major drought, Stephen can see that people learnt valuable lessons from the experience. For example, many people started destocking earlier, rather than waiting until they were forced to sell and livestock prices were rock bottom. On Bunginderry, they are down to 8000 sheep, instead of the usual 15,000 or so. 'We are back to the core breeding herds, and we have put everything out in the mulga scrub. It's not highly productive country but it's what saves you in a drought. We can push the trees down to feed the sheep and the cattle—it's not a great diet but it gets them through, and it's a lot cheaper than carting feed. But it's another battle that we have had to fight against government regulation, so that we are still able to do it.'

Receiving practical support, like money to build a fence or install water infrastructure, is something most graziers much prefer to being given social welfare handouts. Aside from creating a permanent asset that will make them better able to withstand future droughts, it has other benefits that may seem less obvious. Even before the first stretch of fence is completed on Bunginderry, it has boosted everyone's spirits because it's given them something constructive to do, rather than sitting around waiting for the drought to break. Stephen is also relishing applying his inventive mind to refining the design of the fence and the system for installing it. The smallest efficiency might save many days.

Out in the paddock, he is in charge of a skid-steer loader, fitted with a bucket attachment, which he uses to pull out old fence posts. Once the posts are out, he switches the bucket for an auger and sets to work drilling holes for new strainer posts which are being installed every 500 metres or so along the fenceline. Bunginderry's only full-time stationhand, Josh, stands by to clear away the large stones that occasionally make it heavy going. He then drops the new post into place, checking the hole is deep enough.

Meanwhile, Derek is up on the back of an old truck mixing concrete. A Canadian backpacker, he is helping out at Bunginderry to fulfil the terms of his working holiday travel visa. Derek has to spend three months doing a specified kind of work in a regional area if he wants to stay in Australia for a second year. It's a long way from Toronto but he is loving his time on the station, even when it involves shovelling sand and gravel into a concrete mixer. Once the mixture is ready, he pours it over the edge of the truck's tray.

Annabel keeps her head down as the concrete splatters into an old metal wheelbarrow she has lined up below, and then wheels it over to where Josh is waiting beside the new post. She upends the load and together they tamp it down into the hole, fixing the new post firmly so that it can withstand up to two tonnes of pressure when the new fenced is strained. When all the posts are in place, the Bunginderry team will roll out a special wire mesh designed specifically to keep out feral animals. One and a half metres high, it will be spring-loaded at the bottom to withstand pressure from wild pigs and dogs. A single strand of barbed wire will be strung above it, to add more height and deter kangaroos.

Unable to resist the temptation, Annabel picks up a small stick and signs her name into the wet concrete, an artist making her mark and a farmer quietly commemorating her first tangible contribution to the project. She loves being outdoors. 'I'm definitely solar powered,' she says. Raising five children and her illness has prevented her from working out on the property as often as she would like until the last year or two.

But she managed plenty of work in the sheepyards while the children played nearby and countless musters, too, working on the ground with Josh and Lachlan, while Stephen spots livestock from above in an ultra-light. With summer rains failing to materialise for a while now, she's also shared the dispiriting task of going out every day to check watering points, and moving the stock on as one dam after another dried out. 'And I had the crappy job one year of fixing all the holes in the fences to get ready for shearing, but that was okay because I got to know where all the gates were,' she adds, admitting that it's still possible for her to get lost on Bunginderry.

It's also been an interesting experience learning how to tackle tasks that Stephen has been doing most of his life, having absorbed the knack by helping his father, who in turn learnt from his father, and so on. 'I've had to learn from scratch. I don't know anything intuitively. When I ask Stephen to explain to me what to do, he gives me instructions one, seven and fifteen, and the rest is missing because he does it automatically. When it's not what you grew up with, it's nice when you learn a new skill and find yourself on the same page and working with the person you love. It's a really cool feeling.'

❖ ❖ ❖

The fence of hope is not the only thing that Stephen has built during a period of considerable stress, when his practical, hands-on nature pushes him to look for something constructive to do, instead of sitting around feeling helpless. Before the fence, there was the studio. He built it over a two-year period after Annabel's cancer came back.

Annabel was diagnosed again with breast cancer in 2009. This time, the surgical response was much more extreme. 'The lump was the size of an orange. It was benign and then it just went nuts,' she says. The surgeons recommended that her breast be removed completely, and Annabel decided her other breast should go, too. She was done with the worry and the risk. So both breasts were removed and then reconstructed using skin, fat and muscle from her abdomen. 'It's amazing what they can do. I make it sound easy, but it was two years and ten operations, and I got some bloody stupid infection that one in a million people get. I was sick as a dog, more sick than I had been with the chemo. It was the same shit all over again, but with five kids this time.'

While his wife was forced to spend considerable time in Brisbane where she could get the medical care that she needed, Stephen stayed at the station and looked after the home front, with help from the governess and a nanny who was employed to provide extra assistance. 'I was better off with him here looking after the kids, and he knew I was being looked after,' Annabel says.

As a final precaution, in yet another operation the surgeon also removed Annabel's ovaries. She had rejected this step when she was younger and wanted more children, but this time her doctors made it clear there was no choice. The surgery triggered another period of full-blown menopause. 'Hot flushes and everything,' Annabel says. 'Everyone thinks they have it tougher than everyone else, but mine wasn't gradual. It was overnight, and from what I can gather the impacts were pretty full on. I'm past it now, but it would have taken a good two or three years.'

All through this time, the exuberant, outgoing Annabel was also struggling with clinically diagnosed depression. 'I've probably gone through eight years of hardcore depression,' she says, wondering whether menopause and the radical changes caused to her body by chemotherapy may have been contributing factors. 'It was almost like post traumatic stress disorder, and I didn't have any strategies to deal with it. I sought help and I took drugs, and once I was physically healthy again, I was mentally better,' she says.

Even her closest friends had no idea of what she was going through. 'I used to go and cook for the artists' camps,' recalls Ali. 'We were sitting in a gully one day. I'd taken smoko down, and she was painting, and it all came out. I was quite shocked. She has become like a best friend, or a daughter, and every time I left after cooking I cried. And then the last time I left, I didn't. I just thought, "You have come so far." But the thing is, if she thinks she needs help, she will go and seek it.'

Annabel gradually learnt to recognise the factors that trigger her depression, and ways to manage them. She goes for a walk in the bush every morning before breakfast, and she has taken up yoga. She knows that scheduling too many outside commitments back-to-back is a bad idea, and that she needs to allow plenty of time to spend with her family and in the studio. 'Art is my therapy,' she says.

Stephen built Annabel a studio knowing how much it would mean to her recovery and staying well. 'That was his therapy. Whenever I couldn't find him, or I'd ring and he didn't answer the phone, he was over there,' she says, looking towards the small but elegant building just a few metres from the house. The studio is set on a slight rise that Stephen formed to create a better aspect in this essentially flat landscape. Facing the home paddock and a meandering line of trees that mark Whim Creek, it also sits above a levy bank that prevents the homestead from flooding. When the creeks and channels burst their banks, the water spreads out for kilometres. In the way of the Channel Country, this phenomenon can happen without it even raining at Bunginderry, with the water sweeping down from the hills twenty or thirty kilometres away, catching people unawares.

Simply designed, the studio has a gently curving roof that extends slightly over the front wall to create a shallow verandah. Huge windows fill most of the walls on two sides, allowing natural light to flood the space where Annabel sets out big tables when she is working. There is a fold-out bed, too, so the studio can double as spare accommodation when needed. Apart from the main room there is just a small bathroom, and storage space for her work and the tools of her artistic trade. 'Stephen built it all,' Annabel says with considerable pride in his efforts. 'He had an extra pair of hands at one point, but no builders.'

The studio is Annabel's bolthole. With three children still at home all day every day, it's important that she has a place of her own, where she can work uninterrupted. 'It's my little spot and nobody else is allowed here,' she says. She tends to work in large blocks of time, and follows a precise process with every painting. 'I like order amongst the chaos, so my poor old brain has a bit of a fight most days, but maybe that's okay because maybe it means I'm using it to its maximum potential. I'm a very organised, rigid person, and the creative side of my life is my spontaneity. It's my outlet, it's my balance.'

She aims for balance in the life of her children, too. Growing up on a station, they have extraordinary freedom and independence compared with many of their city counterparts, but even though there are no school bells or sirens, when it comes to their education there is no escaping routine. At eight o'clock every school day they make their way to the workers' quarters where a governess supervises their lessons. One end of the building is set up as a classroom, which also doubles up as a sitting room for Sophie, who came to Bunginderry about six months ago. There are a couple of desks, and colourful illustrations based around numbers and letters and words fill the walls, just like a conventional classroom.

Off to one side is a small room set up with computers. The days of high-frequency radios which gave the School of the Air its name are long gone. Today students rely on the internet and video-conferencing to communicate with their teachers and classmates. It might sound like progress, but there are more than a few days when the Tullys wonder if they wouldn't be better off going back to the old technology. Conferences of the Isolated Parents and Children's Association in 2015 brought to national attention just how bad telecommunication services are in the bush.

Out here, people rely on satellites to connect them to the internet. In what Annabel describes as a monumental stuff-up, a satellite service that was meant to cater for 250,000 users stopped functioning properly when it hit 38,000. The end result is interrupted access and slow delivery speeds, which make using the internet a nightmare. Harriet, Hugo and Eve use video-conferencing without the video because the system can't handle it. The distance education office at Charleville has to provide still pictures and CDs instead, and Annabel often has to drive into Quilpie to the library to do online research and download material.

Even when the service is working, it's expensive. The Tullys pay $180 for twenty gigabytes a month for the schoolroom connection, and $90 for a separate service at the homestead. 'It's disgraceful and it doesn't even work. We use most of it up by week one or two, and there is no watching YouTube clips or online movies in this house,' says Stephen, the frustration clear. 'When it's dry and you're doing it tough, you get this lecture from people that you should be more educated. Yeah, how? My cynical negative hat says we have grounds for class action, with the amount of dollars we are losing every day because we cannot operate properly.'

The Federal Government has been trying to reassure rural communities that it will all be fine when two new satellites come on line as part of the roll out of the controversial National Broadband Network. That is not due to happen until 2017 and people are worried it will soon be over-subscribed anyway. Desperate for alternatives, Stephen even climbed onto the homestead roof, with a car kit and a big aerial, trying to find mobile coverage.

Even if the satellite service does improve to the point where the children can take full advantage of the distance education services available, Harriet, Hugo and Eve will follow their older siblings to boarding school in Brisbane once they turn twelve. Annabel and Stephen agree that it is the best way for them to broaden their horizons, meet new people and make friends, and then make an informed decision about what they want to do with their lives.

Reminding herself of all those positive benefits hasn't made it easy for Annabel to be parted from Lachlan and Sophia. 'The concept of my kids going to boarding school has been really foreign to me. Stephen's better at it than I am—in fact, he is better at most things when it comes to teenagers!'

To try to lessen the wrench, Annabel aimed for a festive, party atmosphere when the first child left. She took the younger children to Brisbane, too, so they could see where Lachlan was going to school, and the bed he would be sleeping in. Everyone got balloons and she worked at keeping the conversation positive on the long drive there and back. It might have convinced the children but the day after she got home, Josh walked into the house for lunch to find chaos.

Annabel had put a large tub of crystallised honey into the microwave to melt it. Instead of programming it to operate for one minute, she hit ten. 'The tub had spilled its guts out the door and all the way down through every single drawer in the cupboard and then onto the floor. It looked as though the microwave was crying, and I'm sitting in the corner crying, too. I don't know if it was because I was missing Lachlan or the mess I had to clean up.' Josh took one look and left.

❖ ❖ ❖

Annabel is standing on the rise next to her studio, watching the children's puppy, Jersey, disappear into the distance chasing a kangaroo. She tries to call the feisty Jack Russell back but in the excitement of the chase he is ignoring her calls and shows no sign of giving up. Annabel isn't giving up, either. Her husband's family have put down deep roots in the fragile soils of the Channel Country and Stephen is committed to it. In turn, Annabel is deeply committed to Stephen and has come to love this country of extremes, too, weaving her own thread into the Tullys' long outback yarn and finding her own way of expressing that love through her paintings.

This place and illness have sorely tested her resilience. Annabel has known many more dry years than wet since she moved here in 1999. There were three good seasons before the current drought, and the Quilpie district was green for her first summer, teasing her with its luxuriant best. Then came the 'Millennium drought'—ten years that drained the land of livestock, feed and water, and tested the Tullys' skill at managing Bunginderry, while Annabel waged her own battle with cancer and depression.

'I don't think it's bad luck. If I'm completely honest with myself, I think it was a combination of having genes that are predisposed to cancer, and that I didn't look after myself. I really, really didn't and I'm completely honest about that. And I do believe quite strongly that if you don't look after yourself then something will happen to you. It will either be cancer, or diabetes, or a stroke, or heart disease. I ate, drank, partied, smoked. I never did drugs but I was a smoker for eight years. I think I did some irreparable damage. Then there was the stress of having kids, a new environment, and working hard. I think my biggest pressure was trying to find the mix between my old life and my new life, and while I enjoyed the challenge, it was hard to find a way to fit in this new life. Nothing was easy.'

Annabel would look at her mother-in-law and how she coped with losing a child and raising nine others, and she would look at her awesome, supportive husband and think, 'Get your shit together, love. What have you got to be depressed about?' She works very hard to focus on the positives in her life. 'I'm not fortunate to have gone through a crappy time with cancer, but when you come out the other side and you are still alive, well, you know, I am pretty lucky.'

She has also come to realise that she is never going to stop missing her family a thousand kilometres away, or the close friends she made as a girl. It is the same yearning that took Wendy back to Kingaroy after forty years. 'As you get older you realise what is important and what isn't,' Annabel says. 'When you live in a man's world, the number-one thing that you miss is being close to your girlfriends and your family, and I will never get over it. I have tried, and I will never get over it. I just have to suck it up. It would never be reason enough for me to leave, but I have never found a friend here that comes close to the friends you make in those formative years between sixteen and twenty-six, when you live, eat, breath, sleep mates.'

She calls an old teaching friend on the Sunshine Coast two or three times a week for a chat, although she finds the phone a poor substitute. She also takes advantage of school holidays, and delivering or picking up Lachlan and Sophia from boarding school to visit her parents. And once a year, she goes on a walking holiday with a bunch of girlfriends, including Ali. They have even tackled a trek in the Himalayas.

At the Creative Cowboys workshop she told participants that everyone had faced challenges in their lives and had stories to tell. 'I'm just crazy enough and loud enough to stand up here and share my story but, please, remember, it is really no better than anyone else's,' she stressed, with the self-effacing modesty that colours her entire approach to these workshops and the message they carry.

'I had this drive to be super human and I don't any more,' Annabel says. 'I love to be busy but what I've learnt is that if you fill your life right up to the top, when something else comes along, it all falls apart. You are kidding yourself if you think you can keep pushing and something isn't going to give. The container will not only pop its lid, it will smash. So you have to leave a little buffer at the top. Give yourself a bit of a break, and do it often. I still push myself, but I'm doing it for better reasons now. I'm doing it because I want to get the most out of my life and out of every day.'

In the same vein, Annabel has started studying nursing part-time by distance education. It's going to take six years and a lot of juggling with family, station and community responsibilities to finish the degree, but she is determined. In the back of her mind is the potential to marry her qualifications when she is done with her interest in art as therapy. Meanwhile, she is very conscious of the words of wisdom passed on by Wendy, who in turn received them from Stephen's grandfather. 'You have to learn to live with drought and look forward to the good seasons,' Wendy says, quoting her father-in-law, before adding her own words of wisdom. 'And you have to laugh at yourself. That's how you survive the hardships.'

ACKNOWLEDGEMENTS

Writing this book has at times proved to be a real struggle, not least because the woman who inspired it died while it was in its early stages. So for that reason, I begin with an extra special thank you to my patient publishers, Allen & Unwin, for understanding that sometimes life just gets in the way, and to my family and friends for their extra love and support when I needed it most.

Special thanks to Claire Kingston for her ongoing faith in me as an author, and for reuniting me with the wonderful team that brought *Women of the Land* into being: my thoughtful and diligent editor Aziza Kuypers, always encouraging and considered copyeditor Susin Chow, and also to eagle-eyed proofreader, Simone Ford. Once again my agent, Fiona Inglis, was there for me too, with wise advice and words of encouragement when needed, despite her own challenges.

For the wonderful cover, I have to thank the singular talent of photographer Nigel Parsons. Working with you is always a great pleasure, Nigel, and I promise to buy you that drink sometime very soon! And to Rick and Tania Gladigau who not only allowed us to shoot the image on their beautiful Adelaide Hills dairy farm, disrupting milking and end-of-year school commitments, but managed to organise perfect weather, quiet well-mannered cows and a dog, even if he was a bit reluctant.

Most of all, my deeply felt gratitude goes to the women who agreed to be part of this book—my mum Elaine and Aunty Grace, Wendy and Giuliana, Marnie and Sherryn, Daljit, Annabel and Wendy—for trusting me with your stories, and your willingness to share your lives. In particular, thank you to my family for allowing me to cross the Rubicon in this book and tell something of our own story. It was no small thing to ask any of you, and I take none of these privileges for granted.